Groovy Bob

grOOvy bob   HARRIET VYNER

The Life and Times of Robert Fraser

faber and faber

First published in 1999
by Faber and Faber Limited
3 Queen Square London WC1N 3AU

Photoset by Intype London Ltd.
Printed in England by Butler and Tanner Ltd, Frome.

© Harriet Vyner, 1999

Harriet Vyner is hereby identified as author
of this work in accordance with Section 77
of the Copyright, Designs and Patents Act 1988

A CIP record for this book
is available from the British Library

Front flap: *Portrait of Robert Fraser* by Jean-Michel Basquiat
from the collection of Brian Clarke, © ADAGP, Paris, and DACS,
London, 1999. Front cover: photograph by Hans Hammarskiöld.
Back cover: Richard Hamilton, *Swingeing London II*, courtesy of the
Tate Gallery, © Richard Hamilton; all rights reserved, DACS, 1999.
Back flap: Jean Dubuffet, untitled sketch, © ADAGP, Paris,
and DACS, London, 1999.

ISBN 0–571–19627–6

10 9 8 7 6 5 4 3 2 1

Contents

Prologue

MICK JAGGER Robert in a way was more like a man from the fifties. But this is what was interesting about the sixties, like every decade or time period . . . I was thinking about this – I'd just come back from Morocco (which Robert loved), where I'd sat on the bank of a river watching a man ford the river with his donkey, and another man on the other side waving, who'd walked across carrying his bicycle, which looked as if it had been designed in 1890. There I was, with my Japanese car at the top – we were not living in the same place.

And so if you're talking about the sixties, Robert was in a way more like one of those fifties people you see in photographs who used to deal in art or dabble in it then. He was like one of those John Deakin people, with the pinstripes, nice ties, blue Turnbull and Asser shirts, his hair always perfectly combed, always well shaved and so on, that sort of person. Public school; Eton, you know. Bit of money. Falls into another world. He wants to be on the edge of the *demi-monde* – but he's not happy with the *demi-monde*. He wants to be on the outside edge, where there's criminal activity. That's why he's attracted to Spanish Tony, and other criminals probably. He's gay, but not with a nice hairdresser boyfriend; gay in the rent-boy way – doesn't want to show he's gay. He's a drug addict – doesn't want to show he's a drug addict. When cocaine's fashionable, he's like an early avatar of that, which of course goes back to the dashing thirties days as well. But what else is he doing? He's presenting this new kind of art. Who to? Well, not so much to gay gentlemen living in the Albany on family money, making good investments, but to young upstart people in this brash new world of England which hadn't really existed before.

So there he is, sort of representing old-world England, though we know he isn't really, but he presents himself as that without belabouring it. He couldn't claim anything more than public school, after all, but he obviously had that aura, and there he is, not only selling to but taste-making, which is the best way, for these brash pop singers and others. So he's bridging two worlds. And having a great time in the process, a very hedonistic time. And that was his blaze, his quick swathe through London. He found a part. And the interesting thing about the times was that it had never happened like this before. A big social change. An interesting social change.

And so there he was. But then he got involved in this Rolling Stones thing and got busted. Then he was sent to prison, which was awful . . .

Introduction

When Robert Fraser is thought of nowadays it is usually as being one of the subjects of Richard Hamilton's iconic *Swingeing London*, the image that became symbolic of the sixties, showing Robert and Mick Jagger, holding up handcuffed hands, as viewed through the police van window and on their way to prison.

By 1967, when this happened, Robert was already famous, in certain circles anyway, as being the owner of London's most exciting modern art gallery – one that had not only built up a reputation for serious and groundbreaking shows, but one that seemed to move with the free-floating spirit of the times. It showed the latest films by Kenneth Anger and Bruce Conner, its opening parties were famously glamorous, and being in sole charge Robert had the authority to act on a whim: for example, in September 1966, for five days only, he had the gallery window taken out and a psychedelically painted brand-new AC Cobra sports car exhibited in its place. His catalogues were laid out by the best designers and would have a profound effect on future graphic design. It was thanks to his powers of persuasion that the Beatles employed Jann Haworth and Peter Blake to create the now famous cover of *Sgt Pepper*, and later on used Richard Hamilton for the *White Album* cover. His gallery was also the first in England to show many of the latest American artists – for example, Jim Dine, Andy Warhol and Ed Ruscha – and in fact, being connected with it at all was enough to be caught up in the glamorous spin of swinging London.

Robert's enthusiasm had never extended to the financial side of the venture, though, and the artists were always having to wait for cheques that would arrive late, unsigned or not at all. When they'd go to complain there would be every sign that Robert wasn't short of money himself – he lived in lavish splendour in Mount Street, had a chauffeur-driven Rolls-Royce to take him the few streets to his gallery (though even then he was always late) and often wasn't around at all, but off on foreign jaunts with his glamorous friends.

By the time he found himself serving four months for possession of heroin following on from the infamous Redlands drug bust, he was a heroin addict, his gallery was on the verge of bankruptcy and the artists were not only owed money it looked unlikely they'd ever receive, but now had to watch as their works were palmed off for nothing by the receiver. However, in the continuing generous spirit of the times, they rallied round, organizing exhibitions in Robert's absence to keep the gallery going and featuring him in protest paintings, including the variations of *Swingeing London*.

However, in many ways Robert was a strange figure to be at the centre of this wild scene, one of the discrepancies that lends a certain poignancy to *Swingeing London*. Even throughout the razzmatazz of the sixties, his most dazzling moment, and in spite of the sharp multicoloured suits, the drugs and the way-out language that gave rise to his nickname, his grooviness sometimes had a touch of the old-fashioned about it. There was a formality to him that seemed more akin to his earlier life – Old Etonian and officer in the King's African Rifles. He seemed, in many ways, a vivid embodiment of England's transitory time between the old age and the new.

The sixties was a time of social change in which the desire was to break away from the older generation's values, but Robert was reluctant to let go of all the signs and symbols of an aristocratic old England that had seemed so glamorous to him from a young age. His father Lionel had been a highly successful banker who had radiated a certain self-satisfaction at having worked his way up from nothing. Both parents, his mother Cynthia especially, were devout Christian Scientists who had their generation's acceptance of a certain snobbery and, as Lionel's 1965 obituary pointed out, "a determination to do right". Although Robert's wildly promiscuous and self-destructive lifestyle seemed a far cry from theirs, he couldn't escape shades of their influence, including an old-fashioned dislike of familiarity. He had no wish to discuss his private life or feelings – would have thought that rather vulgar. It meant that many people knew very little about certain aspects of his life: his homosexuality, his promiscuity and his drug taking. His relationships also suffered from this dislike of intimacy, so were rarely on an equal basis; during the height of sixties egalitarianism, his lover Mohammed served double duty as his manservant. None of this indicated any sort of caution on his part; Robert had always had a most high-handed disregard both for authority and for the opinion of others.

The high-handedness is one of the reasons why he is not remembered with great fondness by those in the art world who lacked his unlimited recklessness. They point to his irresponsibility towards his artists, most of whom would agree, but who themselves had other reasons for loyalty to Robert and the gallery until its closure in 1969. In spite of his reticence, Robert's manner was always mysteriously inspiring and compensated for many other shortcomings. He radiated a sort of confidence or clarity that was very flattering to those at whom his attention was directed: it implied that he appreciated the subtleties of their work without the tiresome need for analysis. Furthermore, the artists knew that they would be showing in the most prestigious gallery in London and that the shows he promised them would be consistently stylish and beautiful. In a perverse way, his aggravating and erratic approach was sometimes part of his appeal, even to these long-suffering colleagues; indeed to those for whom it had appeal at all, it reflected some of the peculiar charm of London at that time – such a grand man leading such a groovy lifestyle.

With the passing of the sixties, the gallery and its owner have lost much of their significance. Only in people's imaginations and memories has the Robert Fraser Gallery made any lasting impression. However, it reflected the genuine enthusiasms of that short-lived moment and was certainly needed – a gallery that consistently showed the best of what the period was producing. No other art dealer in history has been the subject of so many of his artists' works, and this reflected not only his elusive charisma and charm but also the impact he had on the times and his hand in many of the major contributions to that decade's memorable look. Robert not only created stars within the British art world for the first time, but was himself a star, and this at least caught the attention of the usually indifferent British public. The gallery seemed to suggest a world of possibilities, thanks in no small part to its owner's reputation for wildness. Art students, who saw it as a place of pilgrimage, approached it with a sense of trepidation that they would hardly have felt had they been visiting merely another significant modern art gallery.

The artists he showed have all become famous and their works of that time valuable and sought after. If Robert had managed to build up a safe collection of the artists he promoted he would have been very rich. Had he had any sort of business sense his legacy would have been more longstanding, for, as with many other idealistic beginnings at that time, the art world soon moved in a more financial direction. Modern art prices began to rocket, and proof of a good eye was in the resale price a few years on. This was not a bandwagon Robert felt inclined to jump on, nor did he have the ability. In spite of an initial burst of enthusiasm and some excellent and memorable shows, including the graffiti artists whom he introduced to a sceptical London, his second gallery, which opened in 1983, suffered not only from his continuing financial incompetence but also from the fact that England had reverted to the conservatism from which the sixties was but a brief departure.

Robert died of AIDS in 1986, one of London's earliest victims. He was one of the first AIDS sufferers to insist that he should be allowed to die at home, and he chose not his own but his mother's. So in spite of the complications of their relationship, at his end (almost with a feeling of peace in spite of the terrible circumstances) he found himself back in her Knightsbridge flat, surrounded by her Christian Science books and her decent modern art collection, purchased mostly from him in moments of his own need. Cynthia had always been ambitious for her favourite son, hoping that he would turn to her religion for direction in his crisis-ridden life. Although she was never to see this happen, at least in the end her own unshakeable beliefs came somewhat to her rescue – in the spirit of Christian Science she was able to ignore as unreal the imperfect side to his life and focus on his achievements, his undeniable and considerable contribution to the art world.

Groovy Bob

1 An Aesthete in the Making

*By the time Robert, the youngest of
three, was born, in August 1937, the
Fraser family had settled into prosperity.
It had not always been so. Lionel, his
father, was the son of Gordon Selfridge's
butler. However, having raised himself
at least to the level of his father's
employers, Lionel was now able to provide for his family the very things he'd
seen around him and desired since childhood.*

*Both Robert's parents had a faintly
puritanical approach to life, a kind
of Victorian reticence which they
attempted to instil into their children.
Lionel, however, also had a flamboyant
side, and if the other qualities had less
appeal this trait at least was embraced
by Robert.*

Fraser family at Buckingham Palace for Lionel to receive his CMG.

LIONEL FRASER Letter to Nicholas Fraser

Investiture at Buckingham Palace on 27th February 1945. We started off bright and early in a huge Daimler car, Grandma, Mummy, Robert and myself, and got to the Palace at 9.30, although the investiture did not start until 11 o'clock. Grandma, Mummy and Robert were installed in the very first row only about two or three yards away from where the King would do the Investing.

When my name was called out, I must admit that I felt a little nervous. We had to walk a few paces to the King from his right, then turn left to face him, give a bow and then take one step forward towards him. He then put the Order round my neck, said what a pleasure it gave him to invest me, shook hands and smiled.

The King was quite superb and most dignified throughout. Although the Investiture lasted from eleven o'clock until 12.45 he never looked bored for one single second and always had a nice word to say on the right occasion. We were all very proud indeed of him. ■

BRIAN CLARKE Robert used to talk about his father a lot. There was one occasion I had to get somewhere and he said if I waited I could go in his father's Bentley, because, he said, 'My father never rides in the Bentley, he walks alongside it. So it'll be empty. Save you walking.'

NICHOLAS FRASER My father was a mixed figure. He was very Victorian, came from frightfully respectable country people and was a very respectable figure. He is impossible to pigeon-hole, but he did come from a humble background. His sister told me what an ambitious person he was. And he did get on, to some extent by conforming – outwardly anyway.

He wanted to be part of the establishment, no question about that, but every now and again he'd kick out against it, especially in the City, and occasionally won. He was certainly pleased to know the odd Duke here and there, and to be a member of White's club. The gloss of conformity is the Victorian bit really, but he always had his own views.

At 64, Lionel Fraser can look back on a colourful career. He is the outsider who won his way inside. He was not a member of 'The Establishment'. He did not go to Eton. 'I am comparatively uneducated,' he claims. (Newspaper article)

NICHOLAS FRASER My mother's mother was married to Walter, a very unreliable person who spent a lot of his life in Brazil. My mother was proud, curiously, of being born in Brazil. It was slightly exotic. It meant getting new passports, etc. Anyway her father was a very live wire, a rather unexpected character, who formed the Rio Football Club, but was always either frightfully rich or bankrupt, and I think my maternal grandmother found it all rather wearing.

After he died she then subsequently married Hugh Reeves. He was a very successful, very old-fashioned solicitor, known as Pop Reeves. They married in about 1928–9. He lived in some splendour. He had a very large house in Norfolk, then a large house in Sussex, where we were during the war. It was a very conventional marriage – he'd get on the train and go up to the office every day, and my maternal grandmother carried on the life of a country lady.

OLIVE COOK Cynthia had the most appalling childhood. I think her father died and the new stepfather didn't want her as part of his family. They used to make her stay in her bedroom and have her food sent up, instead of sitting at the table with them. Her cousin, Daphne Henrin, the sculptor, is a very great friend of mine and she's told me how awful it all was.

NICHOLAS FRASER I've so many pictures of her, in Vienna, in Grenoble, etc. She seems to have been sent off to all these foreign universities – courses here, courses there – from age 16 to about 20. She was constantly abroad.

I don't think my mother liked the establishment. She made comments like, 'I was so pleased when I met your father. I'd never met anybody who was different.'

LIONEL FRASER Hugh Reeves was a great character and had many facets: generous benefactor to his old school, Cheltenham, famous rowing man, dabbling in politics and farming and a supporter of lost causes. He was the finest judge of port I'd ever met and could tell the shipper and the year from a quick sniff at the decanter. This may not be so unusual, but at the time it seemed amazing to me. Whilst I had been welcomed as a weekend guest in his country house, it was a different matter when this unknown person was asking for the hand of his stepdaughter. He summoned me to his presence. Who was I? What were my prospects? Where had I been to school?

SARAH SESTI Cynthia was my father's stepsister. When Cynthia married Fraser, it wasn't considered proper. I know it was always considered by the family that she'd married beneath her. He was always referred to as a 'self-made man'. However, then they were all absolutely amazed to find that he became absolutely brilliant, and made *so* much money! It was then rather difficult for them to backtrack!

LIONEL FRASER Our first child, Janet Mary, was born in July 1933. We did not mind whether it was a boy or a girl – we never did when the two boys were born later, Nicholas Andrew in March 1935 and Robert Hugh in August 1937. Had it not been for Hitler and approaching war clouds, we should certainly have had a larger family, for we know of no greater joy or interest.

. . . We were deluged with offers from thoughtful friends in the United States to send the children over there, most of the cables reading, 'When can we expect arrival Janet, Nicholas and Robert?' This was very touching, but my wife and I quickly decided not to avail ourselves of these generous offers. We felt that if this was to be a war to end all wars, our children, if they survived, would be thankful to us for not depriving them of sharing the experience. We also saw the danger of estrangement and a change of habits and outlook, especially for children of such impressionable ages. So, we expressed our extreme gratitude and instead of the United States, we moved our children out of London to Sussex to stay with my mother-in-law. There they remained until the guns of Dunkirk could be heard.

Dear Mummy and Daddy

Thank you for the letters, how is the cooking going on. How is Ginger? We had a beautiful tea in the little house. I had a beautiful piece of snake skin, we had a lovely game of hiding-seek the pigs are very lovely. I saw the smoke from a doodle-bug.

this is a list of Revolting things, snell stuck a hay-fork in a grass snake, the next day cut his head off. I saw some chicken's liver. It looked like a choclate blancmang.

I have a bentley I will take you for a Ride in IT

BEST LOVE FROM ROBERT

NICHOLAS FRASER It was the strong puritan ethic, a strict, humourless attitude to life, that shaped Robert, rather than Christian Science. That gave him something to kick against. My father was a very 'good' man, tried to do good to everybody. But he had these Victorian principles. I think Robert was deeply fond of both our parents without sharing their views.

I have been reading – The Adventures of a Black Girl in her Search for God!! – I didn't enjoy it much, I must say.

MRS MORRIS Robert never showed signs of religious feeling. It's not for me to say, but I think it was a bit shoved down their throats when they were young. I'm not sure really. But that happens in a lot of Christian Science families.

LIONEL FRASER I must put on record my unbounded gratitude to Mary Baker Eddy, the founder of Christian Science. Mrs Eddy was by any standards a quite remarkable woman, a thinker who has had a more ennobling and spiritually uplifting effect on mankind than any other woman.

I have seen the possibility of bringing into effect in daily life the First Commandment, the Golden Rule and the ideals of the Sermon on the Mount, which I had always regarded as out of reach, and inapplicable, especially in business dealings. I have found that God has no material appendages.

From You Don't Have to Be Poor *by Warren T. Brookes (The Christian Science Publishing Society, Boston, Massachusetts, USA):*

True, Jesus did love the poor. He loved everybody. He did preach to the poor, and he did tell the rich to give up love of riches for love of God.

But, just because he loved the poor, we can't say that Jesus loved poverty. And, just because he challenged the rich man, we can't say he was against plenty.

How do we know?

Well, for one thing he told us, 'I am come that they might have life, and that they might have it more abundantly.'

Does that sound like a man who was preaching poverty?

MARK GLAZEBROOK I did think that the thing is – my feeling about Christian Science is that it's very much a religion for rich ladies. And it was founded by a lady who became rather rich through it . . .

MR BENDON Cynthia was very ardent. Lionel was not as ardent as Cynthia but he was keen. And the boys were meant to have been brought up as Christian Scientists, but neither of them stuck to it. Nicholas had this bad leg; he'd always had it, and this was a great sorrow to them because in Christian Science terms you're not supposed to have anything the matter with you, and that's why they don't go to doctors, you see. You're supposed to be as God made you, and you've just got to say that it's not true if anything appears wrong with you.

I had rather a big stye on my eye but I did some reading on thursday and friday and then the erroneous belief fled before the holy truth – also Mrs Holland left me a bag of sweets and an orange!

OLIVE COOK Cynthia used to teach the children in Sunday School and was very, very good at it. I was forced to go to a terrible meeting once. It was interesting how many well-known people were members. Cynthia spoke at the meeting and was excellent, speaking with real conviction. She was admired in that circle.

Dear Pa and Ma,
    It has been pouring all day, and we have not had cricket. La La. Hope you have had nice weather. I went to a party yesterday and had a conjuror and punch and judy. Granny and Pop are coming to eat a picnic lunch tomorrow, everything all right. Rain did a lot of good, now for some sun.
    From RH Fraser S.M.C.G.

NICHOLAS FRASER Fan Court was a Christian Science school – not pushed down one's throat exactly but prayers in the morning, and if you were ill, no doctors.

All the boys at Fan Court came from Christian Science homes, so school strictures weren't something new. In the Christian Science doctrine you're not ill unless you're mentally ill, and once you get that right your physical self rights itself. Fan Court probably wasn't all that different from other prep schools, except perhaps reading from Mrs Eddy rather than the Bible and no doctors.

Instead of doctors, one had to go to 'practitioners', who gave you tracts to read from the Bible and so forth.

Mrs Wilcox who takes us for Science Read set me a few pieces for my stuttering.

We had Mr Elliott for Sunday School he was talking about the Lord's Prayer mostly. He says we must express these qualities in class – Attention. Unselfishness. Patience.

NICHOLAS FRASER Robert must have been an intriguing figure for my father. My father was quite a strong person – in the end perhaps not as strong as my mother – but Robert said things in letters to my father that I'd never have said. Quite cheeky stuff. I'd have been far too nervous. I think Robert was totally unfazed by him. He didn't want to hurt him, but he wasn't frightened of him as I was.

In some ways Robert was very keen to be part of the establishment. He was immensely snobby in some ways, especially when he was younger. I've been looking through his letters. He wrote a jolly good letter at a very young age.

Dear Mummy and Daddy,

Thank you for the nice long letter. You seemed to have had a very busy week, what with luncheon partys at the Ritz etc. Did Daddy wear White tie and tails at the City Ball, I hope you look lovely dancing. I hope you enjoyed yourself there.

We went to 'Britain Can Make It' on Friday which was very interesting. Mr Elliott took a Busload of boys to the Exhibition, Mr Leslie the Chairman of the Board of the Exhibition invited us up. The great thrill of it was <u>THE PRINCESSES</u> were there and we saw them. I hope you will have a good journey to Paris, Which hotel are you staying at this time, The Ritz?

JUDITH ELLIOTT I was at Fan Court with Robert, a girl in a boys' school, and we knew the whole family very slightly. I have vivid memories of his parents and brother, his sister as well. But Robert was my contemporary.

What I remember chiefly about him, and I was terribly attracted to this, was that he formed a splinter group against games. In a footballing environment it was a rather striking thing to do. Obviously an aesthete in the making.

My opinion of rugby football is that its thoroughly unruly. My hate of it lies in its utter futility. It is a riotous, ridiculous, incredulous, futile, muddy and entirely out of keeping with any civilization whatsoever game.

JUDITH ELLIOTT I remember Robert's parents very vividly, because although I don't think I saw Robert again, I certainly saw them through the years. His father was a tremendously imposing presence – this wonderful shock of silver white hair, the bow tie. A very powerful, good-looking man, I suppose. One was aware of him as being quite somebody. And his mother was a very striking woman, elegant. To me Cynthia was as much a figure in her own right as Lionel. They came down sort of grandly. There seemed to be a lot of style about both of them.

How daring, no not daring, what shall I say, how forward of that backward paper 'the Sunday Times' – to have acknowledged Henry Moore as a great sculptor – even a genius! Improving!
I now feel I am well on the way to an appreciation of Modern Art.

LIONEL FRASER Although for many years my wife's and my interest in pictures had been growing, I think our appetite was really whetted before the war when on visits to Paris we had the unusual advantage of accompanying our great American friends Ruth and Gordon Washburn to many of the galleries there. Gordon Washburn was prowling around in search of suitable purchases for the Albright Gallery in Buffalo, of which he was then the Director. Dealers hid nothing from him. Sharing these visits we were able to feast ourselves on examples of the works of some masters of modern painting, such as Renoir, Rouault, Soutine, Klee, Cézanne and Picasso. It was a delightful experience and my wife and I gained much in knowledge and discernment. Our eyes became attuned to these revolutionary exponents of the art of our day and we began to acquire a warm appreciation of them.

I trust Paris is as beautiful in November as in April. I hope you have bought the most sublime picture at the most sublimely cheap price, by an artist who is going to be sublimely famous in future, altogether too 'deevine' for words!!

NICHOLAS FRASER Robert was very interested in visual things, even as a boy. Not pictures, but he was mad about the cinema, the theatre. He noticed visual things when you were with him – buildings and things.

I'm afraid that you did not like or understand the new Picasso pictures. I was looking at some last week and found them to have great rythm. I have just been lent a little book on Picasso by Andre Leclerc, which was more revealing than all Gertrude Stein's 55 pages. I know so much more about art now – since the end of the Holidays.

OLIVE COOK He could be very cheeky as a boy, and also very sophisticated at an early age. It was just his nature.

I am rather pleased that you are not going over to Paris, because you might get mixed up with communists and get shot (then we'd be orphans)!

LIONEL FRASER We always encouraged the children to express their individuality, but never to be precocious. One incident which occurred when our younger son, aged eight, had gone to his prep school was almost too much even to us. My wife was suddenly telephoned by the anxious headmaster, requesting her to come down at once, as our son was having an upsetting influence on the other boys. My wife hurried down to Chertsey as best she could, to find that the boy had been preaching Communism with such great effect that the other pupils were being tainted.

I listen to 'The Week in Westminster', every Saturday now. I heard that Communist man Piratin the other night. And

I
HAVE
GONE
RED! (Socialist!)

That does not mean I wish the pleasure of the rich to be abolished. It is in my course to believe that many self-styled Tory aristocrats are frightened out of their wits by workers becoming rebellious (and probably rightly so at working conditions and wages) also they are at the rise of Socialism, and anti-capitalist feeling! That is why I've seen red!

Best Love, Robert

Letter from **LIONEL FRASER**
My dear Robbie,

Congratulations on getting as many as 9 credits so far! That is not at all bad and I hope you will go on. This time I will not mention the word 'co-operate' but will leave it for you to report on any improvement you may have found in the team spirit as far as you yourself are concerned.

You are using a lot of very lengthy words in your letters but on the whole you seem to understand what they mean, from the sense of your writing.

Mummy and I had four rounds of golf at New Zealand over the week-end. The whole course was completely white in the mornings, but in the afternoons, especially Sunday, it was quite lovely. We rushed back on Sunday afternoon to have tea with Mrs Heywood-Dove.

Incidentally, I do not think I should let politics worry you very much at the moment, for properly to understand them I can assure you they need a tremendous lot of study and time, neither of which you can give at present. For instance, I could tell you a great deal about nationalisation from the practical angle, and I am wondering too whether you are not rather inclined to change about very quickly and accept the point of view of the last person who spoke to you. It is very important in life to give serious consideration to all statements before they are made, especially if one expects others to regard them as profound. The one thing which one does want to avoid is any impression of ranting, otherwise nobody will take any notice of what one says. I feel you ought to give as much attention as you can to your studies, and to loving your neighbour as yourself. If you do the last-named, you will find all sorts of revelations and intelligent ideas will come to you.

Glad you beat Gareth at golf. Did you do a hole in one?

Best love,

Daddy

Dear Daddy,

Thank you for your letter which I received this morning. I am concerned only in this letter with the last paragraph.

You seem to be bent on dissuading me from pursuing one of my major interests in life. Your request that I should relinquish interest has fallen on completely deaf ears.

You say I change quickly, perhaps I do, but I have been on the verge of this act for over a month, I have thought it over, read speeches from Hansard (of which has been lent to me), looked up definitions in the 'Encyclopedia Britannica' and done everything that might help me on this subject, and having studied have changed. You say Politics is too big a subject, maybe but you have to make a start somewhere, & somehow.

And altogether I deplore every statement in the latter part of that letter. However I will be writing again on Sunday along with some news of a more substantial basis!

Love

Robert

Letter from LIONEL FRASER

My dear Robbie,

We *are* having a wonderful correspondence on political subjects, aren't we?

I was glad to see from your letter that you were really taking the trouble to study politics to the best of your ability. All I wanted to say was that just at this time, with Eton looming ahead, I did not want you to devote too much time to outside things. I had just wondered from your previous letter whether you had really given full consideration to the matter. If you have, jolly good luck to you. I am looking forward to some nice friendly talks to you on the subject, and you will then see that you read something into my remarks which was certainly not intended.

You marked your letter 'Private', which I shall respect, and I hope you will do the same on your part.

See you on Sunday afternoon.

Best love,

Daddy

NICHOLAS FRASER He was said to have disrupted Fan Court school with his Communist propaganda and the headmaster asked for Robert to be taken home, which he was. I think it was just for a cooling-off period.

Drawings included in Robert's letters home, aged ten.

JUDITH ELLIOTT I do remember him as an exciting person. I understood in later years from my parents that he was in fact an extremely difficult boy, not surprisingly.

the sweet young man, handsome, and delicate !

The Art Lover

does he look like this !— is he the old Bohemian hardened by many years drinking absinthe ? and cafés of Montmartre

new intellectual dude ?

or he the

the petle professor's Darling ?

MR ELLIOTT (headmaster) Letter to Robert's parents
He enjoys the belief that he is 'different' from other boys. If he could lay this aside, he would find that many more of his fellows could and would share his interests than he supposes. I believe we can help if in thinking and speaking of him we do not think of him as 'different' except in so far as he expresses individuality by reflection of the one infinite God.

1950–1955

Lionel, like many other Englishmen, held the belief that Old Etonians possessed some indefinable grandeur besides a good education and now, having managed to have his sons accepted there, he could settle back and wait for them to reap its rewards.

He was not alone in expecting a lot from Eton. Robert, with his early interest in society matters and taste for glamour, had his own images of its mystique. Both were to be somewhat disappointed.

Robert's first Eton photograph in 1950.

J. PAUL GETTY Robert's grandfather was a butler, wasn't he? But I think Robert transcends class, very much in a sixties way. But somehow he got sent to Eton, which is what formed him to a great extent. Formed his style, his personality. It's still one of the best places to learn arrogance.

From 'Adonis at Lords', story written by Robert for the Eton Chronicle, *aged 15*

A dowager, in tweeds, with a small green hat set at an aggressive angle on her head, was talking in strident tones with a man of uncertain age. But it was his clothes that belied the man. His top hat rested firmly on his ears, and seemed to swamp completely his minute features. His tail coat riveted the attention by its very ghastliness. An ancient pair of sponge-bag trousers formed the crowning indignity.

'Up from the country, it stands out a mile,' murmured Adonis. 'These people are like rats in their holes. They only come out once a year; where exactly they crawl out from Heaven only knows.' ■

We had quite a good Luncheon at Bray Windsor – Liver Pate. Curried Chicken & Rice. Vanilla Ice. Cafe Noire. – We talked of Eton, France, Politics.

LIONEL FRASER Now why did I take trouble to get my two sons into Eton, I who lacked the education and social standing of an Etonian? I think I was influenced in the main by the natural wishes of every parent to ensure for his children something at least as good as he himself had, and if possible better. I saw in Eton the best club in the world and I was convinced that if my sons could become members, they would be able to enjoy the advantages of the unequalled traditions of the school. At the same time they would meet on level pegging contemporaries who were likely to become prominent figures in industry, commerce or politics.

But I have to confess there was at a certain period another, and quite formidable, influence in my 'literary' life – boys' weekly magazines. There was one called *The Union Jack*, which each week recounted the hair-raising adventures of Sexton Blake. There were also two other penny weeklies, one named *Gem* and the other *Magnet*. These last-named had quite an effect on me, for they dealt with the lives of public schoolboys. They brought brightness into my rather humdrum existence, giving me an insight into the hitherto unknown life of upper-class children.

TOM MILLER Fraser was something of an admirer of Cyril Connolly's *Enemies of Promise*, a good source on Eton in the early twenties, not too different from the school in the early fifties.

From Enemies of Promise *by Cyril Connolly*
I had a moment on Windsor Bridge; it was summer, and, after the coast, the greenness of the lush Thames Valley was enervating and oppressive; everything seemed splendid and decadent, the huge stale elms, the boys in their many-coloured caps and blazers, the top hats, the strawberries and cream, the smell of wisteria. I looked over the bridge as a boy in an outrigger came gliding past, like a water-boatman. Two Etonians were standing on the bridge and I heard one remark, 'Really that man Wilkinson's not at all a bad oar.' The foppish drawl, the two boys with their hats on the back of their heads, the graceful sculler underneath, seemed the incarnation of elegance and maturity.

There was no doubt that this was the place for me, for all of it was, from the St Wulfric's point of view, utterly and absorbingly evil.

GILES ST AUBYN (tutor at Eton) Robert was there from '50 to '55, before the rebellion of the sixties, but he was very much a precursor of that kind of mood. I expect that's why he liked *Enemies of Promise* – from a schoolboy's point of view, a pretty rebellious book. Robert was an early rebel, more individual than most, not going to be led by anyone, and that book would have harmonized with his outlook on the world.

NICHOLAS FRASER Robert was regarded as an unconventional figure at Eton. However, Etonians take things in their stride. To them, I had the bad luck to have this curious brother.

GILES ST AUBYN I thought him rather amusing – what will he do next? I wouldn't have lent him more money than I could afford to lose, but he was unusual, and he had wit. But the tutor, as I was to him, didn't have the responsibility of the housemaster, so I could afford to be amused.

NICHOLAS FRASER Because of the system at Eton, the housemaster is massively more important to you than any other master. He runs the house where you live. You didn't really have a choice of what house you were in at Eton, unless you were an Old Etonian – possibly then you could send your son to a friend of yours. As we didn't have an Old Etonian father, we took what we were given.

TOM MILLER Fraser's Eton career would have been different had he been sent to another, more orthodox house. His performance at Eton must be seen against the backdrop of the disintegration of Watkin Williams's house.

W. W. Williams ('Fishy') (d. 1985), a deep Christian but a bloody fool, succeeded C. R. N. Routh (d. 1976) as housemaster in September 1949. There also lived in the house Fishy's mother and unmarried sister ('Mum' and 'Death'). Having these eccentrics around stimulated derision. Fraser arrived, I think, in the summer of 1950. He was *never* an admirer of Fishy.

GILES ST AUBYN Fishy was a very good man and any mistakes he made with Robert – and Robert wasn't easy – he would have made with the best will in the world. He would have been deeply concerned, done all he could, but Fishy was a fish out of water in dealing with Robert. They simply weren't on the same wavelength at all. If Robert had been in some other house with more worldly-wise men, he might have had a more successful life.

Mr Williams escapes my attraction completely, in fact he flounders on the horizon miles away. But he is abounding in 'bonhomie', of course too much, and is much 'le brave'.

W. W. WILLIAMS Letter to Cynthia Fraser (28 June 1950)
Dear Mrs Fraser,

I had intended to answer before now your letter of the 20th, to say that Robert seems to be settling down happily and that I am pleased with him. He apparently works quite well and his life is abundantly full of interests; he is not hostile towards cricket and supports athletic activities in a vaguely patronising way! He got rather mobbed about some remark he made about 'life being enveloped like a blanket in a fog of philosophy', but is quite capable of standing up to his seniors in friendly argument, and I was rather amused to hear him shout out at one of the Dawson twins the Parthian shot 'You'd better take extras in philosophy!' I am so glad that his letters home are happy, and I certainly get the impression that he is settling down well, if a little unconventionally.

Yours sincerely,

W. W. Williams, Carter House, Eton College, Windsor

I fag every other night for Wormwald which includes valeting his clothes and making everything look neat and tidy. It might be more interesting if he had some papers or something in his room. Everything lacks atmosphere here, – or rather – romance, things go so far but no further.

M. R. SNOWDEN (tutor) There is something most unboyish about Fraser minor, which has puzzled me. A charitable explanation would include such adjectives as 'thoughtful', 'unassuming', 'intellectual', 'preoccupied'; an unkind person would use 'self-opinionated', 'cynical', 'detached' and 'uncooperative'.

I have now been here long enough to be able to read the character of Mr Snowden – a very gratifying state of mind though not one of difficult attainability, all one needed was some diplomacy, and then both the door and key of the labyrinth were in your hands. One of course is as yet unable to figure the inner intricacies of his soul.

M. R. SNOWDEN
Dear Williams,

Here are the reports on Fraser minor's schoolwork this half. As I have watched him sitting at the back of the pupil room engaged upon his Latin, or, if he's finished that, engrossed in reading of his own – in Eastern religions or the like – I have been forcibly reminded of a mot attributed to one don at the University, when he was asked about the boyhood of another . . . 'Oh, yes! Old G. and I were boys together – at least, I was!'

There is very little to write because everything is the same each day, however tomorrow until Saturday may be more eventful. Altogether Eton is a facsimile in miniature of the world, and one can have endless fun throwing red herrings etc about.

Love, Robert.

'L'amour c'est tout.'

18

GEORGE RICHMOND-BROWN Robert was always different from the rest of us, seemed older, more mature than his age. He had a lovely cynical smile and laughed at all the petty school rules and customs. He never took authority remotely seriously. He didn't so much fight against it as completely ignore it.

TOM MILLER Not really a considerable figure, not taken seriously as a brain at Eton. But amusing, though unscrupulous (one wouldn't have lent him half a crown). Fraser knew a fair amount about the arts and did tell me something that I didn't know – that Oscar Wilde went to prison for queer behaviour.

CHRISTOPHER GIBBS Opposite the record shop there was a gate with some steps going right the way up that said, 'Private. Don't Enter.' And that went straight up the side of Windsor Castle and through to the cloisters by St George's Chapel. Eton boys were allowed to use this gate, and we all did. So it meant that you'd arrive on Sunday afternoon, lots of people milling about, and you'd walk straight through the red ropes, etc. Smart kids . . . you know – I'm going to look at some Raphael drawings, etc. We all did that.

Thursday being a 'Non Dies', I have escaped the pleasant game of bat and ball for a whole week. On the day in question I went to look at the Old Master Drawings in Windsor Castle.

How low ebbs the tide of artistic appreciation in Britain, for although the castle was thronged with people there were only two people in the Old Master Drawings Room – they foreigners!

CHRISTOPHER GIBBS But real success in school, as far as the beaks were concerned, it was being frightfully good at games. Those that were became heroes to the beaks as well as the boys, and that was an area Robert never got into at all.

On Saturday we played cricket. They battled and I bowled, we felt very lazy, and the maroon ball meandered between the yellow wickets, and the click of the bat, and the sun beat down always . . . So we went to sleep under the sun . . . Then i got my man out, – they said, 'Take him off, he's got his wicket.' How I hated them! How I hated the boy who got mine. A big strong fellow with blue-green veins that rippled on a brown arm, and beads of shiny sweat clinging to his face.

Love, Robert.

TOM MILLER I never met any member of the Fraser family, though I saw his elder brother about the place. Fraser did, however, talk about his father with considerable respect. Fraser was of course identified by others as *nouveau riche*, but no one held this against him. Eton is really a meritocracy. Fraser a bit ahead of his time in the sense that he didn't take games seriously and was quite prepared to say so.

I have scored once this week for a house Junior, but this is emphatically the last time that I shall yield to the Captain of Cricket's persuasive smile, it bores me so!

By-the-by I have discovered that my mess-mate, Edward Greene, is a nephew of Graham Greene, the novelist.

Robert

EDWARD GREENE I don't think I was a friend of his. I only messed with him for one year.

JOHN SEMPLE I didn't terribly like him. I seem to remember he gave the impression that he was a tremendous social climber in the sense that he was very impressed by people who had titles, and used to seek out their company. I always assumed this was because he came from a rather outsider sort of background. He always took the *Tatler* (or was it *Vogue*?), and was always claiming he knew everyone in it.

There is another, Sykes, who was a complete hooligan, and then on Thursday I came across him far away in the lonely fields, and I found he was going to be a writer. Then I asked him, 'Are you the son of Christopher Sykes?' He answered, 'Yes.' Sweet fumes rushed to my head, I danced with joy. He told me lots of stories about the London Literary circles, what's more he is great friends with T. S. Eliot! calls him Uncle Tom! and told me a lot about him!

Do come on Wednesday! bring the food please! also the money!

R. A. Butler's son is in my division – he tells me good stories about W. S. C.! Also I have Lord Salisbury's nephew – a really rather uninteresting boy.

JOHN SEMPLE I always got the impression that he wanted to be very well known among the aristocracy. He was always very much seeking the company of people outside our house – people in Pop or the fringes of Pop or people who were, and this is sort of rude, that he considered socially distinguished. Our house was rather splendidly undistinguished.

And you couldn't get anyone more unsophisticated than Fishy. He used to take a local group of Boy Scouts. After Eton he got a job in the St John Ambulance Brigade.

CHRISTOPHER CLOGG I was a very, very good friend of Robert's. Robert was great fun. He'd come into my room in the evenings and we'd play jazz records. We both loved Dixieland. Greene was the odd man out, he was difficult and didn't participate. And so was Semple, hardly ever talked to him. He'd never come and play records, whereas Robert came every day.

GEORGE RICHMOND-BROWN Robert definitely had a cynical sense of humour, but I wouldn't say he was social-climbing, more an art snob.

CHRISTOPHER GIBBS I first met him when he came to my room, which you weren't supposed to do if you were a low boy in somebody else's house, and said, 'I'm told you've got some Landseer drawings I'd like to look at.' I didn't have any Landseer drawings. I was terribly impressed. I can remember first this glistening patent-leather sort of Dago-looking person, hanging around in Howard Roberts, which was the chic place to have your cup of cocoa and your club sandwich, in Eton High Street. He always had a nose for the hip scene, going round boring people.

ALASTAIR LONDONDERRY I can tell you exactly what my first memory of Robert was, it was in the drawing school at Eton. When I heard Wilfred Blunt, the brother of the traitor Anthony Blunt, who was a drawing school master at Eton. I remember him – I'd submitted some work to him and I heard a laugh, and then I heard him saying, 'That's a loud Fraserish laugh.' That was when I first became aware of Robert. We were probably about fourteen. I don't know what drew me to Robert, but we became friends after that. There was something about this loud laugh, you know. And then we sort of drifted together and then one thing led to another and the rest is history, as you might say.

CHRISTOPHER GIBBS Robert was much more socially alert than most boys. When you arrive you know people from your prep school, your brothers, your cousins and that's it. But Robert was always saying, 'I didn't see you at the children's party at the French Embassy before Xmas.' Being terribly grand. At the time it seemed glamorous and exciting.

Robert always had a finely honed kind of snobbery, which I have too, but it was all-encompassing. It would cover musicians, politicians, bankers, athletes, bookbinders, criminals, etc. A sort of personal aristocracy. And a nose for the raffish too, even then. The pull was equal for the low life and high life, but away from the straight life.

Nicholas' outlook on life over infects me when I go to see him. My only fear is that he is becoming too much the pattern public-school 'good man', – of course completely unconsciously, and he begins to hail everyone by their

Christian names, 'Jamie so-and-so', 'old Pete da-da', 'Philip something-else', which is thoroughly amusing, again his latest idea is to have all his friends in for Tea, next holidays, completely impracticable, thank Goodness, knowing all the laggards, and blaggards, with whom he knocks around with, in his soccer games, above all he wants to rope in a lot of harmless beaks, like M. R. Snowden, who would be hopelessly ill-at-ease, and embarrassed, in the atmosphere of our house. However he himself is a thoroughly 'GOOD-MAN', in the best and most exclusive sense of the word.

NICHOLAS FRASER With Alastair and Robert you always had that feeling they were up to something, whispering and giggling, whether they really were or not. I had done quite well, I was in cricket, I was in Pop, etc. It must have struck Robert that he and I were quite different. His obsession with Pop shows there was a dichotomy in him. I didn't notice that so much myself though. Of course Pop, in the little world of Eton, is the most glamorous thing to be in. But basically Robert was fighting against authority, and that included Pop. I don't think he was exactly a runner for entry into Pop.

Nicholas is very well. Maintaining a marvellously even standard of constant successes, yes just what I lack. I am destitute of determination. Either I don't know how to try, or I'm not trying. Anyway I'm profoundly depressed as I don't know what to do. I am now experiencing a great and lasting difficulty in another very important matter i.e. the feeling deeply rooted in the slow mind of my classical division master, that I am not trying as hard as I might. TRUE! they all echo, and busily commit it to memory, for triumphant production in their next order-card comment! By the powers, may I here and now denounce it all as BOSH!!!, bilfering, unimaginative, ludicrous, gigantically idiotic, – BOSH!!!!!

Is it likely in the precarious position of remaining or not remaining at Eton, – unless I try, is it likely in that position that I slack off, admittedly my place in the fortnightly order has dropped 5/26, 17/26, 20/26, 17/26. Nevertheless it is *not* idleness that is the cause of it. But, by God, how can I tell them so – I can't, what a hideous dilemma, what am I to do?

W. W. WILLIAMS Letter to Lionel Fraser
My dear Fraser,

Many thanks for your letter, and for showing me Robert's letter, which I return and which I shall of course treat in absolute confidence. Even though we are going to meet and talk things over on Sunday afternoon, I thought it might help you if I made a few immediate comments on his letter, so that you could think them over before we meet.

I agree that this is a most disconcerting letter to find awaiting you on your return from several weeks abroad; but from what I have seen of Robert lately I think that a good deal of it is a bit of exhibitionism – not so much to prepare you for bad results, as to prepare you for *my* thinking that the results are bad . . .

Williams, a thoroughly good fellow, must agree, though my behaviour in Pupil Room has on his own confession been satisfactory, yet I have no lasting proof, but my own word, (and what is that?) that I have not been, – he points to the story indicated by the figures, and what am I to do? There is nothing, its terrible, dreadful.

W. W. WILLIAMS He says that his behaviour in pupil room has been on my own confession (*sic!*) satisfactory. Behaviour, yes; but competent effort, no. I wish I had been able to keep one or two of his recent weekly exercises or copies of Latin verses to show you; they contained mistakes which (as I told him) were utterly unworthy of a boy of his intelligence; and I can only ask you to believe that that is because he has formed the habit of spending hours of unintelligent effort.

Yet another failure, I have logged the English Literature Prize – I came 3rd, beaten by two miserable boys whose names I can't recollect clearly.

W. W. WILLIAMS I think his description of his third place in the English Literature Prize as a 'failure' is totally out of proportion. Before the results were known I asked him how he got on, and he said that the paper was disappointing and he wasn't interested in it and wasn't expecting a good result; so when he was placed third and the examiner went out of his way to tell me what a very remarkable paper he had entered, I thought he had done very well. It is quite absurd for a boy who, while still in Lower Remove, has gained second prize in the Lower Boy Rosebery, second place in the ECC story competition for Lower Boys, and third place in the Literature Prize, to imagine or describe his performance as a 'failure'.

How nice it must be to be back in this place, England, so quiet after that screaming tornado, ugh! the American colonies. How I love this place, if only I could succeed, oh but it is not in me! I hear Janet is living in England now, how nice for her, even France seems inferior to us.

P.S. I have conceived a fit of violent dislike for that Demoniac, Devilish, riproaring, red, revolutionary, Bob Birley esq. C.M.G. who incidentally wants to run Eton upside down for I am told it is in his mind, to not only stop school-press, and Pop, but to build a by-pass around Eton, so that we're just a school, instead of a free, forceful independency.

FOR KING AND COUNTRY!!!!!!!!!
FLOREAT ETONA!
FLOREAT; FLOREBIT.

Robert.

P. T. O. P. S. etc I have concluded that the most important thing in life is money. <u>Please wire me your opinions, and reverse charge, as I've plenty of it. This is no joke.</u>

NICHOLAS FRASER Robert spent quite a lot of time at the Tate when he was a boy and would write essays about the pictures. And once he'd seen a picture once or twice he could always recognize it again, know that artist. He grasped it all very speedily. He didn't intellectualize pictures at all. That didn't interest him at all. It was just he liked a picture or he didn't. Very much more emotional than intellectual.

MR SNOWDEN Letter to Robert's parents

It seems to me that his thinking is naturally intuitive and associative; his thought tends to range widely and to favour general principles rather than particulars. Metaphorically, he perceives and argues from the wood, but fails to distinguish the specific distinctiveness of the trees. He *can* analyse a problem into its parts, but he finds it very difficult to isolate one part and deal with it to the end – his thought keeps turning round to the other parts. This is neither laziness nor stupidity but the mode of a natural faculty which, when properly and consciously used, can prove most valuable. It is not adequate to say 'lack of concentration' when, in fact, he is concentrating on the pattern instead of the element, the whole instead of the part. It will take time to develop an eye for intellectual detail; but, provided he remembers that this is what he particularly needs to do, he can and should achieve it.

NICHOLAS FRASER Robert read very widely, was a great bookworm. He was always reading books, then going off to see pictures. He didn't actually study art history, but his recognition of good art was very rapid. He had an intuitive understanding of art, not an intellectual appreciation. And he had great visual memory.

JOHN SEMPLE The other thing was, he appeared to me to have absolutely no interest in art – this was an adjunct. He liked to drop names of painters, but I don't remember him having pictures around him. Well, I mean, he had lots of posters of Toulouse-Lautrec, or he would find a name of some painter that no one else had ever heard of and liked to drop that into conversation, but I felt again that this was a terrific pose.

JOHN McEWAN At Eton Robert was incredibly glamorous, because he was such an old shade (i.e. shady character). Being called a shade was a great compliment – it meant you were really beyond the pale for any school institution like Pop. Above Pop in a sense. Shades were also dark glasses of course, but I think that's what the boys were called then.

TOM MILLER Though not obviously a fashionable social figure, he took clothes and the business of being well dressed seriously. Fraser presented a jowly, five-o'clock-shadow appearance. I think that he used an aftershave powder. He often wore dark spectacles and tended to set the fashion for them. On one occasion, almost certainly in September 1952, Chris Clogg and I saw the film *Lovely to Look At*. When the character actor Kurt Kasznar came on, Chris and I said, as one boy, 'Solly!' This was because Fraser, who resembled Kasznar physically, invented for himself a subsidiary personality, that of a dishonest Jewish businessman, Solly Fraserstein, and he was generally referred to around the house as 'Solly Fraser', or 'Old Sol'. If a chapter is to be devoted to Fraser's Eton career, it should be called 'Solly Fraserstein'.

My room 'lui-meme' is nice enough, I have stuck all my pictures up, including lots of photographs from the 'Man About Town'. Among them is that splendid photograph of Wilbur Evans in evening rags. 'Fish' Will is in his usual 'world-shattering' form, breaking all records for the biggest bore of all time.

GEORGE RICHMOND-BROWN Fishy hadn't a hope with Robert. I once saw Fishy close to tears with anger and frustration, shouting at Robert about something he'd done or failed to do, and Robert just standing there with a benign, quite untroubled expression. Completely unworried. Our house was in a state of total chaos – all discipline had broken down. The housemaster hadn't any idea how to cope with teenage boys, and we ran circles around him. Fishy was a terribly sad figure.

Yesterday night we had a sock supper, viz. Founder's tenor, y'day was Founder's Day holiday, very rowdy as can be imagined, in fact the revelry was on a Bacchanalic scale, so much so that it was found in the morning that someone had plugged an apple through the window of the dining room. Also several glasses were shattered during the roasts, and what with une chose et un autre things were stormish. After we had carols – typical Fish – and the old man sang songs like 'When the sergeant major is on parade' and a 'Bachelor Gay', with evident scouting gusto, giving a slice of the real camp-fire spirit.

GEORGE RICHMOND-BROWN I felt Robert was too grown up to be at school, desperately bored by it. But he had a wonderful sense of humour, a lovely guy. I only knew him at school though, afterwards our paths went different ways. Londonderry was a weirdy at school – typical of Robert's friends, a rather way-out creature. I can remember this creature looning around, about as enthusiastic about school as Robert was. They hunted together, I think.

ALASTAIR LONDONDERRY Robert and I were forbidden to see each other at one time because we were considered a disruptive influence on each other. I do remember that. I can't remember what – it must have been some escapade, either we were caught smoking together or the still-life episode in the drawing school when Robert ate the still life. Something to do with that. I know it was a fact we weren't allowed to talk to each other for a few weeks or months.

CHRISTOPHER CLOGG Londonderry used to come around a lot and we used to smoke up the chimney. They did it quite a lot, I couldn't afford to. I didn't want to get involved in that sort of thing. I just did it for fun sometimes. Alastair and Robert were much more confirmed smokers. Robert may have got pissed on cider once, but I don't remember him drinking much.

CHRISTOPHER GIBBS He also had a certain sneaking liking for certain very dashing athletes, and he had a desire to seduce them in some fashion – make them smoke cigarettes, get drunk or do something disgraceful. They fell for that. Robert was pretty thorough when he set out to do something.

Dear Mummy & Daddy,

As you may or may not know I was caught smoking last night; for which transgression I was awarded a Georgie. It doesn't seem to have been regarded by Fish & the Head Man as a very heinous crime, partly because the type who was caught with me, – Christopher Prideaux was in my room after 10.00 at night, which is a more serious offence in itself apparently, because of the various implications. Secondly the cigarettes belonged to him. Like a damned fool he chucked a lighted butt into the road, which as luck would have it was populated at the time by the Fish himself; naturally Fish noticed the firework display which occurred as the end hit the ground, and thus drew the obvious conclusion. He was more annoyed with Christopher than he was with me obviously, partly because he was in the Library, and partly because he was at least technically the guilty party.

As you probably know, quite a bit of smoking goes on in Eton, and thus it is more irritating to be caught in this way, irritating for me and embarrassing for Fishy who is very tolerant about such things. Not that I am implying that I am a regular smoker at Eton, because I am not.

I hope you will not be too annoyed about this, and I think you will agree that being caught is worse than the offence. All I can assure you is that contrary to the usual, it was not my fault only that arse Christopher who precipitated the whole affair, and without whom it would not have come about. Anyway I expect you will be hearing from the Tutor in due course.

All Love, Robert.

See you on Friday, – what time?

GILES ST AUBYN Robert must have had a very candid relationship with his parents to write to them about Prideaux being caught smoking in his room. It might have been to break the news first of course, before the master told them. But I think most boys would not have discussed it, just hoped that it wouldn't be mentioned. The degree to which Robert was worldly-wise at that age was unusual.

As masters we were aware of homosexuality, naturally, and were rather frightened of it. One way of trying to stop it was to be very firm if you found a boy out of his room after lights out. The worst interpretation would be put on it. It *was* a serious offence for two boys to be caught together in a room after lights out.

I got into the House Debating Society (Debate) last Sunday. This means you can fag boys etc.

PAUL McCARTNEY I used to talk about Eton to Robert and ask, 'How was it?' Because I went to a grammar school and was intrigued to meet someone honest from Eton. He told me about the fag system. I said, 'Do you think it made you gay?' He wasn't sure. But from the stories he told me, it would be conducive to gayness, just the whole idea of serving an elder boy, fagging for him. And I understand it went much further than that.

GILES ST AUBYN As a master I wouldn't have known about his homosexuality, but the other boys would have known. Tom didn't think he was. Robert's group was slightly arty, enjoyed being different. It might have been smart to boast about it, but most boys would be boasting about female conquests in the holidays, and a lot of that would have been fiction. It's the sort of thing Robert might have thought it smart to boast about.

JOHN SEMPLE I rather remember him being the other way; boasting of tarts he'd picked up in London. Never heard of him being interested in boys – lots of people were, it wasn't as though these things were kept under wraps.

GEORGE RICHMOND-BROWN Shows how well they knew him. There were definite signs of Robert's homosexuality at school, absolutely. No question. He was quite grown up about his sexuality. In a single-sex school an awful lot of homosexuality went on. Robert was definitely that way inclined and likely to remain so, whereas others were just experimenting. There were no sexual incidents where Robert got into trouble, just great activity. It was such an easygoing house. Much against the rules, you could be sacked for homosexuality.

CHRISTOPHER CLOGG The only time I've been set upon by another man was by Robert. We went out to Agar's Plough to play cricket. I'd forgotten my pads and had to go back to my room to get them. He came with me and then suddenly jumped on me on the bed.

His making a pass at me didn't change our friendship. He certainly wasn't embarrassed about it. I don't know of any other passes he made then, and we had quite a number of good-looking little boys in the house, but I don't think he was particularly interested in them.

ALASTAIR LONDONDERRY I remember once when he wrote one essay, it may have been in the 'O' level examination, that he compared the enjoyment of seeing a bullfight. He said, and he actually put this in the essay, 'The enjoyment I derive from a bullfight is comparable to the joys of sexual intercourse.' Well – at the age of fifteen or something!

I am wondering perhaps if it would be a good idea to leave earlier than next summer, – perhaps next half, or the half after. I don't think I can stand the pace for so long. What do you think?

LIONEL FRASER For some boys school is like the Elysian fields, for others it is a perpetual trial and a drag. This probably sums up the different sentiments of our two sons.

GEORGE RICHMOND-BROWN Robert led his own life at Eton, but he was liked, wasn't unpopular at all. He was just different. He shouldn't have been there. He did break out on odd nights . . . What he got up to I don't know.

JOHN McEWAN He was always at nightclubs. The Eton tails looked fairly natural on him. I think Robert just spent the whole bloody time in London. He'd turn up at Early Schools wearing a dinner jacket, slightly rearranged. Therefore he didn't stay long in the senior year. He was very sophisticated and must have found school a nightmare, just waiting to get on with his life.

All my fags are ill in bed, which is rather annoying, as you can imagine.

GILES ST AUBYN It was not all that long after the war that Robert was at Eton and public schools hadn't changed all that much, not at all really. They were still training people to run the Empire, which hadn't quite vanished by then. So there was tremendous emphasis on leadership and character – completely gone now. So you grew into the responsibilities you were given, mainly in your own house. When you became a prefect (which they call the Library), you were meant to show you were of sterling Empire-building officer-like quality. So however naughty you'd been before, that was forgotten and forgiven. Now you were meant to be on the side of authority, play it absolutely straight. It was your job to keep others in order, so you kept yourself in order, you behaved yourself. That was tremendously deep in the ethic.

ALASTAIR LONDONDERRY Robert was a bit of a character then, you know. Certainly never fitted in to what the Etonian establishment demanded of its students. I'll say *that* again! The Groovy Bob side to his character only appeared later, but I think Robert was regarded with suspicion even then. He was often in trouble of one sort or another, but then he was caught smoking and it was reported. There may have been an accumulating number of reasons, whether it was that particular thing, the smoking – that might have been the last straw that broke the camel's back. In those days Eton was sufficiently rooted in the past to want to cut him down to size.

GILES ST AUBYN I think word had got out that Watkin's Library was not what a Library should be. It's very, very difficult for a headmaster to pull a house together which is going off the rails. I think that Pop, who were the supreme boy authorities, were egged on . . . They might have done it off their own bat – Watkin's house needed a real shock. There was a rumour that boys were smoking on the roof of Watkin's house. The smell doesn't go away of course. It was a terrible crime and you had to take a lot of trouble not to be caught doing it. Hence smoking on the roof.

Anyway a watch was put on them and a tremendous example was made of them. Perhaps also as an oblique shot across Watkin's own bows. That was a rather large episode in schoolboy terms.

ALASTAIR LONDONDERRY It was a time when boys were allowed to beat other boys, like *Tom Brown's Schooldays*. And it was pretty awful when you think in Robert's case he was Pop-tanned with that awful cane which is double the width of a swishing bamboo cane and it had ridges, what I call SS ridges, all the way down.

The cane was probably about two and a half feet long and very nearly an inch thick – (thickness played its part in Robert's life even then). It was the President of the society of Pop, in Robert's case it was a scum-bag called Ricketts, who administered the Pop-tan, which was not only undignified but sadistic. Some very unpleasant person saw him smoking from the roof of College Chapel, who equally deserves a premature death, and reported him to this odious creature, Ricketts – whom I saw in the street about fifteen years ago and very unfortunately I resisted the temptation to run over him in my car; talk about justifiable circumstances . . . At the age of eighteen, the thought of one eighteen-year-old Pop-tanning another one. Now anyone who had the slightest trace of civilization in them would have said, 'Well, sod it, he's leaving anyway,' and that's it. But this chap Ricketts was an odious, conventional character and sadistic, obviously, as well. And liked to abuse his power. And Robert was a bit of a bohemian character, rebellious and just the sort of person to be cut down to size. There was always the temptation for one boy to be cruel to another – cruelty amongst children is well known – and for boys to abuse their power. Luckily they usually get cut down to size once they leave school. But this chap – I ought to have cut him down when I saw him in the street, but I think he wasn't worth going to jail for.

NICHOLAS FRASER Robert was then sent down in the very last half or asked to leave two or three weeks before the end of the half. It was done deliberately, that once and for all we'll get rid of this turbulent boy. It was meant to have a chastening effect on Robert. Didn't work.

GILES ST AUBYN Robert was a bit of a mystery to everyone I think. You were never quite sure you'd got to the bottom of him. He was the sort of person who attracted legends. And some of them may not belong to him. Certainly the army, which was to follow, would not have been a good choice for him, because he wouldn't have liked the discipline.

NICHOLAS FRASER I don't think my parents talked about this episode, I don't remember it being discussed. In his book is the phrase to the effect that sending us to Eton was to join the best club in the world so I think my father may have found Robert's antics a disappointment, but at the same time Robert was a very interesting person and my father was devoted to him.

LIONEL FRASER Yes, I am glad I made the effort to send my sons to Eton, so rich in history, so mellow and, I believe, quite as well geared to the modern conditions as other less traditional schools.

On the whole I venture to think Eton passes the test well and that my experiment has been successful, although I speak merely as an observant father of two Etonian sons. I do not anticipate that, even in this rapidly changing world, an Old Etonian tie will work to the detriment of the wearer.

Robert's official leaving photograph in 1955.

JONATHAN HOPE I remember a lunch in Brasserie Lipp with Bruce Chatwin and Robert and myself. Robert started talking to me, very pointedly, about Eton: did I remember this or that? He obviously loved his time there. Bruce was getting more and more uptight: 'So maddening, the way these people go on and on about their public schools!' But that didn't shut Robert up, more like a red flag to a bull. He just went on: 'Do you remember the colours test? Do you remember what colour the boats were? Maroon with green quarters. Do you remember the field colours?' etc., etc. Bruce was apoplectic, his eyes popping out: 'Oh, shut up! *Shut up!*'

J. PAUL GETTY This is his Eton leaving photograph – he gave it to me and I keep it up here. Yes, he does look very confident in it. Don't you think perhaps a little *too* confident?

3 A Bit of an Amusing Character

As Lionel and Cynthia stood with the other parents watching their sons in the passing-out parade at Caterham, though perhaps disappointed with Robert's exclusion from the most prestigious Guards regiment, they were at least glad that he had passed his officer training and hoped that he would learn a few sensible lessons during his time in Africa, so that his failures at Eton could be forgotten. This seemed unlikely, though, as Africa would provide little in the way of his sort of amusements and Eton had not impressed upon him many of the qualifications needed for leadership.

However, it was unavoidable, so he was prepared to make the best of it, though his boredom in the face of his companions' enchantment was to set a lifelong trend of offending those with less sophistication than himself.

2nd Lieutenant Robert Fraser in the King's African Rifles in Uganda.

COLONEL PEDDIE I think Roger had seen somewhere that Robert was running this art place. And so he went in. There was Robert Fraser looking at him. He went up to him and said, 'I'm Roger Perkins and we served in the King's African Rifles together.' 'Oh,' he said, 'well, that's a phase of my life which I'm trying to forget.' Which seemed to me to be rather sad really, because for the average young man it would have been the most fantastic phase of his life.

ALASTAIR LONDONDERRY A picture I've got of Robert is of him with his regiment. I had it enlarged. It's absolutely wonderful. Robert and all those black men. He was always supposed to have a great weakness for black men. A sort of male version of Lady Mountbatten. ■

ROGER PERKINS National Service – well, in those days, on their eighteenth birthday, everyone would have to go and do their ten-week basic training; everyone mucked in together. Robert would have gone in as a squaddie to Caterham, which was a Brigade of Guards basic depot. He would have gone through the first few weeks polishing his boots, learning how to keep his locker tidy, that sort of thing.

Dear Mummy & Daddy,

Well here's how! Still alive. Although you haven't a moment you can call your own the whole day, there are plenty of laughs to be had. Can't spare much time as I have got to get back to my brasses! Drill starts tomorrow, up till now it's been all spit & polish. My address is Recruit R. Fraser N.Y.A. A Brigade Squad, Guards Depot, Caterham, Surrey.

ROGER PERKINS They would say, 'Right, well, you've been to a good school, got your school certificate, you will be going to a Potential Officer Course.' He would then have gone to Hartley Whitney for the War Office Selection Board. For three days he would have been put through essentially leadership challenges, leadership tests, initiative challenges. You were split up into groups of seven: e.g. Objective – how to cross bottomless chasm, here's a bucket, a piece of string, etc. 'Right, chaps, here's what we'll do,' etc., etc. All the time watched. Do you panic under pressure? Do chaps listen to you? Have you the ability to formulate a simple little plan? After three days you were called in to a final interview with a colonel and a group of officers. The first question was always, 'How do you think you got on?' A tricky question! Then, 'Why do you want to be an officer?' Again, a question loaded with perils!

If you passed you were sent back to Caterham, then after about a week you were given kit and sent off to an Officer Cadet School. In those days there were two: the Brigade of Guards guys went to Eaton Hall outside Chester, at one time ancestral home of the Dukes of Westminster – a vast Victorian Gothic pile – horrible!

Dear Mummy & Daddy,

Here is the letter I promised you over the weekend. We have not been able to go away this weekend, because our weekend was stopped by the Platoon Commander because our rooms weren't good enough, which was rather a bore.

Did you read that rather amusing article by Cyril Ray in the Sunday Times last week about Eaton Hall; good up to a point, but then he could hardly be expected to convey the horrific side of the place!

I haven't received any intimation either way whether I am in the Grenadiers or not yet, but I should know in a few weeks.

I have no idea whether it will be yes or no, but I have done my best so I hope I shall come through O.K.

ROGER PERKINS Towards the end of the four months at Officer Cadet School you were given a piece of paper on which you had to set down preferences for what you wanted to do after you got your commission: e.g. Do you want to serve with your own parent regiment (in Robert's case, the Grenadier Guards)? If no, what would be your preference to be seconded to?

CHRISTOPHER FINCH Robert told me about going into some Guards regiment, that he hated it and requested to be transferred out. I think he felt the Guards was just a continuation of school, that's why he wanted out. So I don't think he got into trouble. He just found it very boring, school-like.

ROGER PERKINS There would have been only two reasons why somebody in Robert's position would not have gone to 1st or 2nd Battalion Grenadier Guards at that time. The first reason: some elderly or not so good regular soldiers would have needed an easier option. That wouldn't have applied to Robert. The second reason: they may simply not have needed any more officers at that time. The National Service machine was bringing in tens of thousands of young men. Didn't always have need for all the officers with all the well-educated young men coming in. It was an expensive business being a Guards officer, the pay was better in the King's African Rifles. But that wasn't a problem with Robert, was it?

COLONEL PEDDIE My feeling was that Robert wasn't really good officer material. I suspect influence or bad judgement got him through the whole procedure. I wouldn't say he wasn't disciplined enough to make the grade – that's putting it rather strongly. But I don't think he was dedicated enough. Let's put it this way: Robert Fraser came first in his priority of things.

LIONEL FRASER Robert, having to do National Service, was posted to the Grenadiers as a guardsman. Finding the Brigade unwilling to adapt itself to his personal idea of discipline, he was commissioned to the King's African Rifles and served a cooling period in Uganda with that first-class African regiment.

Tomorrow morning very early we go off to Jinga, where I will write again when I have settled down and am able to assimilate things more in this strange country. Love Robert.

ROBIN DUTT: *You were in the Army, weren't you?*
ROBERT FRASER: *Yes, along with hundreds of thousands of others.*
ROBIN DUTT: *Ah, but you weren't any old trooper. I believe you were in Africa. In the East African Rifles?*
ROBERT FRASER: *The* King's *African Rifles!*
ROBIN DUTT: *What was that like?*
ROBERT FRASER: *A fucking bore. Have you ever been in the Army?*
ROBIN DUTT: *No, conscription was before my time.*
ROBERT FRASER: *It was thirteen months of purgatorial boredom.*

COLONEL PEDDIE And I got the impression that he thought it was all just a little bit of a bore, but why it should have been I can't imagine, because it was brilliant for a young man going out to Africa and seeing all the game and the wildlife and training with African soldiers, being part of a jolly good battalion, a very happy battalion. I can't think why, because the Uganda we saw was the most wonderful place.

The work does not seem to be very demanding; as this is a peacetime battalion, the only danger seems to be that of getting very bored. At the moment of writing this I am sitting at my desk in the company office, writing this as I have got no work to do. Such work as there is is mainly office work, as the officers do a lot of clerks' work which cannot be trusted to the Africans.

From Jambo Effendi *by Iain Grahame (Army contemporary)*
Tall gum trees shimmered like aspens in the cool breeze, cattle grazed contentedly in the meadows, and a sweet smell from the wattle trees pervaded the air. Everywhere the arrival of the train was greeted by impish grins and happy laughter.

I came up last Friday by train from Nairobi; quite a pleasant sleeping compartment provided by the army, food likewise socked. The train however was agonisingly slow, taking a day and a night to do 400 miles or so. The scenery is very tropical and quite unlike Kenya. About my money . . .

COLONEL PEDDIE My experience is if you can speak the language you get to know that their sense of humour is the same as ours, they laugh at the same things, they cry at the same things, and you will really get to understand people. But I don't think that Robert Fraser made any effort to get to like the job he had, or really got to understand who he was serving with.

My Swahili progresses slowly, mainly confined to stumblingly articulated instructions to my servant Albert by name, such as 'Anja happa san moffa na oobo' (wake me at 7.15 o'clock) and 'Tangancza kitandu upesi' (make my bed and get on with it!).

COLONEL PEDDIE We looked for a fairly high standard amongst the young officers, and although he never put a foot seriously wrong he just had that chip which quite a lot of young men had sometimes . . . Well, this was the thing, he had too much money.

Our ex-C.O. who has gone back to England as a full Colonel has now been replaced by one Col. Peddie who has just come back from Malaya. He seems a nice enough chap, although it is too early to form a distinct impression.

COLONEL PEDDIE As a commanding officer you don't get down to know the subalterns, you only get to know the superficial. You aren't sitting alongside them, listening to what they say and laughing at their jokes and taking part in their pranks and so on, so you don't really see . . . you only see half a picture.

   Robert was a subaltern, and he was a little bit troublesome as a subaltern. I think one wouldn't want to be unkind, but . . . Of course, I'm in my declining years, and he would have been half my age, and one tries not to be pompous, and I have never tried to be pompous with young officers because I think one has to get to know them, and the way of getting to know them best is to go and sit with them in the mess . . . But he wasn't one of those people one felt one could chow down with. As I say, he was slightly standoffish, slightly – what's the word I'm looking for? – slightly removed in some way.

ROGER PERKINS I've known a fair few Old Etonians and there seems to be no middle ground with them. Either they are absolutely cracking people, really super-dooper people, or they're really not very nice. It's either one or the other, and I think Robert came in the second category, as far as I personally was concerned.

ALISTAIR FLEMING There was obviously a bit of jealousy. Whereas Robert might have gone off to the top hotel in Kampala just to have dinner, the others would stay in the mess and would just go down to the club for a drink afterwards. They probably thought, Brigade of Guards, well, he's worth hundreds of thousands of pounds or whatever. It was probably just jealousy, actually. I enjoyed his company. He was a bit of fun. He was just a hell of a nice person.

I am taking my driving test here at the end of the month, and wondered if you could see your way to helping me get a little 2nd hand car, which I could get for between £200 and £225. I have seen a Morris Oxford for £225. The thing being that without something one is completely marooned in the barracks; too far to walk to Jinja and 60 miles to Kampala.

COLONEL PEDDIE About the car, yes. Firstly he quite correctly came along and said he could buy a motor car, and because he had his father's permission to do so he could get the money for it. And so we said, yes, fine, no reason why you shouldn't have a motor car. And then of course the next thing one heard in about a month's time was that he'd pranged it in some escapade or other.

Now to some very bad news. Since I last wrote I have had a smash up in the Consul. I was hit by an African driver driving up the crest of a hill on the wrong side of the road without dipping his lights . . .

ALISTAIR FLEMING His car – in my book it was a sports car. When he drove I had to make sure I had a few drinks inside me before we actually took off, because it was foot hard down all the way, and, well, he wasn't the *best* driver in the world.

He didn't stop, and I went into a bad skid, and made the fatal mistake of pulling the wheel round instead of driving into it. Subsequently the car overturned completely and righted itself. As you can imagine I am very distressed and angry. But I am lucky to have escaped without injury of any sort. Still, there we are.

COLONEL PEDDIE Then the next thing that happened was everybody expressed a certain amount of displeasure about that and his father wrote to me and said that an old friend of the family, a man called Holland-Martin, which is a well-known banking family, was coming out to see the Governor and he would like it very much if he could see Robert at the same time and tell him of his father's displeasure. So I wrote back to Dad and I said that he had no great cause to worry, we were experts at looking after bolshy young men, and I didn't see any reason why Holland-Martin should come down really.

LIONEL FRASER Letter to Colonel Peddie (12 November 1956)
Dear Colonel Peddie,

I am indeed grateful to you for your letter of 7th November. You certainly have the position well in hand and my wife and I have derived considerable comfort from your most sensible summing up of the situation.

If you felt I could ever be of help at any time, please do not fail to refer to me. In the meanwhile, may I express my deep appreciation for anything which you may be able to do to guide my son Robert. As I said to you in my previous letter, he is not a bad boy but rather fond of sowing wild oats. I try not to forget that I was young myself once.

I now depart for West Nile, the land of sand, grass, sand and grass, and naked women, and grass and sand. First a three day trip up the White Nile from Lake Albert – shades of 'The African Queen', through crocodile and hippo infested waters, and then we start on 350 mile walk across the Uganda–Sudan border, with a good chance of a 'shoot up' at the end as there are plenty of bandit refugees in hiding up there. Then back by truck.

COLONEL PEDDIE Yes, he drank a lot. To coin a phrase, he would . . . I think the polite phrase is he would take the mickey, and he wasn't above taking the mickey out of his senior officers, and I can give you an example of that. We used to have the task of patrolling the Sudan border. I sent Robert off with a man called Jeff Jones, who was all right, but also a bit of an 'amusing character'. They sent through a signal message one day to the effect that they were very pleased to note that they had had a very pleasant night and that they had had pheasant, or whatever it was they had . . . No, what was it? Guinea fowl! And he gave me a detailed list of what they had been doing and so on, and I could see quite clearly that they were taking the mickey. That didn't concern me, because it gave the signallers exercise. But what did concern me was that they sent it in code, and this meant that some wretched man at their end had to sit down and put this wretched thing into code, and it arrived in the middle of the night at our end and somebody had to get up and decode it. And so it wasn't really very funny, and I ticked them off about that.

Fraser was just a slightly troublesome young man. I mean, one can't really say more than that.

I feel suicidally depressed coming back to this ghastly place after the most interesting and carefree time on safari. The last two weeks was the best when I was out on my own with my platoon in the bush on the east side of the Echoli, which is one of the best game areas in Uganda. I saw every kind of animal including lion, and even managed to shoot a Kongoni buck myself, which was eaten with relish by the coons.

We had our exciting moments, such as when I shot a cobra through the head at five yards with my revolver; and when a rhino came out of the grass in front of me at about ten yards, luckily it just looked and went away.

I had a very boring christmas, went out to lunch and dinner with officers' families in the camp. Roll on August. I'd like to go back into the bush for another 8 months until it is time to go back.

ROBIN DUTT: *What are your other African exploits?*
ROBERT FRASER: *I was introduced to the Kkebbabhh of Uganda.*
ROBIN DUTT: *The Kebab of Uganda?*
ROBERT FRASER: *The* Kabaka*! His Highness, King Freddie – probably the most civilized person I have ever met.*

FRANCIS WYNDHAM The Kabaka was the local King of Buganda, which was part of Uganda. He was mad about Robert, talked about him all the time, just loved him. The Kabaka was very sophisticated, rather decadent possibly. He was terribly attractive, Freddie, and I think bisexual. Robert would have been a godsend to him. He was terribly bored and really rather snobbish about the sort of colonial English people out there. Thought they did up their houses in a very middle-class way.

ROBERT FRASER: *I went to his country house. He had eight cars, two of which were in working order.*
ROBIN DUTT: *So what was his country seat like?*
ROBERT FRASER: *It was the grandest hut you've ever seen – about the size of Cork Street. The weaving of it was exquisite. After a shower I came down to the reception to meet King Freddie in a superb Savile Row suit or Guards blazer, with a drink in a huge pot. But you couldn't see what the drink was. Probably a pot of gin, though – drinks just flowed. I was only eighteen at the time, so conversation was pretty limited. We talked about clubs and food was brought.*
ROBIN DUTT: *Doubtless a grand feast.*
ROBERT FRASER: *No, but suddenly a lot of women came into the room – about twenty-five of them, all giggling. There was another light pressure on some part of my anatomy informing me that it was time for me to go.*

I went over to Freddie's last Sunday. He was very interested that his brother had been to see you. It is rather a pity because he asked me over for this coming weekend, but owing to this thing I shan't be able to. He had some quite interesting people coming, Francis Wyndham, the 'Observer' critic, and Nicholas Mosley, Oswald's son.

FRANCIS WYNDHAM Robert wasn't there when we went – off on manoeuvres somewhere, I suppose . . . There was a hippopotamus hunt on the lake. We all went out on these rickety rowing boats, and the guns were machine guns. It was absolutely terrifying. Thank God we didn't kill any hippopotamuses – I love them, don't you?

COLONEL PEDDIE Freddie was, I think, a Grenadier guardsman, but he was also, on the other side of life, quite a harum-scarum chap, because when he went over to the big city in London he had one or two rather doubtful girlfriends from Soho and other places, and one of the activities or one of the concerns of Special Branch was to prevent these ladies from stepping on an aircraft, which they were quite free to do in London, and landing in Kampala and announcing their presence.

We were a little bit concerned. By that time we had had one or two sort of brushes with Robert. We were a little bit concerned about Robert having the run of the Kabaka's household, so to speak, without a restraining hand on his collar.

ROGER PERKINS The Kabaka was neither one thing nor the other, and I don't mean sexually. I mean sort of black or white. I mean, he was a sort of King in Uganda and he was honorary Captain in the Grenadiers. Psychologically he must have been thoroughly messed up, I think. But he was certainly worshipped by his people

ALISTAIR FLEMING Robert suddenly said, out of the blue, 'How would you like to have dinner with the Kabaka, King Freddie?' And I thought, well, Robert, you know, I'd be delighted! So we set off in this red-hot sports car, and by the time we arrived in Kampala I was shaking like anything, because Robert wasn't the best of drivers.

Anyway, we were all dressed up in suits, regimental ties and everything. And of course they all had these wonderful servants in their various robes and everything else. Anyway, this servant said what record did we want to listen to? It was the first time I had seen a radiogram in East Africa. We looked through them and said whatever it was – old King Freddie had all the latest records of all the musical shows at that time running in London. Then they asked us what we wanted to drink, and I think in both cases we had very large gin and tonics.

Robert and I were talking and smoking away, and then the next thing I heard was the most perfect Oxford English being spoken: 'Hello, Robert, very good to see you again,' or whatever, I turned around and I just couldn't believe it! I thought it was going to be another white guest, but not at all – this was old King Freddie!

After a fantastic meal, old Freddie put on a dancing show for us out in the back – his tribe. They had all these dancers and all these bongo drummers, everything. We must have spent about four or five hours there, I suppose. We had the most entertaining time and he really was a very, very nice man.

ROGER PERKINS The only time that the likes of the rest of us saw the Kabaka of Uganda was on ceremonial occasions, such as, for example, the Queen's Birthday Parade, which was held each year in Kampala.

But it's as Alistair said it was, for him, a unique occasion to be entertained by royalty and to see how Ugandan royalty lived.

BRIGADIER KARSLAKE Bob Fraser was very laid-back indeed. Very shortly after I arrived in Uganda an extraordinary incident took place on the Sudanese frontier in which some rebels ambushed and massacred a number of Sudanese officials. It was a very long way from the frontier, where we were based. The British Army in its usual marvellously understated way sent one company of 100 men to throw this brigade out of Uganda, of which I happened to be one. Bob Fraser was also certainly on that expedition. I remember him being very much the old soldier – you know, he'd seen it all before. Which I'm sure was quite untrue, but that was the line he took. I was rather excited. I thought we might actually see some action. Blasé and laid-back were really what I'd say about him. I should think he actually was quite lazy.

It might be quite amusing, at least there is something to do, and the off chance of a fight. Funnily it is the same area as I was patrolling last December so I know every blade of grass.

ROBIN DUTT: *Your sergeant major was quite a man, I understand?*
ROBERT FRASER: *Yes, Idi Amin. There was a boxing championship and one of the fighters was Idi Amin. He won and King Freddie presented him with a trophy.*
ROBIN DUTT: *A prize fighter?*
ROBERT FRASER: *An enormous thug.*

COLONEL PEDDIE Idi Amin was a splendid sportsman, and he was also a very good sergeant major. He was a very good boxer, a very good rugby player and he played a very good game of hockey. In fact, my wife, Doreen, was watching a hockey match at one time and dear old Idi arrived with his blazer on and said, let me get you a chair, and seated her down, which was quite unusual for an African, because, as charming as they are, they weren't into that sort of courtesy.

BRIGADIER KARSLAKE Idi had been sent on a course, and I would have thought Bob Fraser would have overlapped with him both before and after the course, but I don't think he would have been particularly closely associated. There may have been more to it than I know.

MARIANNE FAITHFULL Idi Amin was a sergeant, Robert was a 2nd Lieutenant. Robert had a fling with Amin and he spoke about it years later. I didn't actually ask him if Amin was good in bed, but it was obviously an interesting relationship. Probably just a one-night stand. If he'd said he'd had an affair, that would be quite different. He saw Amin for what he would have been at the time – a nice, big, strong – well, don't know about nice, but a big, strong lad in the Army, under him, ready for a bit. Robert would blush, look pleased with himself, whenever Amin was on TV.

ROGER PERKINS I think the short answer is, homosexuality – Robert Fraser – East Africa – nothing, no evidence of any kind, and it would be quite unfair and wrong to hypothesize. And living in such a tight little community, you know, all bachelors in one mess and sharing the same bathroom and that sort of thing, it would, I think, very rapidly have been spotted if he had been making himself available, as it were.

And he would have been on the plane so fast back to London it wouldn't have been true. I don't think a bent bloke would stand a chance of staying there more than five minutes as that *wasn't* part of the scene – cause too many problems. Must have remained the same as we all did then – celibate.

This week is fairly full, as there are two big parades; I hope my last in the army, one on Tuesday as a farewell to Brig. McNab, followed by a party in the evening, then the Queen's Birthday Parade on Thursday in Kampala, with drinks at Government House in Entebbe afterwards.

It was quite amusing, but very strenuous standing erect with sword for endless minutes, while guns boomed and addresses were read. But my Caterham training did not fail me!

ALISTAIR FLEMING Just to let you know how badly we behaved – after the Queen's Birthday Parade a whole lot of us afterwards were invited by the ADC to go up to the Governor Freddie Crawford's house and have a few drinks. In fact, all the single officers were invited, including Robert. To keep us company, the ADC had also invited a whole lot of air stewardesses from BOAC or whatever. Of course, we all had quite a lot to drink.

On our way back, we dropped into this hotel which had a swimming pool and dancing. All I can remember was that suddenly people were taking on outrageous bets and I can remember a whole lot of us jumped into the swimming pool, which was floodlit. All the diners could see what was going on. We'd be accepting all these challenges – so many shillings a length fully dressed. I remember waking up the following morning with the most monumental hangover and my wet clothes *full* of all these shillings!

I think that I shall be leaving this place in about 6 weeks time. Yes – 6 WEEKS!!!!!

MICK JAGGER He would talk about being in the King's African Rifles. It must have been the last ten minutes of the KAR, because it was disbanded soon after. He found that very amusing. I think there were a lot of goings-on and he gave the impression that it was all a bit of a lark. Africa was famous then for being a den of vice and iniquity, and it was the last days of colonial rule – it must have all been falling to bits, all a bit of a shambles. Those were the days!

B Company march-past – visit by H. E. the Governor (Robert far right) photographed by Roger Perkins.

COLONEL PEDDIE I got this job in Chelsea and I used to go up every day by a train from Oxted to Victoria. Walking down to the railway station with my next-door neighbour, we were talking about the Common Market, which was then all the thing, and I said, 'I can't understand, old boy, why don't we just stick to the Empire?' And he stopped absolute – dead and he said, 'Where have you been for the last twenty years?' I had to say . . . well, I felt I was doing something to uphold the Empire but I came back home and there was nothing. I mean, the idea of an Empire had gone by that time. It was quite extraordinary.

ROGER PERKINS There's also a rather fine irony, isn't there, that here you have a representative of Her Majesty the Queen leading brave African warriors in front of a Governor-General with bands playing and Union Jack flying and so on – it was all the end of nearly 200 years of Empire – and he finishes up dying of the most modern disease you can think of. There's a kind of, I'm not sure how to put this, but my gut feeling is that there's a jolly good caption to go with that.

4 Garden of Enchantment

Robert had not managed to think of any way forward during the interminable months in Africa and so was condemned to a further two in Spain. However, the suggestion which came next, that he travel to America to improve his working knowledge of the art world, was one that met with his wholehearted approval.

For some time, New York had been the centre of the modern art world, much as Paris had been at the turn of the century. Although Robert's initial taste of America may have reinforced his early prejudices, once he'd touched down in New York, he was for the first time to find a city that neither bored nor disappointed, for once a place that lived up to every expectation.

Ellsworth Kelly in his studio with Robert, New York, 1960.

BILL WILLIS The time Robert was in NY was a very exciting period of history. America was very prosperous after the Second World War and it was a new era. The sixties was an era of social liberation, social barriers were falling, very creative. Those were glamorous times, but we didn't realize it. We were just so curious about life, feeling young, feeling our oats, the world was our oyster. We were learning in every way – sexually, intellectually, every way possible. It was wonderful, absolutely wonderful.

JIM DINE I had a birthday party in my studio for my wife Nancy in March 1960. Her brother was in college then, very handsome, and came down with a friend of his. Naturally everybody was really drunk. We all got into cars and went to a Greek restaurant to eat. These two young college students were very unsophicated, from Ohio, and they kept saying to Robert: Are you queer? And he'd say: Yeah. But he was still coming on with them. They kept saying: Come on, are you really queer? What does that mean? ■

I have simply no idea at the moment what I would like to do in life. I feel badly that I need qualifications in some line now. However, as to your arrangements about my going to Spain although it is quite a nice idea, what could I gain by it in the end? You say you think I could learn a great deal in Bilbao, but what exactly? I am not qualified in any field whatsoever, and Bilbao is a city more or less like Manchester in UK. It is not a particularly amusing or interesting town; in fact its limitations are considerable. However, I am taking a correspondence course in advanced Spanish.

NICHOLAS FRASER Robert had a great facility with languages, I think he picked up Spanish quite quickly. And he was almost semi-Spanish if you like in attitude. I always remember once when we went to stay in this sort of villa near Bilboa, I must have been about sixteen and he must have been about fourteen. Looking after us were – I think – twenty servants in the house. Robert certainly loved having these thousands of servants to order around, he rather went for that sort of thing!

Anyway, this time he went, I think he spent a few months there, mostly up in Bilboa.

I have now graduated to the diesel plant, which is Babcock's newest thing out here and really only in the experimental stage. I find myself interested though sometimes it is soul destroying watching, watching, – I long to be *doing* something. I went to a novice bull fight here on sunday afternoon, which was quite amusing as the torreros kept being tossed all over the place, none killed however. I was presented to a genuine matador in the hotel after the fight on Sunday – great thrill! With reference to my return journey, which I shall be starting exactly a week from today, I got the confirmation this morning. The boat leaves Dieppe at 12.00, arriving therefore at 2.30–3.00. Love to Nicholas and Janet and by the way, many congratulations to Janet on her sputnik-like ascent in the journalistic world! Looking forward to seeing you all on the 18th.

OLIVE COOK Robert didn't seem close to Janet. She was very conventional in what she said, but I don't think she was really. She was a bit like Robert to look at, but she talked like a girl who'd just been presented and I never felt it was her real self. She had this extraordinary vitality too and you felt it was seething there underneath. But she never said one thing that revealed her true self.

LIONEL FRASER Our eighteen-year-old daughter Janet, who had been applauded at her school for a stage performance on Parents' Day, earnestly wanted, like so many young girls, to make acting her career. The newspaper–magazine bug, however, caught hold of her and she returned to London full of determination to make her way in Fleet Street. Finally, after some disappointments, she achieved her desire and joined the staff of the *Daily Mail*. I shall never forget her joy. Then falling deeply in love with a fine young man, Richard Proby, she became engaged and was to be married on 8 May 1958.

OLIVE COOK Cynthia was delighted with the engagement. His parents were terribly nice, lived in a delightful small country house, very comfortably situated in life. They would have been very good friends for Cynthia later in life.

LIONEL FRASER But a few weeks before, when driving home one night together from Windsor, they were killed instantly in a collision, she twenty-five years of age and he a few years older. It was tragic for the Proby family and for us. They both gave such promise. Our daughter's ideals and standards had become so strong, yet she maintained a gaiety and purposefulness which radiated throughout the family. She was so full of life. Things were very different for us without her, but we shall always be grateful to her for what she gave us. We have consoled ourselves with the thought that the qualities which she displayed in such abundance are still available to be drawn upon and to be enjoyed and that we cannot be deprived of them.

NICHOLAS FRASER I think Robert was really very sad about it, because Janet and he really got on. I suppose, because I was in the middle, Janet and he were really better friends than, say, I was with Janet. Because he was the younger brother, no doubt I was always kicking him about, things like that. I always remember when Janet died and we went to this amazing hotel in Bournemouth called the Branxham Towers – the sort of five-star hotel in those days. My father wanted to catch his breath. And he took Robert and me and my mother of course to stay in this *huge* suite in this hotel. And we took with us loads of these letters that they had received about Janet having died. And we all sat down there reading these very affecting letters and I remember we all got very upset and emotional about it all. I always remember Robert being very affected by those letters. Although neither he nor I saw an awful lot of Janet during that period, we were very sad. I think Robert was quite affected by it.

I think Robert was attached to her as a sister, but I don't think that their way of life was similar in any sense at all. So I think he felt more sad about losing her as a sister than as a person, if I can put it like that. I don't think life stopped for him, or for that matter for me. I think for my parents, well, it affected them more.

OLIVE COOK Nicholas through all this was a pillar of strength to his mother. The only good thing in this dreadful story.

MRS MORRIS (family friend) She adored her daughter – Cynthia so adored her daughter, she couldn't mention her name for decades after she died.

ALASTAIR LONDONDERRY Well, you know, the artistic side of Robert, I was never aware of it at Eton. He went to work in a factory in Barcelona or somewhere, I can't even remember what they produced there, and then he told me afterwards he was going to America, because he was always interested in art. That's where I ran into Robert. After Nic and I got married we went to America in the winter of 1959 and we met up with Robert there. Robert didn't actually have a gallery there, but I think he was working in a gallery. No doubt that's where Robert was introduced to his 'dark side'! We won't go into that. But when he told me that he'd always been interested in art and was going to America, it was news to me. I'd no idea he was interested in art. I was absolutely – well, you know, in some ways, going to school and meeting people in school, you never get to know them until years later.

Naturally I have been thinking about my career. As you say I cannot vizualise myself in business. For myself I feel I would like to do something in either publishing or particularly some form of picture or antique Dealing. Though I realise the latter would require a lot more specialised knowledge than I possess at the moment.

KAY GIMPEL We knew his parents, you know, to wine and dine with. We were very fond of them. They used to buy things from us. One day, his father came into the gallery and he seemed very worried about his son. And he said, 'You know, the only thing he's interested in is art. What can I do?' After all, it's one thing, art, as a rich man's hobby, and another thing as a career. Charles said, 'I suppose for *me* it would be as if I suddenly had a banker in the family. I wouldn't know what the hell to do with him.' He suggested, why not surround him with books and let him go to museums and galleries to his heart's content if that's what he wants? And travel too, to other museums and other cities.

NICHOLAS FRASER Robert then went to Pittsburgh to work for Gordon Washburn. Washburn was married to my mother's closest friend, Ruth, whom my mother had met in Grenoble when they were both studying French there in about 1928–9. He was the director of the Carnegie Institute in Pittsburgh and ran the Biennale there.

JOHN RICHARDSON The Carnegie traditionally had this job – I don't know if it paid very much – but they came and worked on the Carnegie International. It was a very good way for an Englishman to get right into the thick of the contemporary art world. You met all the painters, all the dealers. It was the best possible introduction to the art world.

Since I arrived in Pittsburgh I have been practically all the time at the Museum, or out at a round of receptions and dinners with which the robber barons and tycoons of Pittsburgh have greeted the International.

KAY GIMPEL It was manna from heaven for Robert because he saw how you organized a huge international exhibition. He really managed to pull his weight terribly well.

. . . One's lasting impression here is that with all the money that has been made in this place over the last 100 years they have so little to show for it; and that is so ugly! This week the Jury have been awarding the prizes, and I have been with them the whole time, it has been a fascinating time and I have learnt an immense amount.

One and all are sickened by the choices of the Jury – who were forced into their decisions by the loathsome J. J. Sweeney from the Guggenheim Museum in New York, and everyone is agreed that the Henry Moore should obviously have got 1st prize, small consolation though it may be now.

It is heartbreaking to see the cold reception which a brilliant show gets in such an artistically retarded spot as Pittsburgh, and Gordon has every reason to feel frustrated when the products of his talents are wasted on such stony ground. This show of course is incredible in both its breadth, and selection, and in the brilliance of its layout, and everybody of discernment is realising this.

Pittsburgh society is of course as grotesque and ridiculous as rich Americana always must be beneath its veneer of bonhomie; but it is a fascinating experience all the same. It seems to me that any attempts at 'beau monde' existence bring out the most laughable features in the great American civilisation. Having only been in Pittsburgh it is difficult to find something new or stunning. New York is as yet an unattainable Nirvana.

. . . Well, I am nearing the end of my time in Pittsburgh, and on Friday will be moving to New York via a weekend in Washington. In many ways I shall feel sorry to leave Pittsburgh, although it has alternated between excruciating boredom and great interest, and has been a unique experience.

On the whole my ideas on America remain fairly unchanged, though my appetite to see more is whetted.

What a wonderful city is New York!!! I feel I shall stay here for ever and ever! So it looks now as if I shall be going to Knoedlers . . . It will be a job selling contemporary sculpture. The important thing is Knoedlers is a good step-ping stone, universally respected, having firms in London & Paris. So far noth-ing fixed on places to stay, but plenty of ideas.

DAVID HERBERT When I first went down to Pittsburgh, Robert was with Gordon Washburn. I had shown Louise Nevelson in my own gallery, and she and her son and I were invited down to Pittsburgh for the opening of the Pittsburgh Carnegie. There were about thirty tables and at each table was a Pittsburgh host and hostess. I met Robert that night and then we got along. I had six and a half rooms over here in 87th Street and I said, 'Why don't you come and live with me?' He said, 'OK, great.'

I am now living on 87th Street with a man called David Herbert, who is assis-tant to Sidney Janis at the latter's gallery. He is very charming, and of course knows all sorts of people who one must meet connected with the Arts in N.Y. How long this will last I do not know, as it is such a trial trudging around looking at dingy apartments.

DAVID HERBERT I always respected Robert. He respected me because I had an eye for art, and so we got along very well. And we'd go around to artists' stu-dios and it was just wonderful, because we both zeroed in on what was good. It was great to talk to him.

My living in arrangements with David Herbert are proving mutually satisfy-ing, so much so that I have decided to stay on here as the quest for fur-nished rooms is so arduous and unrewarding. He has a nice space, though it is not very palatial as he is very poor.

DAVID HERBERT The first week he lived with me we'd go to the store and he'd get this small change, pennies and nickels . . . Know what he'd do? He'd throw them on the ground! They were just too inconsequential! It was great! That appealed to me. I felt like doing that myself, but I wasn't quite as outrageous.

New York continues to be a garden of enchantment, though after the first flush of contact one's lyricism wears off as one feels it necessary to find one's bearings etc. However, suffice to say that I am very happy here, and there are *many* possibilities and plans for me in this place.

IRVING BLUM The most remarkable thing about Robert was his almost instantaneous understanding of what was going on in the art world in America. He understood in the sixties that there was this groundswell of real activity and he was able to sort through it in a very precise way and get right to the core of it.

JOHN RICHARDSON This time wasn't for him, like so many dealers, a pretext for hanging out and making new friends. He really did go after artists. Probably his friendship with Ellsworth Kelly stood him in very good stead. I assumed they'd had an affair, but I didn't know for certain.

IRVING BLUM Robert had an abiding and ferocious interest in Ellsworth's work. They may have had a thing. Robert brought early Kellys to London, even before opening his gallery. He was selling out of his apartment as I recall.

I send you by way of an offering a Birthday Collage done for you by Ellsworth Kelly, the famous New York artist, who is one of my best friends, and who you will meet in September.

ELLSWORTH KELLY I liked Robert immediately I met him. He was very likeable, friendly, and there was a certain immediate bond between us. I was just beginning my NY career, shows with Betty Parsons etc., and things were beginning to sell – very slowly then. Robert was a very courageous and flamboyant dealer. He had a big collection of my early drawings.

I hope when you pin it up on the wall, it will amuse and exhilarate you. I think it is amusing, don't you? Ellsworth likes doing these, just for fun.

ELLSWORTH KELLY There were nice moments when he came out to my studio on Long Island and we spent the day driving and joking. He made me feel good. He was lively. I introduced him to a lot of friends and he liked them. Robert was a good spirit.

IRVING BLUM Ellsworth lived in the same building as Jack Youngerman, who was married to Delphine Seyrig, as she became later of course. Then she was just a housewife, and they had a little boy, Duncan. And Robert Clark, who changed his name to Robert Indiana, the painter, he lived in that building too. And Agnes Martin. It was on a street that no longer exists, Coenties Slip. Right in the fish district, Fulton Market. It was one of the buildings torn down to refurbish the fish market. Kelly used to take dinner at a seamen's club just a block away. They lived there for some years at the end of the fifties, beginning of the sixties.

DAVID HERBERT Robert also had a little money and he actually made purchases, which was wonderful, because there were a lot of people who couldn't zero in, who were afraid to make a purchase. Robert was not afraid and zoomed right in there, and we went up to Kelly's studio and he said, 'I'll take that, I'll take that.'

A word about my plans; Knoedler do not want me for the summer so I decided to go to California for a while. I shall be staying with a man called Paul Sorel, who I met here recently, in Santa Monica, which is just outside L.A. He is an artist of sorts and 'au courant' with all the collectors around Los Angeles and Beverly Hills.

PAUL SOREL Robert Fraser was a fine, exuberant young man fascinated by the art of painting when I knew him. We met at the Ferus Gallery of Los Angeles in 1959, introduced to each other by Irving Blum, one of its owners.

During that summer, he stayed in my beach house at Santa Monica and spent most of the time not sunbathing and swimming but lying on the couch, his bed, in my living room. I had turned it over to him, and there he was, as my guest, entirely free to clutter it with books about painting and painters and various periodicals devoted to the fine arts. Indeed, he was devoted: culling out of that scrap heap of papers scattered on the floor all sorts of information that he presumed would aid him establishing his own gallery. From time to time, he would pose for me, indulging my wish to draw him while he lay reading, or he would sit for me when I wanted to execute a watercolour portrait of him on large thirty by forty-inch paper.

Paul Sorel, who I am staying with, is very agreeable and as he is painting and playing the piano all day I can use his car and get around. Actually he is pretty much of a recluse and doesn't socialise much. Santa Monica is a Nirvana of Palm trees, yellow sands, blue skies, hot days, and cool evenings – everything New York isn't.

PAUL SOREL That autumn, I rented a flat in Manhattan. He, with Irving Blum, David Herbert, Tom Wasserman, Delphine Seyrig, the actress, and other of his associates, would call on me from time to time. Being of the younger generation, his select group was not mine. But our meetings were always cordial: the curiosity of their generation to see my work.

During that winter, he invited me to make an excursion with him to the Barnes Foundation outside of Philadelphia, where we relished the excitement of being in that jungle of contemporary art. Like tourists in a safari, we were, viewing the wild beasts at a safe distance.

DAVID HERBERT Paul Sorel tries to make a myth out of himself. He says Robert lived with him for all these months, and through him met all these people out there. How true that is I don't know, but he's a fascinating man. He claims to have been very close to Robert, but I know for a fact that he wasn't. Not the way Robert and I were.

PAUL SOREL After that winter, we seldom met. I recall once, later, when I was again at the Plaza, inviting him to run over to Philadelphia. This time he was curious to experience the gay night life there. We went in a chauffeured limousine which I rented, and with a young, professional companion to the homosexual bars. The next day, after getting back to New York, when dawn had cleared the night away, he was most impatient with me for showing him that steamy area of American's deviance. He protested that such activity might destroy his reputation and prejudice against his opening a gallery. The difference in our ages and experience caused me to take his reaction lightly.

Once, when his distinguished parents visited him, I had the honour of meeting them at a party given by them in their hotel. It was on that evening that I also met Madame Marie-Edmee Escara de Ribes, a roving curator for Lord Beaverbrook's Canadian museum, with whom I became most friendly. She posed, indeed, for several portraits in oil. But that, although it is the most fascinating result of my brief friendship with Robert, is another story.

FRANK KONIGSBERG When I first knew Robert in New York he was incredibly attractive. He drank quite a bit, he was incredibly wild, both drinking and doing outrageous things. He was very puckish, with an elfin sense of humour.

He was independent, on his own, so he would drift in and out of things, very much like a bumblebee – he would land on one flower, then land on another. He'd cross-pollinate! You'd hear a lot about Robert – he'd be visiting artists and stuff. He was not afraid to place his bets on people. He felt quite strongly about certain artists. The art world then was different. It wasn't so money-orientated. Robert was a little celebrity-orientated though.

JIM DINE I met Robert around 1960. My stepmother's brother, Stanley Posthorn, brought him to my studio. He was an art collector. Robert bought $1,400 worth of work, which was enormous then. And he was the first person who put down some money for me. Here's this guy, twenty-two years old! That was more money than anyone had laid on me up to then. We instantly became friends. He was part of my life until he moved back to London about two years later.

Quite frankly I feel my future may well develop in this direction, i.e. that of a private dealer. I can gradually work up my turnover until I can get together the capital or subsidy to have a *buying fund*. Every day, by being on my own I am learning more about the art business than I could in an office. Right now I have nearly $50,000 worth of pictures consigned to me, and I can gradually work this up. That's not too bad for 9 months in New York.

JIM DINE During that time here he was a private dealer. He was like a gentle-man dealer, but not really. He was hardly a gentleman and not much of a dealer.

FRANK KONIGSBERG He had plenty of money, I guess, and lived in bursts of lavishness. He was very free with money, not always his own. Then he would have these periods where he had no money at all. He'd be scrounging in a sense, in that you'd have to pick up the check, otherwise you'd be washing the dishes. But that wouldn't stop him from ordering great wines or lavish meals. He did-n't have an accountant's view of money. If it was there, you spent it. If it wasn't there, someone else would provide. He was always doing terrible things. He would borrow money and you'd never see him again. You'd give him the money and he'd disappear!

David (Herbert) and I, and Frank Konigsberg, a young Jewish lawyer in C.B.S. and good friend, hope to fly to Puerto Rico on the 24th staying until about January 1st.

FRANK KONIGSBERG He liked to push the boundaries of acceptable behaviour. He was promiscuous in a polymorphous way. I was living with this woman who later became my wife, and Robert would have been just as happy to lie down with all three of us, or two of us, or none of us, or whatever hap-pened to come around. He was a great aesthete. He was a great sybarite too, indulging himself sensually. Then he was the object. Later when I knew him, he was the older, more experienced one. When I first met him he was like a flower.

JACK YOUNGERMAN I knew Robert from about 1959. He was young, handsome and charming. I met him through Ellsworth Kelly. He brought Frank O'Hara down to our house and studio. That's when we lived down a street called Coenties Slip in New York, near the Staten Island Ferry, the fishing dis-trict. That's where myself and Kelly, Bob Indiana and other artists lived. I sup-pose the main thing about Robert was his charm; a kind of poetic charm. And a very real interest in the arts. I dunno, I think maybe the arts were more a vehi-cle for Robert. I think his real interest was more the zeitgeist, the poetry of the times. I mean the street poetry and the social poetry.

DAVID HERBERT At least once a week we went up to Harlem. In those days there wasn't any fear at all, not much anyway. I had some black friends and we always went up with them and so we were part of them, so we were accepted. Sometimes we went up without our black friends, but there wasn't the fear as there is now. Robert loved to go to Harlem . . . and the audience response at the Apollo! Oh, my God!

But it wasn't only for the music, it was also he sensed a freedom in those people, a style he admired. Robert and I, we were great aficionados of style, and to see those people! How they dressed, how they carried themselves, it was just heaven. And that's one of the reasons I got along so well with Robert, because he did have flair. He had *style*, he really did.

JACK YOUNGERMAN He had a sense of the city. On a number of occasions we would go down to Harlem, to the Apollo theatre there, or to Count Basie's restaurant. I remember going to a number of places like that with Robert. We were friends, yes, I guess that's what it comes down to.

JOHN RICHARDSON One of the odd things about Robert was that he always dressed up. The rest of us were in blue jeans and leather jackets and up to no good in the Village, but Robert always had an impeccable blazer, very Old Etonian, consciously so. I suspect he had slight chips on his shoulder about his father. There was a streak of the old-fashioned servant in a way.

JIM DINE Robert was always fanciably dressed, always done up like a Guardsman, with very structured English suiting, and those wide shirts – fancy from the forties and sixties, the way upper-class people dressed.

JOHN RICHARDSON You could see that he was a butler's grandson. That's what one liked about him, this flash side, which he never tried to gentrify at all.

Just lately I have suddenly become madly social. This is mainly due to Jane Stewart's being here, as she has been toting me round with her to all the Society Balls and dances, which are a dime a dozen at this time of year. Actually they are more fun than the equivalent affairs in London, because they are more lavish, and the flavour is much more 'international', viz. film stars, South American millionaires etc.

Jane is so marvellous, we see each other every day. I am trying to persuade her to stay on in New York for ever. She illuminates the scene.

FRANK KONIGSBERG Robert always liked exotic types. He compartmentalized his life quite a lot though. He liked to slum a lot, he really liked the gutters, but he also liked the Park Avenue circuit.

KENNETH JAY LANE I met him in the south of France. He was staying with Angelo Ponce De Léon. I was staying in Fiorentina, which was a very posh house belonging to Edith Kenmare and Rory Cameron. Robert would appear with Angelo – very pleasant, very nice . . . you know, funny. And he'd wear the English idea of sports clothes – the trousers to a pinstripe suit, black shoes, white socks and a white shirt with the sleeves rolled up, or a T-shirt. He was just starting to be involved in art.

Rory Cameron wrote travel books and his publisher was Heinemann. Robert was at lunch one day and rather at the last minute Rory's publisher was coming, the head of Heinemann. And I remember that Rory was a bit nervous about the way Robert looked, in his not-very-chic clothes. He was astoundingly unchic, let's put it that way! As soon as the publisher came, the first person he went up to was Robert! I think it was, 'Mr Fraser! How are you? How's your father?' So Rory was sort of, 'Ohh, mmm.' You know, a new aspect – snobbism raises its head . . .

CHRISTOPHER GIBBS Kenny Lane will know about that time – they certainly had a romance, worshipped at some of the same altars – boys, social aspirations, wanting to be at *the* hip party, etc. Robert disdained it, but at the same time it was frightfully important to him. It's a well-known syndrome in those 'bachelor' circles – I mean the idea of tottering from Drue Heinz's to some louche bondage bar. He loved all that. Robert didn't tire easily. Bored easily, though.

KENNETH JAY LANE Next time I think I saw him was when he came to New York. We became fast friends . . . He had an apartment, a brownstone in 72nd and Madison. We became inseparable friends. He was great fun. I remember he had never seen a great snowstorm and there was this *huge* snowstorm, and we were playing leapfrog in the snow down Madison Avenue! We were young.

I have at last got the apartment under control – I think. I bought a very handsome Louis XVI 'commode' for the sitting room, and some little tables, and an upholstered chair, six 'Sheraton-type' dining chairs . . .

JOHN RICHARDSON I met Robert about 1960. I remember being friends, but where or how I can't remember. My impression of him was bright, attractive, rather glamorous, not totally to be trusted, on the make, very elegant, fun to be with, a bit secretive.

I don't think I mentioned that I have become very pally with a man called John Richardson, English but now living in N.Y. He lived with Douglas Cooper in Provence, and has written several books on Cubism etc. Perhaps you know who I mean. I have become quite close to him. He knows the American outback intimately.

JIM DINE I went to one party at Robert's and met John Richardson, who came with Drue Heinz and all these fancy people – Betty Parsons the art dealer was there – and Robert had two dry-cleaning delivery boyfriends. They were Puerto

Rican boys, and they'd do Latin dancing. They stole everything from him, absolutely everything. He loved that. Everyone could see this was going on.

BILL WILLIS I met Robert in New York in 1960. We went to bed together the first night, and then after that became fast friends. I can't remember, my dear, where I met him – in some gay bar, whatever. Robert was always trying to talk me into investing in something wonderful. He offered me a Francis Bacon then for $15,000! If I'd bought that picture, my dear, I'd be a millionaire! But he also tried to con me out of the two pictures I did buy from him, and did so.

This brings me on to a discussion of the future. I really feel that the direction I should work in is that of building up my own business, as I can't see any future in working for galleries on a salary basis.

JIM DINE One night I met him with his parents at an opening at MoMA. Robert was with Michel Warren, and he was stammering so much in front of his father. It was so obvious what the deal was, the power of the father. It was really amazing, Robert could hardly get a word out.

I thought I would sit down and write you an Easter letter, as I have the day off and am this morning sitting in front of a bowl of carnations, which I have just bought, and am feeling quite happy, although New York is rain-washed and dull-looking outside.

JOHN RICHARDSON Fairly early on came this extraordinary affair with Michel Warren. Michel was completely self-invented. He was a working-class boy whose mother was a sort of housekeeper. His story was that his mother won a prize for being the best manager, the best housewife, in France – handed out by some magazine or newspaper – and was very formidable. She must have been a very dominating woman, ambitious for her son.

JIM DINE Michel Warren was on the scene before Robert was his lover. He had a gallery with Ekstron and Cordier. I thought he was a very nasty, slippery character, a really slippery character. Rather pretentious and phoney. It was like a Central Casting view of a sinister Frenchman art dealer.

ARNE EKSTRON I don't think about those years. I'd forgotten about Robert. He wasn't a friend. He was the boyfriend of Michel Warren and that caused a lot of trouble in my life, because he departed to join Robert romantically. Michel just left me high and dry.

You see, my wife had given Michel a gallery in Paris and he made out very nicely there. He had become attached to us. We were a nice normal family who gave him very good advice and had great fun with him, because he was an extraordinarily brilliant and amusing young man, and was devoted to my wife. And after we moved to this country [USA], after a year or so, Michel wrote and said he missed us, we were really his family, and would we finance a gallery operation here.

We were so fond of him, and I suppose I shouldn't doubt completely his sincerity, but looking back over forty years you reach the conclusion that he made a great show of affection but was after whatever he could get out of us. But I don't want to withhold my belief in him totally. He was so funny, so lovable and so touching with my wife. He designed her clothes. For Xmas and birthdays he would bring these beautiful fashion sketches. I gave a lot of my wife's clothes to the Fashion Institute. At the age of twenty Michel was the chief designer at Lanvin. He was absolutely incredible – charming, good-looking. But he came from a very simple milieu – his dress and table manners! He turned up for a party at our house once, a black-tie affair, wearing a dinner jacket but a long white four-in-hand tie. We had to guide him on to the right lines.

JOHN RICHARDSON Michel was always adding little flourishes to his persona, and Robert gave him a whole new repertory. The English gentleman came into play, which was a riot. This French queen suddenly became very English, in tailored suits, a member of the St James's Club, etc. All thanks to Robert. The pair of them were faintly grotesque. Michel was madly in love with Robert and wanted to copy him, wanted to *be* Robert. Michel was very extravagant.

I have been giving a lot of thought once again to the problem of my future, particularly in relation to whether or not my present mode of operating can bring me the best returns. My thinking in this direction has led me to wonder if under the right circumstances London could not be a very good field. Dealing in the sort of 'merchandise' I have at the moment may not be able to sustain the interest for ever, by which I mean – Is it absorbing enough?

One cannot help but notice the tremendous stirring of interest in American art the world over, and that despite its 'réclame' how little it is seen in Europe. One cannot help noticing either the high prices that this art brings and how those prices seem to be continuing to rise for certain artists. Many of these artists with already established reputations have never shown in Europe, and although they are under contract here would be delighted to show in London under favourable circumstances.

This leads me on to the next stage: to mention that I visualise the establishment of a gallery of this type in London as not only a tremendously attractive way of getting in on the ground floor of an ever burgeoning market, but as being the only way of being able to show the top American painters. This would also mean that as a long term possibility (say 5 years) one might be able to either merge with another New York gallery or be strong enough to open up here on one's own account.

Does this make sense so far?

All this boils down, however, to the very basic fact that all this would need capitalisation, some of which might be forthcoming here, but the majority of which should be English. Looking at the costing, albeit roughly so far, I think between £50–65,000 would be needed over a 5 yr. period (subject of course to various securities, lease, fixtures, etc.). These as you see are only ideas, do you think though that on this basis so far, there is anything to this? And if there is my chance of capitalisation when and if the matter is more crystallised?

Letter from LIONEL FRASER

My dear Robert,

We got your long and expansive letter on Saturday morning and I am hastening to reply as speedily as possible.

We quite see that you must be straining at the leash and desirous of making very rapid progress all the while. All this we fully understand, and indeed applaud the attitude immensely. And broadly speaking we are convinced you are thinking along absolutely the right lines in feeling you can cash in on American art, which together with all that is to be found over here, means that it is really big business.

I do just wonder, however, whether it would not be preferable for you to consolidate your position more powerfully in the States before you make any further moves. Funnily enough if you have any disadvantage, it is that you are young, and although learning very fast with impeccable taste on the whole, are comparatively inexperienced.

There is so much to learn and so much to absorb and so many people to see and to handle, skill in negotiation to be imbibed also, that honestly if I were you I would sit on my haunches, even though very restlessly, for the time being and just concentrate on making your presence felt and appreciated more and more with those who matter in New York and elsewhere in the United States.

Please do not think I want to dampen your ardour in any way, but I feel you are not really wasting time, that if you took a step such as you contemplate too prematurely and without perhaps sufficient background, you might regret it later on. Meanwhile you can be visualising, and playing with, any prospects which may arise, such as the two which you mention. If you have got the talent, and we believe you have, there will be quite sufficient applicants for your assistance. You have just got to go on in a most thoughtful and concentrated manner, never losing an opportunity to further a new connection, however remote it may seem to be at the outset. Contact after contact, impression after impression, that will be the way to expand, so that in the course of time you will be able to work your associations as if you were playing a piano.

If you have any further thoughts you would like to explore with us, do not hesitate to drop us a line, we are at your disposal all the while and we fully understand that you are limited in those with whom you can expose the position delicately and objectively.

I am afraid I have got awfully little time for more chatter just at the moment. No doubt your Mother will provide this. We are very excited about the prospect of our new flat and we are collecting some very nice pieces of furniture for it. We climbed up there on Saturday morning and liked the outlook very much.

New York to London: I have a booking on the 'Liberté' at the moment for May 28, arriving in London on June 2.

NICHOLAS FRASER I imagine that Robert then came over to London specifically to bring Michel Warren to meet my father. The object of that would have been to persuade my father that now would be a good time to set the gallery up. Michel was in the gallery game in Paris and in New York and I think that Robert would have thought that to show Michel to my father would show my father that he had some experience behind him to start the gallery.

ARNE EKSTRON It was Michel who bravely faced Robert's father, the banker, and told him there ought to be some sort of gallery, so the old boy put up the money. Michel was crafty in a way; he knew on what side the bread was buttered . . . Michel's story was that he exacted a price from Robert for getting his father to finance the gallery, and picked out an elaborate stork from a Bond Street shop, all gilded and absolutely useless, as his reward for doing something for his lover. Michel was very generous but also calculating underneath.

London–New York: Arrived yesterday at New York, after what had seemed an almost interminable 6 days on the ocean. Had it been alone however I think it would have been far worse, as the N Amsterdam emanates a deadening combination of Protestant purity and Dutch propriety!

ARNE EKSTRON Michel also described to my wife and myself a visit Robert had made to his father. His father had been sitting behind a very big desk, with a certain distance to travel across this impressive office. Robert had apparently confronted his father, shaking with fear, and admitted he was homosexual. This had taken real effort on his part. He had been told by his father, much to his relief, that as long as he was a *good* homosexual it was all right.

CHRISTOPHER GIBBS His parents encouraged him with everything he wanted to do. You know, went out of their way to try to be understanding, accepting, learn about his things. I think it was a bit of a disappointment to him that his father was so understanding. I think he felt it deprived him a little of the agonies of being misunderstood . . .

NICHOLAS FRASER I'd heard that Robert was gay, so that wasn't such a shock. I never thought that anyone would have minded particularly about it, because he didn't have the ways of a gay, absolutely wasn't camp. I don't know how he struck other people, but I never felt he was gay in a conventional sense. If you met him you wouldn't think he was gay. None of the physical characteristics. There was absolutely nothing gay about Robert whatsoever. Nothing. I suspect I was taken in by that for years. We never discussed it. His friends probably knew long before I did.

I had a godmother I'd see at weekends and she would always want to discuss it with me. She was a sensationalist. I think she knew enough people in the art world to have discovered that. Rather embarrassing. She was the sort of person who was always trying to force people into making revelations into what they thought about this and that. That was the sort of thing that didn't appeal to me particularly. She'd say things like, 'What's your mother going to do about him?' That kind of thing. I expect I sort of retreated with a slightly pink face. Robert couldn't *stand* her!

Michel is well, and sends his best. You will be amused to hear that he sold out the Lindner exhibition that you were so sceptical about!

JOHN RICHARDSON Michel had enormous magnetic charm. He glowed. He was rather odd-looking. He could just *get* everybody in the room. He'd look round in a weird crafty way. He was very funny and the most marvellous cook. I remember him making a soufflé without flour, of whites of eggs and raspberries, which puffed up, obviously learnt from his mother.

We had a quiet thanksgiving in fact, dinner cooked by Michel; John Richardson came too.

JOHN RICHARDSON Robert was always promiscuous, a sort of discriminating, gourmet promiscuity. He'd tell you about this absolutely amazing young Puerto Rican, or this black with the biggest cock he'd ever seen. He'd talk about them as if they were a wonderful bottle of claret. Some of them became regular tricks, not really romances. I think Michel was the only one, and that was so much from Michel's side.

ARNE EKSTRON Robert opened the gallery in . . . 1962? That must be when Michel left New York to join him. That's how we were thanked for our help, by him buggering off, leaving me with my name on the door and the contracts of the gallery. Of course, the relationship with Fraser was all-absorbing. This was an intense love affair and I don't think Michel wanted to stay in New York. But Michel told terrible stories about us. When my wife died, we had been married fifty-six years. It had been an extraordinary marriage. And we'd done so much for Michel.

Anyway, after he left to go with Robert he was telling the story in Paris that my marriage was breaking up and that I was sleeping with my son. You have to be pretty sick to come up with a story like that. Imagine me carrying on an affair with my own beloved son – so fantastic. Michel then went wild, leaving me with this enormous gallery, huge rent, years of contracts with all these lousy second-rate painters. It was a challenge for me, but I had no preparation for it. I'd never bought a picture or hung a picture before. I felt so vulnerable, with everybody looking at me, expecting me to fail. Instead of which, I carried it off. My gallery was renowned from the outset.

That kind of betrayal, because so excessive, it's acting out some sort of guilt. I mean, we'd done everything for him, including providing him with a gallery in New York – I mean *everything*! And for so many years. He was the man who came one night to dinner and never left! We were just practically parental. And when someone turns on you like that!

NICHOLAS FRASER I thought Michel was absolutely creepy, a terrible person. Snake-like, someone you'd want to get away from. But, he delivered. The important thing is that when Robert was starting his gallery, Michel delivered Dubuffet, and no doubt a few others, and introduced him to people. He was the power behind the throne for perhaps a couple of years.

Dear Ma & Pa,

This is to say I am <u>definitely</u> leaving New York on the morning of Saturday Dec 9, arriving Sunday morning 7.30ish.

I am staying the full week because Michel has a big party at his gallery on the night of 8th, and wants particularly for me to stay. As it is only a couple of days more anyway, I said I would. Actually, it will be a very good <u>lancement</u> as very many strategic people will be there.

Robert, Lionel, Michel Warren and Cynthia at Robert's opening show, 1962.

JIM DINE I had an opening at Martha Jackson's gallery and Robert came and Yves Klein was there. Robert went up to him – I think they probably knew each other in Paris, maybe had a little action together – and was talking about the tailors in Nice (Klein was from Nice). I think Robert also knew the artist Armand, who was a friend of Klein's. Robert knew everyone in the world at one point.

I am, every day, more anxious to get home, and see you all; also to get started on the gallery which is going to be marvellous.*

All love, Robert

* I feel sure.

1962–1965

*Now back in London with his own
stylishly modern flat and gallery, both in
the old-fashioned heart of Mayfair,
Robert looked set to take advantage of
London's burgeoning appreciation of
modern art. There was generally beginning to be a new mood of energy in the
air, a desire for change, and this, along
with the absorption needed to keep up
the high standards his gallery set from
the outset, was almost enough to
counteract Robert's ever present restlessness and dissatisfaction.*

Robert photographed by Lord Snowdon at the Duke Street gallery.

CHRISTOPHER GIBBS My bond with Robert was Eton, behaving badly in every sort of way, going to sleazy clubs in Soho, etc. One of these times Robert and I were storming about Soho we went into Muriel's club. As we went in, Francis Bacon looked up and then to everyone there said, 'Here come the *Belgravia pansies!*' Robert was furious.

MICK JAGGER We have all these pictures of Robert-type people, along with famous artists like Francis Bacon – you know, gay, art-loving, Soho, Mayfair and all that. Robert fitted in very well with these people and, in fact, represented the end of that era – London in the fifties before these pop singers came along. Except we had pop singers even then – we had coffee houses and Cliff Richard and so on. It might seem laughable now, but it was part of Soho life, and part of fifties London. No one likes to remember this because the sixties seemed to obliterate any previous popular culture in post-war England. But the sixties of course didn't come out of nowhere. And these people like Robert who came from the end of that fifties time – were there, educated and prepared enough to pass it all on to the sixties people. ∎

ROBERT FRASER OPENS GALLERY IN DUKE STREET

Robert Fraser, the 25-year-old son of City banker and director, Lionel Fraser, is setting up as a picture dealer in London, with a gallery in Duke Street.

'I will be dealing entirely in modern paintings and sculpture. This will possibly include American artists, and English ones when I can find any I like – I have a couple in mind at the moment,' said Mr Fraser.
(Evening Standard)

CEDRIC PRICE I knew his dad rather well, and his mother. They were a lovely pair. I assumed his father put up the money – but it was dangerous to assume anything with Robert! This is what Robert wanted to do and his father was proud of it. You know, it was something new. There was no nervousness. It was very successful very quickly.

I got to know him through Nicholas, then I got to know him better than I knew Nicholas, whom I had known through Cambridge. The thing is, Robert didn't actually know of the work I'd done, together with a lot of people at the 'This is Tomorrow', so that didn't affect him. The exhibition was at the Whitechapel and was some years before the Fraser Gallery. At the time it was rather a startling design I think, startling as it didn't have any colour – very stark. Black and white sounds pretty natural for galleries nowadays, but at the time . . . There were some reasonably plain galleries, but there were far more plush ones. But then the work was far more plush, eighteenth-century horse prints and so on. Actually, they weren't so much plush, they were generally rather dingy. There weren't any comparable galleries in London certainly, in architecture or colour.

Robert had very definite ideas and he was also my ideal client in a way. He said when he wanted a thing. He agreed what he wanted and what he'd like me to do, or what he'd leave to me. He was the ideal client. He'd worked out his first exhibition. But what he was very clear about, a very good businessman, was how much money he had, and he told me how much he could spend, the dates he would want the things, and when he would get an initial idea and then a final idea of my design, including the fittings. He was perfect! He didn't do my work for me, and he didn't expect me to do his work for him. It was wonderful. In fact, I wrote about it somewhere: if clients know what they want, they don't need me – they need a builder. I'm too expensive. If they don't know what they want, but know what they want to achieve, then that's different.

An example is, we designed an illuminated sign in black and white for the gallery and it didn't arrive on time. He said, 'I can't wait for it, I'm opening tomorrow. It hasn't arrived, therefore we don't want it. Shall we do a sign?' I think he decided this – a square of wood painted white and the same lettering as on the illuminated sign. And we did that and we never paid. They'd broken their contract. That was marvellous. So many clients go soggy at that time and think, oh well, we'll put up a temporary sign and we'll get the other a day later. We kept the wooden sign. He never panicked, he was very hard – marvellous. He knew the dates, how much things cost, always paid me on time. The whole thing was beautifully run.

BRYAN ROBERTSON So, he came from a rather good family, he'd been abroad, he'd worked abroad, he knew the art scene quite well in Europe and America, and he certainly knew enough about England, about London, to know what they would and wouldn't take and what the market might be and who was selling what and where. And he had a great style. Hence using Cedric Price to do the interior of the gallery. Cedric Price, of course, being one of the great geniuses of this country, unrecorded and unsung mostly as he is. Wonderful. Of the first order. Maddening how he is tagged with others, because he has done so much more. However, there it is, that was Fraser. He started off very well.

DUBUFFET DRAWINGS AND GOUACHES
Mr Robert Fraser has opened a new gallery at 69 Duke Street with its high, wide, and well-lit upper room given over to a remarkable exhibition of recent drawings and gouaches by Dubuffet. Primitivism comes in no more sophisticated guise than from this artist. 'Rude', one could call his figures, in both senses. And even more pertinently, 'earthy'. For the good earth is never far from Dubuffet's conception of that ridiculous and disgraceful forked radish called man . . .

'I only appreciate the finer points of art,' said the man laying carpets yesterday, oblivious of the Dubuffet drawings Robert Fraser will have on show when his new gallery opens with a party tonight.

10 APRIL–12 MAY 1962: JEAN DUBUFFET

CEDRIC PRICE The first exhibition was the first exhibition in this country of Dubuffet in his black and white period. And of course it looked marvellous! I don't think Robert was recognized as much as he should have been.

BUT THAT BIG SALE PROVES THIS ART MARKET IS CRAZY!
London's most distinguished artists and art critics gazed at the graffiti on the walls of the new Robert Fraser Gallery in Duke Street last night and agreed that they were magnificent.

Their creator, Jean Dubuffet, a rather elderly enfant terrible, draws with the vigour of a child.

Sir Herbert Read told me, 'Dubuffet is one of the few European painters who have made a success in the United States. His drawings are vulgar – and they're meant to be. His aim is spontaneity. He is against every form of pomposity and academic art.'

Sir William Coldstream expressed his admiration of the exhibition, but younger painters like Bernard Kay, Harold Cohen and Izan Baz seemed bemused by the problem of how much further any of them could now go on the road to fashionable infantilism.

Artist Francis Bacon held court at one end of the room, while Mr Charles Clore, Mr Robert Melville, the director of the Arthur Jeffress Gallery, Mr Victor Musgrave, owner of Gallery One, and Mr Eric Estorick, owner of galleries all over the place, tried to get a glimpse of Dubuffet over the heads of the crowd.

Mr Robert Fraser, owner of the gallery, is the son of Mr Lionel Fraser, the city banker, whose tall, distinguished presence dominated the room. He told me that his son, even as a child, had a remarkable eye for painting.
(Evening Standard, 11 April 1962)

BRYAN ROBERTSON Well, the gallery made an extraordinary impression, from the beginning, because of its obvious sophistication and style. It had great style. The premises were agreeable and in a rather good part of London. There hadn't been a gallery in those parts, they were all usually further east, in Bond Street and Cork Street. This was a little bit of an outpost, but still a very elegant address. And the interior was pleasant, the lighting was good, the whole feeling was good. It felt serious. And the kind of work that one saw there, pretty well all the time, was of a very high order. Eventually it switched slightly or developed, from a rather more purist, slightly esoteric, slightly tough sort of stance on art to a broadening out, embracing Pop Art and a slightly more extrovert, cheap and cheerful, whatever, style. But still the gallery kept up its feeling of sophistication and seriousness. Also it was on a very good scale, it wasn't too big. You could mount a very decent show and show a work in some detail, in some depth, without going too far or getting too boring.

15 MAY–9 JUNE 1962: KALINOWSKI EXHIBITION

14 JUNE–14 JULY 1962: RICHARD LINDNER

BRYAN ROBERTSON And what good people he had: Dubuffet, Michaux, a wonderful artist . . . Matta, Richard Lindner, the wonderful German-American artist whose work I always wanted to see put on somewhere like the Tate, who had a kinky, strange eye on men and women and clothes and behaviour and all the rest of it, street life and interior life. Lindner would not have been known in England, neither of course would Michaux, neither of course would Alain Jacquet, neither would Matta very much. England had a certain sophistication at the time, but there were big gaps in knowledge. Certain things hadn't come the way of the English. What Fraser did took courage. It took a certain amount of guts.

EDUARDO PAOLOZZI I think he had a tremendous eye. I remember he had a Lindner exhibition, a bit before his time, and I took a friend of mine. We bought one; but I think that was the only one that sold. So, of course, much later on Lindner became much more famous, incredibly famous.

JANN HAWORTH When we first knew him, about '63, I went to his Lindner show, and it was a breakthrough to see something like that. Lindner had hardly showed in NY, was basically unknown except in Paris. Robert was wonderful in that way. He didn't need any credentials, he just responded to the work and got it. Lindner then went from strength to strength. In fact some of his best stuff was in that show.

MICHEL WARREN (poem inside Robert's Lindner catalogue)
Une petit fille sort du Cubisme. Elle en avait assez.
Une autre quitte ses Allemagnes.
Une autre encore, non cette fois c'est un petit garçon, se dépêche à velo (il a même emporté se jouets et voé ses parents).
Une grosse dame en retard termine de s'habiller en route.
Tout le monde s'est mis en pièces!
Ils ont tous abandonné leurs rêves pour s'y rendre, de vieux rêves trop usés par l'emploi quotidien.
Ils ont tous abandonné leur gris réalité dans laquelle ils disparaissaient. Ils ont quitté l'oubli pour se faire remarquer; ils vont, volent, courent chez Lindner.
La petite fille retrouve sa maman arrivée la première, son père est mort. Pourquoi? Personne n'y attache de l'importance. Pourquoi? Chacun est venu apporter une réponse, et ne peut se préoccuper d'autres questions.
En attendant de voir le peintre et de la lui dire, chacun fait ce qu'il veut, même des autres, ou d'autre chose.
Lindner? Cache dans son studio attenant à la salle d'attente, regarde par le trou de la serrure et peint ce qu'il voit.

KAY GIMPEL He had working for him an enchanting youngster, a Thai girl. She was an amusing kid and she had been at the Lycée with my son. She used to pop in to us on the way to the post office and she would say things like, 'We've had twenty people in!' or 'I've got *all* these letters to send!' She was like a kid. Her whole attitude was, 'Aren't we doing well! Aren't we splendid! Aren't we fine!'

BRYAN ROBERTSON He always had very nice-looking girls working in the gallery, and very nice-looking young fellows. And they were always very businesslike, they weren't just decorative young fellows who might or might not have been boyfriends, or decorative debby girls. They were actually quite reasonably professional and rather exceptionally elegantly dressed. Nice clothes. The fellows wore rather good shirts and rather sharp suits, and the girls wore very good dresses.

MICHAEL CHOW I worked for Robert for a bit. I think maybe I walked into the gallery one day as a painter. When I first saw Robert and the gallery he was really nice to me. He showed me paintings, took me downstairs. Once he made me go and pick up a painting, a Dubuffet, from Sotheby's for £10,000. Wow – what a lot of money!

The gallery was very different from the old school of galleries then. It was very avant-garde. Robert was always very hip. I learned a lot about style from him.

15 JULY–15 SEPTEMBER, 1962: SUMMER GROUP SHOW

18 SEPTEMBER–20 OCTOBER 1962: RECENT PAINTINGS EXHIBITION

23 OCTOBER–20 NOVEMBER 1962: HAROLD STEVENSON, `THE HUMAN TELESCOPE'

HAROLD STEVENSON I met Robert with Michel Warren. In 1962 I was invited for the famous Salon de Mai in Paris. I did an enormous painting for it which was kind of a scandal: of Iris Clert, my agent in Paris – it was her foot on the chest of a young man. You only see the chest and the foot in the painting. Anyway, it was a very large painting. Michel Warren and Robert Fraser subsequently went to the Salon de Mai and Michel bought this painting. The next day they went to my gallery and demanded of my agent – well, we want to meet this man who did this painting! So of course we met that day and were great friends for every hour that was left in our various lives.

One thing was, Robert was very beautiful in his youth and of course we were all kind of young and beautiful and carrying on . . . But a lot of fun, and Robert was very generous and it was through Robert that I had involvements with the English artists – Francis Bacon, for example.

'The Human Telescope': it was mostly the paintings of Timothy Willoughby, almost exclusively. And perhaps a piece or two of Alain Delon, the French actor. It was very well received. That is to say, it was controversial, so I considered that and Robert considered that well received. I was very much against the grain and so it was talked about, it was written about – you know, it was hated by some and loved by others. But it was well done and we were all very satisfied. We didn't expect it to become a sell-out overnight thing like that, but it was controversial and that pleased all of us. All of our group.

22 NOVEMBER–20 JANUARY 1963: KALINOWSKI COLLAGES AND GABRITSCHEWSKY GOUACHES

22 JANUARY–23 FEBRUARY 1963: DAMIAN PAINTINGS

26 FEBRUARY–23 MARCH 1963: HENRI MICHAUX

BRYAN ROBERTSON The early shows that he put on were simply marvellous. Because they covered an area that the English simply didn't know about. I thought that Henri Michaux was one of the great geniuses of the age. I had read his books, those marvellous novels and the poetry, and of course the extraordinary drawings: little flurries and flutters of brushstrokes. What he was exploring was totally independent and had a particular sophistication.

DAVID MEDALLA There was a Picasso exhibition at the Tate. I'd been acting pretty funny and got thoroughly drunk, drinking all this red wine and sherry – I was so young! My uncle, the ambassador, had taken me along to this big benefit supper. They wanted to invoke Spain with Flamenco dancers, so I'd jumped on the table and had done an odd version of Flamenco. Robert had really loved it! He and Sir Roland Penrose and his wife, the photographer Lee Miller. So I was just zonked out of my head, that's all I remember.

The next thing I knew I woke up in Robert's bed. I was still so drunk, I still had a splitting headache, and there were all these things by Michaux above my head, and I though, 'Is this part of my headache?' They were calligraphic, he said. I don't know anything about calligraphy, you know. He thought I might be Chinese. I was so embarrassed, thought I'd made a nuisance of myself. He was so sweet, said, 'I'll make you some breakfast. It's good to have orange juice because of all the alcohol in your bloodstream, you know.'

When I said I had a place in Palace Green where I painted, he said, 'Oh, are you a painter?' I said, 'Why do you suppose I was at the Picasso?' He said, 'Well, most of those people are not painters, they're the so-called Friends of the Tate!' Then he showed me all the works in his room. A bit later on he showed me a beautiful painting by Yves Klein, a blue sponge, that's worth a million pounds now.

NICHOLAS FRASER I remember one time when I came back from New York and I couldn't stay with my parents for some reason, so I stayed with Robert. I remember being reasonably amazed when I discovered he was keeping a young man in the bedroom. I was there, but this young chap was there as well. Quite bold. He was hidden away, not produced, but he was in there. Yes, all sorts of grunting and groaning all night long. I didn't discuss it with Robert, but I thought, I won't come here next time I come to London. I was amazed that he should say I could stay, then have these young men there. I never even saw this person. It certainly wasn't Warren.

CHRISTOPHER GIBBS Warren was madly in love with Robert. An extraordinary creature – very good-looking, slightly bovine, dark curly hair, lustrous eyes, strong neck, quite well made but very elegant. Michel was there all the time, in and out, telling him what to do, bickering and bickering. But the more besotted of the two was Warren. Robert was fascinated and intrigued, but Warren wasn't his cup of tea. If he'd been a working-class lout, Robert would have been strongly attracted to him. But he was in fact a piss-elegant queen, and so Robert wasn't.

It was quite a fertile relationship – but they weren't very nice to one another. Robert was always horrible to people that loved him. You felt he must have some terrible malaise deep within him. And he had.

JOHN RICHARDSON Robert was always rather mocking about Michel. He used the feminine pronoun a lot: 'She's so stupid, etc. He was rather funny about Michel, but I don't know why they split up. I don't know if Michel was on drugs. I don't know what he had wrong with him, but you felt he was very ill. He was always dead white and rather sweaty. Like a lot of flamboyant people, underneath Michel was cautious and shy in many ways, hence the passion for Robert, who was neither cautious nor shy.

HAROLD STEVENSON I think it would be untruthful and unfair to downplay the relationship between these two men, because the relationship was very powerful. They had similar interests professionally, that is. However, the final betrayal of the situation was that Michel became intoxicated about the idea of becoming a painter. I think Robert (well, actually I know, because we discussed it any number of times) was rather disappointed in Michel for becoming a painter. So that kind of terminated their relationship. But to think that this was not a passionate relationship would be a mistake. Robert was constantly in Paris and Michel was in London. All that made life very exciting.

I think it was a little one-sided in that Michel Warren was madly in love with Robert but Robert had a fascination with Michel. Around about the time he met Robert, Michel Warren was a very successful art dealer, with partners and all. One thing you can say is that Robert opening a gallery rested entirely on the influence of Michel Warren.

ARNE EKSTRON Michel then became a painter. A very tough gallery woman in Paris was showing his work. He was the most gifted man ever, just fantastic. He was a fabulous cook, he wrote rather well. There was nothing he couldn't do better than anyone else.

CHRISTOPHER GIBBS Warren died in rather dreadful circumstances not very long afterwards. He had a very broad knowledge of art and I got on very well with him because he was interested in all kinds of different things: in eighteenth-century furniture, *cloisonné* cranes – anything you'd care to mention he knew about and was into. And he knew about buying and selling them. A very good hustler, but rather serious. He knew all sorts of old ladies in Paris who had notable collections of twentieth-century paintings and sculpture, in particular Marie Cutelli. He and Robert pursuaded her to part with a great many of her possessions over the years.

He was that sort of French eclectic chic. We were interested in the same sorts of things. I got on well with him also as Robert's crony. And I was doing what I saw as art, Robert was doing what he saw as art and Michel Warren saw us both as being creative and interesting. Somehow I saw more of Robert. We'd go off and do something together, go to a concert, or stay up all night in Soho, or pick up three boys and get them drunk.

Or go out with Paul Danquar all night around Soho. Paul's a very camp black lawyer who lives in Tangier most of the time. He lived with Francis Bacon and Peter Pollock, had a flat over Prince of Wales Drive somewhere. He was a good-time boy, he liked dancing, getting drunk, always taking his clothes off and dancing on tables in restaurants. He and Robert did a lot of storming about in low dives. And quarrelling. Anyone who had anything to do with Robert at that stage had to quarrel with him. He was quarrelsome about things that couldn't matter less – quarrelsome about what you thought about a concert, about the frame on a picture, the way someone had done a party and so on. His behaviour was completely unacceptable in every way and of course especially financially.

PAUL DANQUAR My memories of Robert – charming, good-looking, confident, consciously rich and a bit grand. And adventurous in the arts as well as in 'trade'.

I have a very extrordinary memory of when Robert was getting very much into wild sex. I was with him, I don't know why, and he had somebody coming to visit – I think trade. And to my astonishment, the bell rang, Robert went to the front door and knelt down, so that he'd be ready . . . I said, 'Suppose it's the postman!' It was most extraordinary. He wasn't wild or stoned – I can't remember the circumstances. Maybe it was a joke. I don't remember the boy, what he was or what he looked like. I think it was trade, somebody who had been regularly before and who had come every day at two o'clock or every week. I was a bit . . . not shocked, but I was a bit surprised.

JOHN RICHARDSON Robert and I had very different ideas about cruising. I didn't like spivs – young working class, rough trade if you like – but Robert did. He liked rough young queens. Once we were just driving round, Piccadilly or Park Lane, and Robert saw this boy, obviously a real queen, and Robert suddenly said, 'I'm going to get him and force him to fuck me.' And apparently that's what he did. I think that happened quite often.

I think Robert enjoyed being the desired one. He would manipulate people into desiring him, falling for him. He did that with these tricks. He would get them to do his bidding. They didn't stand a chance once they'd been picked up by Robert. They would do what *he* wanted.

CHRISTOPHER GIBBS Robert was always drawn to the untamed, but like so many people he wanted both sides. He wanted to be standing on his head in some disreputable dive, having taken huge amounts of narcotics, but also to have been to Peter Miller's dinner party and dashing on to see Brooke Astor, all that. This tension remained with him until very late in the day.

ARNE EKSTRON I remember lunching with him once, at his club, and I drew out my cigarette case. He indicated that you did not smoke in that particular room. So he was conservative in that sense, and dressed conservatively.

DAVID MEDALLA In England he had to have a certain demeanour, a way of holding himself in public. He had a certain mask on him. I think in private life he wasn't that repressed. Very concerned with sex, that's for sure. Maybe he didn't turn it on with everyone, but he turned it on with me. He was very slim, tall and well dressed – pinstriped suits and dark glasses. He went to gay pubs without camouflaging his social background. Don't forget he was able to go to Paris and New York quite often, and in those places it was a different norm. You know, anything goes. In those places he relaxed. And then in England he was something else. It was like he was on stage in England – *the* Robert Fraser. He had presence, he had a certain dignity.

14 MAY–8 JUNE 1963: CHAMBERLAIN/STANKIEWICZ EXHIBITION

12 JUNE–20 JULY 1963: 'OBSESSION AND FANTASY'
Bacon, Balthus, Bellmer, Bettencourt, Blake, Dado, Dubuffet, Giacometti, Lindner, Stevenson

CEDRIC PRICE There was one exhibition which had Kiki Burn's bare breasts on the cover. It was 'OBSESSION'. I lived near the gallery and I could walk down and see it.

HAROLD STEVENSON He did this exhibition – I think it was called 'Obsession'. Of the living artists, I was included, Francis was included, Magritte was included.

Whatever I did in England, it would invariably involve Robert, Michel Warren, Francis Bacon and a number of us. We would all hang out at the Colony, which was also called Muriel's. You had to be so in the know. I thought it was terribly funny, being American and all that. All these very sophisticated intellectual aristocrats hung out in this absolute pit! It was such a mess, you know, but everybody loved it.

It was very interesting in that period of the sixties. It was a period in which Francis, for example, didn't paint at all, but just stood at the bar in the Colony and talked for days on end. It was all very fascinating. Francis would take the floor and he would speak indefinitely. There wasn't any such thing as argumentation – you either listened or walked out. Francis drank so much during that period and he was bitchy. Nobody paid much attention to it. I mean – so what?

Robert and Francis were great friends, of course they were. I know that it was in this same period that Francis wanted to paint Robert, but I presume that never did come about.

PAUL DANQUAR I'm sure that he and Francis had a close friendship, not a sexual thing. Francis liked him and admired him. Francis used to hint that I was having an affair with Robert, which I wasn't. I mean I liked him, he was marvellously attractive, and we used to dash around together, but we weren't each other's type. Francis had a wicked tongue, you know. I know they liked each other and Robert was part of that world, in and out of Muriel's and the West End and those places. Francis liked a bit of glamour. I wouldn't be surprised if Francis wanted to paint Robert. Robert was one of the early aficionados of painting to recognize Francis's talents. I can't swear to it, but I'm sure that Robert sought to give him a show at Duke Street – but don't forget, Francis would have been well and truly tied up with the gallery that preceded the Marlborough by then.

HAROLD STEVENSON Robert Fraser and Francis Bacon and myself and several others were all very liberated. Robert had a passion for Arab boys and black-lace ladies' underwear. But nobody thought anything about that. I mean – so what? I think it could be fairly said that we lived in our own world and let the rest of the world enjoy what they could. The liberation was very exclusive. We were isolated from everyone else. It *was* very glamorous!

The end of the sixties and what followed became a parody of the sixties for those of us who were the innovators of – not a movement but a point of view.

Now we live in a so-called liberated world, but all of this was almost unheard of in the early sixties. We lived a liberated life – but the rest of the world didn't. We went about our lives with total confidence, but we were not arrogant or anything. We were all close, and in a very open and jovial way – making no grand statements or issues or anything, just we were all intimate people who enjoyed the life.

I remember I wrote a short story about the group. We were all dressed to go to dinner, meaning in black tie and all, and we met at someone's house and were all sitting around drinking Martinis. And suddenly we all took off our clothes and had a playful orgy. Then we dressed again and went on to dinner.

24 SEPTEMBER–19 OCTOBER 1963: HAROLD COHEN, 'RECENT PAINTINGS'

23 OCTOBER–16 NOVEMBER 1963: ALAIN JACQUET

ALAIN JACQUET I met a lot of people through him. We had a good show, he sold all the paintings and even got a commission for me from the Container Corporation of America. There was an ad in *Time* magazine with that painting, and it is in Washington, DC, now.

Robert's gallery was just perfect, definitely the top gallery in those days. He'd opened it perhaps six months before my show, so I suppose he had support for the gallery at the time. Then he inherited or got some money . . . spent it all probably.

KASPAR KOENIG I went to England about 1963–4. Erica Brousen had the Hanover Gallery, which was a very important gallery in the fifties. I was looking for a part-time job and she suggested I go to Robert. My job with Robert wasn't really professional – more running errands, hanging around, installing an exhibition, that sort of thing. Robert was generous, but very stingy too. I don't think he was so good at paying people who worked for him. He would take you out for lunch, or if you were in a tight spot he'd give you a few pounds, but I think he was always in debt. Sometimes it was difficult for the artists. He wasn't professional enough.

But it was a very formative time for me and Robert played a key role in it. Being much younger, it was possible to have a good relationship and share a professional curiosity, and this was possible without any kind of conflict. Coming from Germany, where the whole class structure had been shattered during the Nazi time, the class system in England was full of intellectual exercises. But it was good to see this beginning to be subverted. The mix was interesting: on one hand the background of moneyed aristocracy and on the other a new aesthetic which was more cockney or working class. I think Robert was a real central figure because of his openness to both.

DAVID MEDALLA Robert liked teasing his establishment friends. He'd say about the art in his gallery, 'I don't think this will go with your Chippendale furniture,' or whatever. I would ask him, 'Why do you say this?' and Robert would say, 'They come in because they're friends of mine – they can't stand this sort of art.' He was also an early exponent of American hip slang, which used to annoy these rich posh friends. They didn't know what he was talking about.

Britain was changing. It was an empire once. Robert and a few other contemporaries changed the culture of England. England was in a transitional period, from being an empire, just about, to being pretty dilapidated. It had to find a new role. Maybe it hasn't even found it yet . . .

There are very few English people who are interested in what one might call modern or contemporary art. I think this has deep-rooted social reasons in that people in England who acquire money do not wish to invest it in art, they wish to invest in social standing. Therefore they are more likely to buy racehorses or country houses . . . and are therefore more likely to buy the sort of paintings that go in country houses.

In America this has not been the case, the people who acquired money have been able to project themselves. They have aesthetic leanings anyway, and have been able to fulfil their lifestyle and social desires by buying art, or supporting music . . . or things like that. Also, they believe in what is going on now, whereas there is not that feeling here in this country.

BRYAN ROBERTSON There aren't many art collectors in Britain. It must have been very hard for him. I don't know who and where he sold – maybe some European collectors, sometimes, that he came across through his friends.

MICHAEL CHOW He was the most amazing art dealer from an artistic point of view, but a very unamazing business person. He was a terrible business person. Someone would come in to buy a painting and he would look at them in a certain way . . . He then wouldn't sell it to them because he didn't like the way they looked. He was quite snobbish. If they were too vulgar, he just wouldn't deal with them. If you have very high artistic standards, it's difficult to be a good businessman.

London was very boring. Suddenly, around 1964, it was all happening. An eruption – a social revolution.

BRYAN ROBERTSON England did change, the cultural climate changed. People's perception of things began to alter and Robert was certainly primary in all this. I think that what he stood for and what he produced at the gallery, what he made people aware of, affected things a lot. He brought a new note into people's sense of art. Also he had a distinctive personal style of his own. It had to do with attitudes to sex, attitudes to travel, attitudes to the sudden ease of just getting plane tickets and going to places. Nowadays on my rather meagre income, plane travel is not all that cheap, I have to think twice sometimes, but in those days it was very cheap. You could go a hell of a way for a few pounds, it seemed. And he was part and parcel of that phase of England. He was among the first, in that he gave out a sense of being a highly sophisticated and well-travelled person. One foot in London, one foot in Paris, and if it were possible to have three feet, one foot in New York. And that was engaging and rather likeable.

The other thing was he was young, in his mid-twenties or something. He was a child. We wouldn't have thought of him as a child then, of course, but he was very young.

Personally, I've been more exposed to American Pop than to English Pop. That's because I was in America from 1958 to 1962, and when I came back, I hadn't even heard of Blake or Hamilton or Kitaj or Phillips. This was after the so-called 'Golden Age' of English Pop, and it was already losing its bloom. Then it took me another year or two to sort things out, and it wasn't until 1964 that I really got going and knew what I wanted.

American Pop is a more deeply rooted thing, born out of desperation with painting and with life, which gave it an intensity the European equivalent lacks. But English Pop is more playful and affectionate, embracing the American way of life. However, it was the first movement in England that was actually brought about by a whole new social attitude. The painters who were doing it were all – how shall I put it? – they were all unrepentantly vulgar . . .

20 NOVEMBER 1963–4 JANUARY 1964: DRAWINGS, GOUACHES, COLLAGES
Bellmer, Blake, Dado, Gabritschewsky, Kalinowsky, Rauschenberg, Stevenson, Twombly

PETER BLAKE When Robert opened the gallery he asked me if I'd go with him, so I was in right from the beginning. I went with him because I liked him very much. He was interesting and he'd got some other good people coming to the gallery. It sounded like an exciting prospect.

Peter seemed to be unattached to any gallery and as I was starting out then, I just asked him whether he'd like to show his work at my place – we seemed to get on so from then on he brought his work in as and when he felt like it. The gallery I was running at the time was sort of kinetic in atmosphere – I guess more or less a reflexion of the 1960s period – unexpected juxtapositions of people and events – I think that inspired Peter and turned him on. On the other hand it took me a long time to be able to take some of Peter's enthusiasms seriously – American illustrators, anecdotal Victorians and so on . . . all this is taken for granted now but then it seemed a far cry from the capital A R T that I knew from Mayfair and Madison Avenue.

PETER BLAKE Robert took Jann on when she was a young student, from the 'Young Contemporaries' show held at the ICA. She was one of the four chosen. It was very early on. She must have been in her early twenties. She was twenty-one when we got married, I was thirty-one.

JANN HAWORTH In the sixties it seemed to me things were very easy. I'm sure some didn't find it so. It was very lively. You could show, get reviews, go straight to the top. Wow! I thought you had to be thirty or forty before you got somewhere.

It *was* different from the fifties. Rationing was finished, people had a bit of money, could move about more, war damage was disappearing, the county was recovering. Young people could express themselves more through clothing, sexual attitudes, etc. There was style in photography and film.

TV began to play a part too, it was coming on-line then, so people's reputations grew exponentially because they were exposed to so many people so fast. You didn't have to be old to be famous. It all seemed so easy then.

My perception was of this place that was the capital, and in America you're never in the capital, you're always in a province. It was all happening culturally. It was alive. There were no provincial galleries then, so the hub was really the hub.

Robert couldn't be all things to all people, he could only have twelve shows a year, but you could say he was a maker of artists. He gave them that opportunity to explode into their art, which might not have happened otherwise. The freedom a dealer can give an artist to create art for art's sake fires them, sparks off ideas, produces a chemical reaction.

The paintbox that Robert's gallery was, the contrast between the colours of the different shows, was so vibrant. You'd have a Lindner, then a Bridget Riley, followed by a Cohen, followed by something else that was very dynamic. It was more like a treasure trove, treasure box, that you're finding different things in all the time.

At the time it was said that there were only two British collectors, so you had to sell abroad or to museums. It's not British to collect art!

Robert didn't make that much money from the gallery. Probably family money helped him. He wasn't a businessman, but he was a damn good salesman, because he was so remote and inscrutable. You couldn't get near him, he was inaccessible, and that's perfect for being a dealer, because you're selling myths. A work of art is utterly mysterious. He was so mysterious.

He could have sold anything. You believed anything he said about something. He was the perfect dealer in that respect. If he said a price you'd believe that was right, because he was so odd. There was a very odd atmosphere about him. And being upper class . . .

Letter from PATRICK CAULFIELD
Dear Robert,

The attached list is, I hope, what you require. Thank you for the cheque, and the opportunity to exhibit.

PATRICK CAULFIELD As far as I remember, he used to pay me a retainer – I can't remember how much. Money didn't seem to matter to him. I suppose that's an unfortunate attitude – that's how he managed to spend it all.

Dear Pat,

I am just writing to confirm the arrangements we talked about on Saturday, and I am enclosing, too, a cheque for £35, which amount we will be sending you each month until your show. As I said, the date of the show should be around December 1st, and I am hoping that it will be possible for you to produce 9 or 10 paintings between now and then!

I would like to say, too, that I am very happy indeed that your show is going to be with us, and I greatly look forward to working with you in the future.

PATRICK CAULFIELD I thought of him as a bit sort of upper class, the way he kind of mumbled. And I was a bit frightened of him, I think. I mean, he was from another world as far as I was concerned. Ex-Etonian. He tried to be hip. Tried to play down that part, but it came through. Because I went to Acton Central Secondary Modern, I could hardly compete with him.

JANN HAWORTH Robert certainly was cool in that way. He responded to art in a very definite fashion. He'd say what he liked, and say, 'I'd like to give you a show,' and that was it. And that happened very quickly – certainly for me it did. And Peter [Blake] as well, I think. So that was good.

But if anybody turned up with a portfolio to the gallery he absolutely would *not* want to know about it. I mean, they couldn't be any good if they turned up in Bond Street with a portfolio, so it was very cold in that way. There was no generosity of, 'I'll have a look at it. Maybe you could do so and so. Why don't you try such and such? It's not right for my gallery, but . . .' Nothing, nothing like that. I don't think that you could say it was anything to do with 'class' or necessarily background or anything, because it was so generalized. I mean, the Beatles did it, too; Peter did it; I did it. I caught it. The people we knew had backgrounds all over the place, working class as well as otherwise. It was the kind of personality of the time, you know. It certainly seemed to run through everything. Though of course he had Eton and all that.

DEREK BOSHIER I first met Robert before '64, because he did my show that year. I'd been photographed by Snowdon for his book *Private View* at the end of '63, beginning of '64. Then there was the exhibition, 'New Generations', curated by Bryan Robertson. So '64 was when all the artists came together: Bridget, myself, Paolozzi, Colin Self, etc. We were all in Robert's stable. He brought us all together.

PAULINE FORDHAM Derek Boshier was at the Royal College, as was I, and I went out with Derek for about seven years. He was my first boyfriend ever. Derek was leaving the college and they had the 'Young Contemporaries' exhibition at Whitechapel. Robert showed interest in giving Derek an exhibition and said he'd like to see his work. At that time Derek and I were living in Gypsy Lane, Richmond.

So Derek hung all his pictures round the big sitting room. To complement the paintings, I covered the entire sofa like a painting and put cushions all around, exactly the same as the paintings – snaky, wavy lines of different colours – so when Robert arrived for dinner, as he walked in, he saw an entire art concept. You couldn't tell where one thing ended and the other began. He was so overawed he took Derek on straight away for a show, which was the whole point of it all.

I gave him a very nice dinner and he said something like, 'The way to a guy's heart is through his girlfriend's cooking.' He stayed the whole evening and they talked paintings, and from that moment on we became quite close friends.

I hadn't met Robert prior to that evening and when he walked into the room my first psychic feeling was that he had a black aura. Over the years that did manifest on occasions – a darker side of him.

DEREK BOSHIER Occasionally one saw Robert with women friends, not girlfriends. There were women on his arm, but I didn't know who they were. He'd sometimes talk about boys. He might see one and say, 'Oh, he's very pretty.' He didn't hide the fact that he was gay, but he wasn't queenie about it. You knew he was gay, but you weren't conscious of it in his company.

He was such a dresser, this strange combination of dress. It's like being a very, very hip ex-Guards officer. If I had to describe the most memorable thing instantly, it would be a very dark blue shirt and a white collar and a tie, and a blazer, and his shoes, which were like a bit Gucci, slip-ons, penny loafers. But he was so elegant, he was so stylish, those dark-rimmed glasses, his hairstyle and his posture. It was so compelling.

He never mentioned the Army, but his shoes were always amazingly clean.

CHRISTOPHER FINCH In those early days England was a pretty provincial town in the art world. Robert was the focus, with Kasmin. They were ready to push this generation of English artists and to connect them with the international scene. I think Robert did it without even really trying. He just loved going around these places and meeting people.

JANN HAWORTH He had this crazy way about him, so he could sell these crazy little drawings of Colin Self's. Now Colin won't sell anything. Robert created situations for people like Colin, who was a Slade student, as I was, who had no credentials, no *savoir-faire*, nothing that would recommend him to a person like Robert, this upper-class Etonian. Robert just looked at the art and something clicked.

COLIN SELF The first time I ever met Robert was when he came to my house at 25 Tivoli Road in Hornsey. I was working on the Victor Valiant nuclear bomber, the Handley-Page Victor Bomber with missiles on, which Terry Southern then later bought, and Robert took one look and said, 'I want that in my summer show.'

He smelt quite nice, very presentable, in a pink shirt, stuttering a bit, a bit nervous, then the stuttering lessened as he got more comfy with us, and he wanted to represent me. I said, 'Well, yeah, I'm interested, I'll put the sculpture in.' After that I switched from the Piccadilly to Robert. One of the main reasons being that he could show my sculpture, because his gallery was bigger and Godfrey Pilkington couldn't do that.

I must mention Robert's belief that I am a great artist. I really must confirm that. I think he really, really did think I was special. It's nice to have someone believing in you. He wasn't just a good-time Charlie or a crook, he was such an entrepreneur, a bit like Diaghilev, who was a bit of a cheat and left people stranded, but put on great shows.

The arts had always been the province of the upper classes, but they don't necessarily make the best artists . . . But, England being what it is, nothing has been changed on the surface by all this. Nor do the people who brought it about exploit the advantage of it all. It just goes on, and unfortunately that is what happens here, everything is simply digested and assimilated.

21 JANUARY–21 FEBRUARY 1964: KALINOWSKY EXHIBITION

25 FEBRUARY–4 APRIL 1964: ALEXANDER LIBERMAN

14 APRIL–16 MAY 1964: MATTA, 'RECENT PAINTINGS'

DUBUFFET STOPS SELLING
Jean Dubuffet, that primitive earthy French painter whom many regard as a major artist, has decided to stop selling his paintings. Instead he will install them in a house he has bought just outside Paris which will become a sort of Dubuffet museum.

His London dealer, Mr Robert Fraser, is bearing the blow philosophically, as he has managed to secure a recent sequence of Dubuffet paintings for exhibition from 20 May. (Evening Standard)

20 MAY–28 JUNE 1964: JEAN DUBUFFET, 'PAINTINGS 1961'

JULY 1964: SUMMER GROUP SHOW

15 SEPTEMBER–18 OCTOBER 1964: EDUARDO PAOLOZZI, 'RECENT SCULPTURE'

EDUARDO PAOLOZZI I've got some rather good memories about Robert, in the way that we once went to see a Balthus exhibition in Paris. At that time you could go early in the morning and come back on what they called the Midnight Champagne plane from Orly. And when I came back with him, having seen the Balthus, he needed some elaborate shopping. Then, after flying back, we went straight on to his flat and he showed some Jean Genet films. Because when we got back at one or two the evening was just beginning for Robert. He was a very sophisticated man. I think in a strange way he was a bit ahead of his time. He would have flourished much better in Manhattan, which, of course, he adored.

No, he was a very sophisticated man. But business and ideas, it was rather like . . . he was almost the nearest in a Londoner to a Diaghilev figure. Great vision and imagination, but poor back-up financially. He was a bit ahead of his time. But I think it wasn't his fault, that there might have been financial problems. I think it was that the audience – and I experienced the same thing myself – the English audience was just not up to it. If you look at what was happening in Europe, or in the world, or in Paris, or if you think what was happening in New York at the time that Robert was active, then you look at English journals and magazines, you'll find they're pathetically provincial and backward. That was the kind of landscape, the kind of climate, that Robert had to work in.

DEREK BOSHIER He was very knowledgeable and so interesting as a person. I loved going in the gallery, went in once or twice a week, had a chat with Robert. He was always friendly. If I walked in in the morning, he'd say, 'Come to lunch.'

Being with the gallery was marvellous, they had such great shows. He introduced so many new, good artists I'd never heard of. He had very eclectic taste. Like Bruce Conner. He did a Hans Bellmer show, very large tinted photographs. A lot of American artists too I met through Robert, like Ed Ruscha. Although Bridget Riley was an abstract artist, most of the others were figurative. Then there was the German he showed, Konrad Klapheck.

3–30 NOVEMBER 1964: KONRAD KLAPHECK

KONRAD KLAPHECK I have very nice memories of Robert Fraser. I regret that our relationship was short-lived, due to the fact that he sold of my show in his gallery in November 1964 only one piece, and this to a collector I had recommended to him, Arnold Maremont of Chicago. So he was not keen on giving me another show. I was introduced to Robert Fraser at the Documenta in Kassel by Kaspar Koenig, who knew him from his stay in London. Fraser liked the three works of mine shown at Kassel and suggested an exhibition. I naturally agreed, knowing a little bit about Robert's gallery programme and that he had given a show to Richard Lindner, an artist I adored.

In order to see the works in my studio, Robert and I travelled together from Kassel to my home town, Düsseldorf, and spent a lovely weekend together. My wife cooked, we went to a Blues concert with black American stars of the genre.

My opening was well attended. I remember David Hockney, Derek Boshier, Paolozzi, Peter Blake, Bernard and Harold Cohen among the visitors. I regret to this day that I didn't approach David Hockney. I only later learned how great an artist he is. Robert, my wife and I visited Ronald Kitaj, an unforgettable meeting. Ronald showed us many paintings, some of them unfinished – just lines, no colours, and today famous.

DEREK BOSHIER Robert would always get you to meet the artist, which was always good. I'll always remember Klapheck – you remember, the guy who always used to paint these strange sewing machines. So I was talking to Klapheck and he told me this amazing thing. If you know what Klapheck's work is like, it fits in. But he told me that for twenty years he had worked in his studio every single day from 8.30 in the morning till 4.00 in the afternoon. If you look at the paintings, they are sort of like that.

KONRAD KLAPHECK They tell me Robert was gay. I never noticed that. He had a very attractive girlfriend, a beautiful and very intelligent creature, who worked as a fashion model, with long legs, which she liked to display in boots with high heels. I once remarked jokingly, 'If I see those boots, I'd like to be masochist and you beeing my domina,' and she answered, 'That's what they are for.'

Robert certainly was not a drug user in those days and spoke of giving up smoking. I remember him as a gentleman, very well mannered, generous to the extreme. In a way he was self-assured and shy at the same time. When he became excited or embarrassed, especially on the phone, he began to stutter. Robert did everything to please us. Our talk ran from Yves Klein – he had a marvellous glass table of his, filled with blue pigment powder – to the American artist Cornell and ended maybe with Cassius Clay, who had just beaten Sonny Liston. He introduced us to Peter Blake and Jane Howard [Jann Haworth], who invited us to their place and studio. We really got a glimpse of swinging London other than the miniskirts and the Beatles.

ALAIN JACQUET When I was passing through London I would see Robert, sometimes stay with him. I loved that. We would go out to good restaurants, etc. I met all that group of Pop artists: Alan, Jones, Peter Blake, etc. I met everybody during that time in London.

ANITA PALLENBERG I met Robert through Mario Stefano when I was going out with him in the early sixties in Rome. He was always talking about the Pop artists. There were galleries with Pop Art in Rome, but Mario always thought Robert was *the* person to go and see. So we did our little pilgrimage to London, and to Robert's gallery, which is where I first met him. I had lunch with Christopher Gibbs, Robert, Stefano and Mark Palmer, at Chez Victor, and I was really impressed by Robert. He wore an aquamarine-coloured suit.

J. PAUL GETTY I think I must have met Robert with either Bill Willis or with Christopher Gibbs. I liked him immediately. I suppose he was canvassing me as a potential customer. I did love him, but I think Robert was the most infuriating friend I've ever had.

I did buy paintings off him. Worse than that, I actually sold him a couple of paintings. That was my worst mistake. One was a Cy Twombly. At that time Cy wasn't worth a lot. I probably paid a few thousand dollars, less than ten thousand for it. Later Cy went on to fetch millions. I think Robert bought it from me for about £40,000. Not that I actually saw the money . . .

Mr N. A. Fraser and Mrs J. Cory Smith: The marriage took place in London on Friday 19 June of Mr Nicholas Andrew Fraser, elder son of Mr and Mrs Lionel Fraser, and Mrs Jill Cory Smith, only daughter of Mr and Mrs Roy Butterfield. (The Times, *Tuesday 23 June 1964*)

NICHOLAS FRASER At that time I'd just got married, was interested in my own life and family. Robert didn't get on with Jill, my first wife, and loathed small children. So we saw him about once every six months. Robert didn't enjoy family occasions, with us particularly. And after I married Charlotte, he didn't like being in a house full of scruffy dirty children, and he'd not say anything. If Robert was bored with the people surrounding him, he just said nothing. He didn't see any obligation to make polite conversation.

16 DECEMBER 1964–9 JANUARY 1965 BRUCE CONNER
*Robert Fraser requests the pleasure of your company at the opening of the exhibition of assemblages by **BRUCE CONNER** on Tuesday December 1st from 5 p.m. There will also be a showing of films made by the artist including **COSMIC RAY, A MOVIE** and others.*

BRYAN ROBERTSON Bruce Conner was a very hard artist to show, a west coast San Francisco artist, a genius, but with a very strange and a faintly macabre streak, yet not decadent at all. He was synonymous, was he not, with the wonderful Ed Keinholtz? They weren't in tandem, but he was part and parcel of the same movement of disturbing, sometimes rather shocking imagery that came about. Bruce Conner was slightly more Gothic, or slightly more Baroque, or slightly more artistic, compared with the rough stuff of Keinholtz.

BRUCE CONNER I think we did the hanging together. It was a beautifully done show. I just took it for granted Robert would do all the right things, which he did. All these people in the art world responded, and he introduced me to all kinds of people. It seemed he had access to almost anybody. Except the Beatles, he didn't know them at the time. I asked him, and he said, 'Oh yes, I see McCartney driving round sometimes.' Then there was a very unusual visit to the Blakes' with Robert. They lived in a flat that was like walking into a stage set for artists' living space in southern California. All the walls white, floors bare, the furniture was that style, they dressed that way. It was funny to be there in the middle of winter, in a freezing-cold flat, in a space that looked like you were in southern California. I kept my overcoat on.

I was at the gallery almost every day, because I didn't know that many people so I'd hang out there. One piece was called *Spider Lady Nests* – stretched stockings – that I used to put or hide things on, forming into shapes the way spiders might wrap things up, to give a feeling of age and decay. One piece had a big bicycle wheel and a belt, the nylons, etc. and other works had similar accoutrements.

One day a dowdy but elegant lady came in, probably around fifty. She looked at everything very carefully and then told Robert, 'This is a very interesting show.' Afterwards Robert said, 'She's very important. She supplies the royal household with all of their lingerie and undergarments.'

ART OF BITS AND PIECES – From Our Art Critic
Mr Bruce Conner's assemblages at the Robert Fraser Gallery live up to their name like few works in this medium.

Old nylons are Mr Conner's characteristic material and the key to the atmosphere of his work. They are stretched tight across a wooden frame in swathes like cobwebs, veiling the litter of objects at varying depths below – ink bottles glowing like quartz, costume jewellery, magazine photographs vague and suggestive, soot, and candle-wax. Remote holes, bags and pockets, half-hidden in the assemblage like the dark mouth of a cave in the woods, tempt the spectator to explore. Yet in spite of the multitude of objects used, each work is not a heap of treasure but the comment of a man obviously involved in the world today . . .

It is true that young American artists have felt it necessary to pollute the rarefied atmosphere of Abstract Expressionism and hard-edge painting in the same way that the original Dadaists felt they had to prick the aesthetic pride of the Cubists. The actual presence of Duchamp, the embodiment of the 'anti-art' position, in the United States has obviously been a spur. A title like Mr Conner's Tick Tock Jelly Clock Cosmotron *recalls the Dadaist way of approaching a 'great' theme like Time . . .* (The Times)

BRUCE CONNER By the time I had the show at Robert Fraser's I was working on a film called *Report*, about the assassination of President Kennedy. Jane and I were living in Berkeley, Massachusetts, where Kennedy was born, about half a mile from our house. I decided to spend a year working on things about that assassination.

It ended up being a thirteen-minute film, the last five minutes being full of fast cutting, changing images to go with the announcer's actual narration of the

Dallas visit. The other eight minutes were all the news broadcasts from the moment he was shot until he was declared dead. I made a print of Jacqueline walking to the coffin in the rotunda, where it was covered with the flag, with her child, and kissing the flag, and turning round to start back the way she came.

The other thing that was unique about it was that I put human blood on it, my own blood, in part of that repetitive sequence. I had the blood taken out of me by syringe, then put it on the film. It was sticky, my hands kept sticking to the film. It dried very quickly. Every time the film was shown some blood would flake off and the projector would have bits of blood on it.

John Richardson reviewed the film and said he thought the blood on it was over-egging the pudding. The film had a strong effect on me as well as other people. Even after years I'd sometimes have to leave the room.

I showed one version in the Robert Fraser Gallery, at night. The room was darkened but a certain amount of light came in from outside. Robert invited a number of people and in the middle of the screening of *Report* I left the gallery, walked down to a phone kiosk and dialled the gallery's number, then left the phone off the hook and returned to the gallery. The phone was still ringing and rang until the end of the film. That was about 1965. There would have been about thirty-five to forty people there. The gallery was not set up for a lot of people.

It was strange meeting people I thought were like those in LA, but they weren't. They came from a class culture, dealt with the world in a fundamentally different way from us. There seemed to be a certain hipness just stuck on top. But on the whole I met some wonderful people there. This was all in '65 and I was coming from the US, totally unaware of the class barriers. That coloured my view of the swinging sixties in London. People were smoking marijuana or hashish and I didn't want to touch it. I did one time, it was a big mistake. I felt very gauche and awkward at that party, not knowing quite what to do. They showed some of my 8mm stuff, and I remember an Italian princess saying, Do we have to watch more of this stuff? I was playing Ray Charles very loud and expecting everyone to party and jump around. I was comparable to some visiting Aborigine.

W. Lionel Fraser
All to the Good

W. Lionel Fraser, a Christian Scientist, leading British banker and industrialist, in his memoirs ALL TO THE GOOD, *writes vividly of his early life and paints an enthralling picture of the City of London, unravelling many of its mysteries and telling of the excitement of the international business world.*

Published October 1964 in Great Britain by William Heinemann, and in the USA by Doubleday.

OLIVE COOK I helped Lionel with his book, corrected the English, helped to get it into better shape. I thought it was a thoroughly rotten book.

From All to the Good *by Lionel Fraser*
I am tempted briefly to retrace my steps. It is a long way back to St Mary Abbots School, Kensington, and to my dear old schoolmaster Ben Jones, who, by his earnest coaching, ensured me a fair education: to my slogging years at Pitman's and to the friendly bus driver: to that exciting but anxious day when I was given my first job with Max Bonn: the 1914 War, and the misery and discomfort of the trenches in that first winter of mud and battle, attack and defence: Room 40 in the Admiralty, pitching me into the very heart unknown things and people: the frenzy of the 1920s and my foreign exchange days: the slump: then my marriage: the children: becoming a partner: the Treasury during the Second War: the Chelsea Borough Council: my first directorship: then Tillings, Tube Investments and Babcocks; finally my Chairmanship of Helbert Wagg and the extraordinary development of this banking house.

. . . The tragedy of the present day scene is that so many young people have little or no standard by which to judge. They seem to find the demands and the discipline of Christianity too high. Nevertheless, young people certainly do show the definite quality of sincerity, and one of their great virtues is their speed at spotting anything in the least bit phoney or hypocritical. Yet spiritual values and the inestimable asset of their attainment, as well as their uses in life, seem inexplicable to them, and, alas, the example of many of their elders leaves plenty to be desired.

. . . Neither my wife nor I ever attempted to 'possess' our children. We guided them, as parents should, and obviously we responded immediately to calls for advice and support, but we saw early that their lives were their own. We stood behind them with all our weight, when necessary, but as soon as we felt they were responsible, we left them to go their ways.

Did my father influence me? I don't think that parents do have influences – the best parents don't have influences. I might be influenced by ideas but not by parents. I never thought heredity plays a great part except that you react against it. It's environment that matters.

OBITUARY: *MR LIONEL FRASER, A LEADING CITY FIGURE*
Mr Lionel Fraser, CMG, who died at his London home on Saturday at the age

of 69, was among the leading City personalities of his generation; all the more so as he made his mark entirely through the force of his own charac-ter and capabilities. His remarkable career of more than 50 years straddled the fields of banking, investment trusts, insurance, and industry.

He was a many-sided man and amongst other things had been a mem-ber of the Chelsea Borough Council from 1945–1950, a Trustee of the Tate Gallery, a Liveryman of the Fishmongers' Company and member of sever-al clubs including the St James's and the Garrick.

A bald recital of his career, though it implies exceptional qualities, is inadequate to portray the man. Endowed with very good looks and a fine presence, he had a warm heart, a gift for friendship and a gay attitude to life. Immensely sensitive, no one enjoyed more than he an atmosphere of enthusiasm and success, but no one was his equal in creating it and bestowing praise on others. He was an ardent Christian Scientist and his deep religious convictions added a fundamental integrity and deep seri-ousness to his character. (The Times, *Monday 4 January 1965*)

OLIVE COOK I didn't really like Lionel, but his death was so terrible. It was dreadful that any human being should have to go through that. The pain was excruciating. They don't even take painkillers, Christian Scientists, no allevia-tion at all. All he had initially was a tiny little cancer of the skin, which could have been removed easily, but it spread all over him and he was screaming with agony. Just awful.

NICHOLAS FRASER From the time my father died, Robert was the rest of my mother's life. She was inordinately devoted to Robert. After he died she did-n't have anything particularly to live for. She loved being a strong person for him to come to. They used to have almost lovers' tiffs, with long periods when they wouldn't talk to one another. That didn't really come out until after my father had died. Robert needed looking after. I was married, didn't need it, so he was there for my mother to look after. She was rather an upright, humourless person. But she was always there if ever Robert needed her. He was a cause as far as she was concerned.

DAVID MEDALLA He was really rather terrified of his mother. He was obsessed with his mother, or actually had a hang-up of some kind with her. He used to close the gallery early to go and have tea with her. I didn't ask him much about this relationship, it was just in the air.

Robert and Cynthia together in Paris, 1964.

JIM DINE Robert and I met Michael Powell, the film director, at a mutual friend's house in the seventies. Kitaj's house. Robert didn't seem to be drinking, but he didn't twig it was *the* Michael Powell at first. I was saying to Powell how much *The Red Shoes* had meant to me as a teenager. It was my favourite film. I loved the quality of the colour. It was like an epiphany for me. And Robert said, 'M-man, my favourite film was . . .' and he told Powell that it was *Peeping Tom* (naturally). He said, 'I can remember going with m-m-m . . .' – and he could not say 'mother' – 'with m-m-mo-mo-mother. And we held hands.'

It was very moving, very touching. He was a kind of confidant to her.

CHRISTOPHER GIBBS Then about 1965 it moved, as far as Robert was concerned, from faggy to druggy. What I mean is that the more broader-based life, like seeing people from all walks and things – which was something that Robert was always into – became more drug-based than fag-based. He still had his conventional life with his old schoolfriends, things like that, but then he always also had had his rackety life of pimps and rent boys and trouble of one kind or another. (Robert's penchance for 'le low life' was with him from quite early days.) But then at this time along came all these photographers and Rolling Stones and writers and such.

Dubuffet opening show,
10 April 1962.
Cythia, Lionel, Nico Londonderry
and Robert; Nico and Robert;
Robert and Alastair Londonderry.

Contact sheet: Robert photographed
by John Deakin.

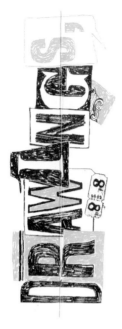

bellmer

peter blake

dado

kalinowsky

gabritschewsky

robert rauschenberg

harold stevenson

cy twombly

november 20 1963

january 4 1964

robert fraser gallery

69 duke street

grosvenor square

london w1

mayfair 7196

Gallery catalogues:
Drawings, Collages and Gouages, 20
November 1963, and *Obsession and
Fantasy,* 12 June 1963.

Nicholas's wedding to Mrs Jill Cory
Smith, 1964. Nicholas third from left.

6 Groovy Bob

Robert by now had acquired the authority that befitted the owner of London's hippest art gallery. His exhibitions, which continued not only to reflect but also to dictate the style of the times, were moving more firmly into the Pop Art category, which fitted the mood of swinging London perfectly, being irreverent, irritating to the uninitiated, deceptively banal and deliberately absurd.

His lifestyle also began to speed up in such a way as to earn him his new nickname. It seemed that his time had come.

OK Robert, OK Negro by Larry Rivers.

PAUL McCARTNEY For me and many others, Robert Fraser was one of the most influential people of the London sixties scene.

DENNIS HOPPER That sixties time in London was the greatest. I knew I was in a place where all the creation of the world was happening. The Beatles and the Stones had just happened. They were still playing in clubs and all these music shows with girls in boxes doing go-go stuff. And the jazz clubs. It was just sensational. The art world, the fashion world, they were exploding. It was the most creative place I've ever seen. I said all this to Billy Wilder and he said, 'It sounds like you're describing Berlin just before the Second World War.' I thought that was strange. ■

TERRY SOUTHERN I first met Michael Cooper in Duke Street, outside Robert Fraser's gallery at number 69. We were both looking for Robert. It was a grey winter afternoon and the gallery was closed.

'What's the time, then?' Michael asked.

I told him it was about four.

'Oh, well then,' he said, sounding like someone out of Lewis Carroll, 'if that's the case, he's most likely dropped over to his mum's for tea.'

'Yes, of course,' I said, trying to get into his Mad Hatter mode, 'that's sure to be it.'

'Yes, he'll not be back today,' he went on, but when he noticed my disappointment, he beamed and added, 'We can wait for him at the flat.'

His expression 'the flat' could not have been more apt for the establishment at Mount Street. From 1960 till 1972, Robert Fraser's flat in Mount Street was a veritable mecca for the movers and groovers of the sixties scene. Calling it 'the flat' was also an indication of the Damon/Pythias tightness of Michael and Robert – an indication hallmarked in spades, so to speak, when Michael produced his own latchkey and let us in.

GAIL GERBER I was there with Terry that night – we spent every night at Robert's when we were in London. Brian Jones and Anita were in love, Michael took pictures, many people passed through, and we would all go for late supper at some fancy restaurant that didn't want to see us. Robert had rigged his car with a record player that played 45s so there would be no break in the music, the first car tape deck I think. He carried the stack of 45s with the big hole in the middle with him wherever we went. Terry and Brian would have long conversations on lofty matters while we all danced and partied.

Robert was a great host.

I met Michael in 1964, through a model. He knew a lot of the Pop artists. Unlike most of the photographers around at that time, he wasn't just interested in doing fashion shows and being a big shot; and so I found him quite fascinating. He sort of attached himself to me. He was interested in painting; he'd been to art school, and he knew Allen Jones. After an ongoing dialogue about the tedium of London and The Establishment, I said we should start a photographic studio together and he immediately jumped at the idea. So he found a studio and I put money into it. It wasn't that much in those days, a couple of thousand pounds or something.

JIM DINE Michael was pathetic, Robert's pawn. Robert manipulated him. They were very close, but Mike was not a great photographer. He was on the scene in the sixties and Robert knew all these people. That's all. Robert sent him to me in 1965 to photograph me for the catalogue for my first painting show, not the alleged pornography one. My kids were four and six then and they said, 'The Beatles are here, the Beatles are here!' That's what he looked like.

He had very idealistic notions. He conceived of his whole life as being one continuous photographic assignment. He was unlike anybody else – he wasn't intellectual but he understood that photography wasn't just a way of making a living. He had a sort of vision and I don't think he was quite able to act out that vision but he did make an attempt.

CHRISTOPHER GIBBS Cooper was very much to the fore in this period of Robert's life. The Stones were coming up then. They used to go to the restaurant we used to go to, Mrs Beaton's Tent, in Frith Street, run by an Australian, Michael Stafford . . . he was very charming. Robert knew one of the waiters there, I think. So we used to go there and the Stones did too. We were all separately thinking, 'These people are having a good time . . .' It was a guarded dalliance on both sides. And it was sort of a change from all the other things one had done before; a long way from dancing round the Hyde Park Hotel with girls from the front page of *Country Life*. When I was eighteen I went to sixty-eight dances in one year, I remember. Even then one behaved badly, though, fell in love with the disreputable of both sexes, but within those confines. And there were no drugs then.

MICK JAGGER Michael and Robert were both friends of mine, but they were very different. I never thought Mike was that great a photographer, he was more a right-time right-place person. That's fair enough, but not a great photographer. I don't know when I met Robert. I didn't buy much from him. I didn't have any money.

Robert was very public school, but not snooty. Not at all. He wasn't after all aristocratic. His father was in industry, a self-made man. Robert was an outsider at Eton and didn't go to university. He didn't use the public school bit that much with me. He might have used it dealing with Americans or something.

Robert had great openings, but I'm not sure I often went. I was very busy at that time, didn't have time to go. I used to go to the gallery a lot and sit and look at the paintings, but I didn't go to the openings, these great social events. Maybe I went to one, a Jim Dine I remember going to. He was always trying to sell me Magritte, which would have been a fantastic buy. I just didn't have the money. If I'd known they'd be worth millions I could have raised it. Robert was a taste guru for both bands, but Paul was someone he could sell a Magritte to.

PAUL McCARTNEY I would have met Robert in the early days of his gallery, and I suspect it was just by going into his gallery, which I often used to do. As a frequent visitor, I started getting invitations to previews and I'd stand around and meet the art crowd of that time. Anyway, I went to Robert's gallery, we started to chat, and then I would often visit him at his flat. Robert's flat was like a second gallery. He had a lot of Dubuffet around that he was trying to sell. I wasn't too interested in him. He had a lot of stuff by Paolozzi, and I bought a big chrome sculpture which was called *Solo*, which was in the big Pop Art exhibition they had about two years ago at the Tate. I just said, 'What is that, Robert?' Fantastic. He said, 'What is it? I don't know. It's a mantelpiece, a bit of a car, who knows?' I was very happy with that attitude, not too academic. There was no dour art talk. It was much more razzy, loose, lively discussion with him. He was the best art eye I've ever met.

ANITA PALLENBERG It was about '65 I came back to London, with Brian Jones. We always hung out with Robert, going to dinner with him, etc. Robert was way ahead of everything that was going on. I'd spent six months in New York and was very informed about that art scene. So I found it comforting to be around Robert. We seemed to share the same interests in art; I was into all that Pop Art stuff. He was incredibly together – young, dashing, his own gallery. He had it all.

KEITH RICHARDS I met Robert through Michael Cooper and Anita, who knew him. We'd been working non-stop from '62 to '66. We'd hardly even been in England. If we were, we were just on tour. No spare time. I think we had ten days off in four years or something like that. Suddenly we reached the end of our tether – even the Stones can occasionally. We were like totally exhausted and we'd done what we wanted to do – we were getting No. 1 records and we'd whacked our arses out on the road. So we went and had some time off – a month, a year basically, '66, off in England, making a record but slowly.

At that time London was changing. It had changed since we'd been away. One of the reasons it was changing was because of the early sixties – the Stones, the Beatles, the obvious thing. We'd gone off trying to change America, world domination being our aim.

I met Robert . . . probably one night I popped round to Mount Street, which was his address, and also mine for quite a while later on. Along with probably Christopher Gibbs, Christian Marquand, Donald Cammell. We were getting back into London, meeting people. At the same time the Beatles were involved. They were also very good friends with Robert. A lot of those early sixties bands came out of art school. So there was like a common thing. It was something you'd given up to do something else, but at the same time there was an artistic connection. He loved music. I guess that was one of the other reasons we all connected. He loved his soul music, loved Indian music – was wide open on everything.

ANITA PALLENBERG Everybody had great respect for Robert. At that time everybody wanted to grow and learn, different from the feeling now. There were the wonderful photographs of Michael Cooper and David Bailey, and in fact a whole range of cultural life mingling together, which was extraordinary and exciting. Robert was really extraordinary. A catalyst, into so many things.

KEITH RICHARDS Robert was someone who owned this apartment where you'd sit around talking and now and again you'd have a chat, without being really interested that much. Then slowly it became more and more of a friendship. Robert was never one to push. Maybe the Etonian thing or maybe it was just innate. He would talk about ideas, then say, 'Why doesn't everybody shut up and listen to Booker T.?' Some Turkish coffee and a pipe. It was a year or so of really eye-opening freedom, even to Robert, in London at that time.

CHRIS JAGGER The Rolling Stones were the centre of a cultural renaissance, the focal point. But there were people like Robert, Gibbs and others who were absolutely key to the process. Robert would have an exhibition and the Rolling Stones would nick some ideas from it for their next album cover. That went on the whole time.

PETER BLAKE You could just as well say that Mick Jagger and the others were interested in hanging around Robert. In that circle were Robert, Tara Browne, Chrissie Gibbs, J. P. Getty Jnr, and they were the gang, and the others were hanging around them. Mick at that time was still a ruffian, although famous. In a way he got more from Robert than Robert got from him. He learned a certain sophistication from those people. The rock people were glamorous too, but Robert was very glamorous. He was handsome, incredibly well dressed. He kind of tutored them in a way.

KEITH RICHARDS He observed and gathered together the best and brightest around. They kind of flocked to him, the most interesting people. In a way it was a continuation or a revival of the eighteenth-century salon. After being locked in solid rock-and-roll roadwork for four years . . . Well, I learned to shoot and play guitar, how to run out of motels and shit. There's been a slight gap in my education here.

He was incredibly funny, incredibly witty. A lot of it went over my head at that time, I've no doubt, because he would be talking about people like Jim

Dine, etc. You could go round there and then, say . . . oh, I've lost contact with the art world, Jim Dine I've heard of, and there he is, sitting in the flat! Or it could be Allen Ginsberg. He had incredibly diverse connections.

20 JANUARY–19 FEBRUARY 1965: PATRICK CAULFIELD, 'PAINTINGS'

PATRICK CAULFIELD I think at that point when I was there the gallery became particularly focused. He seemed to establish a stable of artists – most of them still going strong – and then it really blossomed. He was very good at the gallery because I think he did have style, probably had some innate sense of style, and I don't know where that came from.

Robert had no precedent, like the dynasty of galleries in Cork Street, for example – I don't know what experience he had. But he did it. For example, to make his gallery bright and simple white – now it's old hat, but at that time it was fairly new. And he would take care, he took a lot of care. He would make sure a show looked good. Somehow he never cluttered the place up – everything he put out looked good.

TONY SHAFRAZI His gallery defined the very early sixties for me in London. The most precious part of the sixties really. It was *the* place to be. It had to do with the energy that was there in London, and, of course, with the fashions, the art, the colourful people around the place. And Robert really was a central figure. He'd been in America in the fifties and he'd brought it with him, ripe and ready to be the host and organize it, bring it all together. So it wasn't only the exhibitions, although they were the catalyst. And the exhibitions were of great quality. He did something major there, he helped us to see a lot of wonderful things in art we'd never seen before. Everyone loved him dearly, had tremendous respect for his magic. He really had great magic. Robert used to come by and see my work at the Royal College of Art. I was completely flattered. Getting to know him initially, knowing the gallery, going to the openings, becoming a friend somewhat, looking up to him so enormously, then the gallery being such a hotbed of extraordinary exhibitions – he was the most modern dashing young man I knew.

The levels of exhibitions was fantastic – an extraordinary glittering place for people to meet. But by far Patrick Caulfield had the most special place for Robert. Patrick was very shy – not at all dashing or great-looking, like Robert was. Yet Robert had tremendous insight into the work, because Patrick's work was literally genius art.

23 FEBRUARY–26 MARCH 1965: 'DRAWINGS' – MIXED SHOW

30 MARCH–1 MAY 1965: DEREK BOSHIER, 'PAINTINGS'

DEREK BOSHIER They were exciting times. I taught and Robert sold, so I supported myself. One always sold something from Robert's shows, and he'd sell things in between. I always seemed to have a steady flow of cheques. Everyone liked him. He was an interesting person. Everyone thought he was the best dealer in town.

My connection with Robert was not only the fact that I was one of his artists. I was also very friendly with Jim Dine at the time and so saw Robert socially. I'd occasionally bump into him at a gathering of other social circles, or if Robert wasn't there we would all talk about Robert. He was a common connector.

MAY 1965: DUBUFFET, MATTA, MICHAUX, REQUICHOT

1 JUNE–3 JULY 1965: JIM DINE, 'PAINTINGS'

JIME DINE The sixties was a great time and we're not talking flower power here. There were a lot of really great personalities coming together. In 1965 he got this house for me to stay in in Hamilton Terrace. He was always up there with us, very solicitous. I felt so protective of my friendship with Robert, I was actually jealous when he showed other US artists. He was my discovery, I thought.

CHRIS JAGGER I remember being in Robert's flat with Jim Dine at the time of the first exhibition, the one with the hammer and all that stuff. I must have been about nineteen and I remember him having impenetrable conversations and apparently they were about scoring dope. I didn't know what the fuck he was talking about. I wasn't included in these conversations, I was just 'there'. But there was a lot of hustling going on. He was very good at that.

JIM DINE I thought his views on art were great, although I was never very clear what they were. It was such quirky stuff. He never was interested in Hockney's work at all, for example, but he was interested in the kind of eccentric work of Peter Blake, who was certainly not the artist Hockney is.

7 JULY–15 OCTOBER 1965: GROUP SHOW

20 OCTOBER–27 NOVEMBER 1965: PETER BLAKE

PETER BLAKE Robert might not have known a lot about art history, but he certainly knew about art. He knew whom he was taking on at the gallery, knew their qualities and encouraged them. So he knew the art business at that time, knew who was good and who wasn't. With my work he was always excited. I don't recall him criticizing anything. I would perhaps talk to him about what a show might be, and then just go and do it, and he never was selective or critical. He left artists to get on with it.

I still think that the show we put on at the gallery in 1965, of which the majority were boxers, wrestlers, etc. was one of the best things I put on in those days.

We never talked much about art or anything, it was more boxing, football – which at the time I was interested in – and music.

PETER BLAKE Among the footballers, Bobby Keetch and Robert were great friends. There was an exhibition in The Hague, in Holland, and he brought Bobby with him to that. We met him there and spent the day with him, then Bobby became a great friend of mine.

JANN HAWORTH Bobby Keetch, a footballer at Fulham. He was absolutely glamorous beyond belief, an absolutely gorgeous guy, and whether he was bi or what I don't know, but certainly he was very much at Robert's elbow for a long time . . . He had quite long hair, very blond, and the crowds decided he must be a bit 'iffy'. His hair couldn't have been that long – I mean, it was absolutely nothing, it was short hair by the standards of today. Peter and I have got some wonderful photographs from when they came to a Dutch exhibition of Pop Art in The Hague. Robert sitting in this lovely Dutch seat that they used to have on the beach, sort of baskets, Robert sitting in one and Bobby sitting in one. But Bobby was definitely 'the pretty boy' and he suddenly had suits like Robert and other things. You know, Robert always had these beautiful suits – you've had those described to you, haven't you?

PETER BLAKE Robert and I used to go to Fulham to see Bobby, and Johnny Haynes and David Metchitt. We were really quite close friends apart from the gallery. He came to dinner regularly. We also used to go to boxing together. We went to the Ali–Cooper fight at Highbury, the second one for the world championship. We had ringside seats and we went in a posh car. We were a long way back, even though it was ringside, and someone came around with a tray of half-bottles of champagne, miniatures, rather, at £50 each. Seemed very glamorous at the time.

CHRISTOPHER FINCH The first big push in my career came totally from Robert. He introduced me to Bea Miller at *Vogue* and I started writing pieces for *Vogue*. Although I'm only two years younger than Robert, I felt like his protégé. Because he could do no wrong, I could do no wrong. I had articles in every magazine, and book publishers calling me up, etc. And a lot of that was to do with Robert. More than anyone else he was the initiator of my career.

Robert and I would go to the Albert Hall, several times with Peter Blake, usually with a bunch of other artists. It was wonderful. We were all into the swinging London thing. But the wrestling thing was back to the fifties, women in stiletto-heeled shoes. Great people-watching.

BRYAN ROBERTSON Robert also threw some very good parties, of course, with very, very good drink and rather good food. And plenty of good dope, probably. And they were very enjoyable too, put on with a light touch, you know, and elegantly done. Rather glamorous people, rather good-looking young people of all sorts, were there, and interesting older people. A good mix. It had a classy sort of feel, to use a silly journalistic language, and slightly more adult or slightly more grown up than other galleries. A bit more sophisticated. People that went there wore slightly better clothes, I think. Some of it might have been Robert's friends, or his contacts from abroad, I don't know, but that was the feel.

Kasmin was slangy, informal, you never knew whether anyone was there or not. He might be or he might not. If he was there he was friendly, talkative, or offhand, busy, desperate and on the telephone. But often there was no feeling of occupancy – There was the work, get on with it! It was an immaculately white-floored, white-walled, white-ceilinged space. It had enormous style, Kasmin's place, but it was slightly sterilized. It was rather a challenging place to walk into, you felt *you* were on the spot; women would automatically adjust their seams, or pull their jacket down or hitch up a shoulder strap. And men would almost do the same thing, because you felt the beautiful white light was raking you as well as the work. So that was Kasmin's, rather different.

KASMIN Robert and I frequently found we were having openings at the same time. We didn't pick the same days. He had more rock and roll people, but otherwise not startlingly different. We both had rather a lot of marijuana being smoked at the galleries and openings, and we both played soul and rock music. That was as near as the competition went.

We were friendly rivals, occasionally selling things to each other, living in a rather small art world where we'd meet each other's clients. Our artists were friends. Our tastes never quite overlapped, although there were many things we both liked. So Robert and I were rivals for attention in the papers, for promoting ourselves, rivals for the limited number of collectors.

JIM DINE Robert was such a snob. Probably thought Kasmin wasn't hip enough, which he wasn't. Robert was the hippest person I ever met. Every night at 23 Mount Street there was some pop star, movie star, artist, whatever. You couldn't keep up with that. You just had to be yourself, because you just couldn't keep up.

PATRICK CAULFIELD You felt you had to sort of put on a cool façade. It was a very difficult thing to live up to. I didn't try that much. I used to see him mostly when we *had* to see each other, something to do with an exhibition. I felt I couldn't get through to him on various things. You see, I didn't have this strange relationship when it came to socializing, because I drink a lot but I never ever take drugs. I knew nothing about drugs, so I didn't actually realize that most of the time I was in the company of someone drugged in some way or another.

When he lived in Mount Street he invited me to a couple of his 'events' and you felt you had to sort of put on this cool façade. This is another thing which definitely twitches a nerve. I was at one party where people were smoking and someone passed me this cigarette. I thought, 'That's rather strange, it's not very far to lean to the ashtray,' and I put it out for them . . . That's not what you were meant to do! I just didn't comprehend it, so that shows the degree of ignorance I had. I must have been terribly naïve.

I met some guy, a sort of writer who'd written something quite outrageous – not William Burroughs, Terry Southern. And also I met this football chap, a well-known footballer, sort of blond, who somehow Robert persuaded to get interested in art. He actually bought one of my paintings, which was quite surprising.

1 DECEMBER 1965–3 JANUARY 1966: HANS BELLMER, MIXED DRAWINGS

LARRY RIVERS I think I met Robert through Terry Southern. I was impressed. He was a good-looking guy. He was English in a way that impressed me – coming from immigrant Eastern European parents who could hardly speak English, very battered English.

I spent about six months in London at one time. That's when I saw him the most. I lived in Belgravia in a rented house and Robert came around a bit. We'd go to parties, etc. We were in touch almost every day. At that age, that's what you did. He was friends with Brian Jones. I saw him with Brian one night and we rode all over London at five in the morning, in a chauffeur-driven Rolls-Royce, going from club to club looking for people.

There was something about that time that was a little extra. We had serious conversations about life and love and sex and gossip. He couldn't avoid talking about his sex life with me. He had to own up to it. I don't know what he did with others. But he knew I had so many friends who were homosexual and that I had a history of trying all that kind of thing when I was younger and had no qualms about being affectionate with men.

I don't think this way now, but when I was younger, if someone was attractive to the opposite sex, that added a lot of interest for me. So he was liked by a lot of people and paid attention to a lot of people, because he had to, that was what he was about.

That night we were driving round in the Rolls, one of the Stones was looking for a girlfriend and we were with him. We went all over London, dropping into clubs, but she wasn't there and we'd get back in the car and go on.

He also had a speech impediment. He stuttered slightly. But in a cute way. I liked everything about him. He had a football-player friend and we went to his games. It wasn't a big professional team, some section of London. But we went to a lot of games.

He never made any advances to me. For whatever reason – I was older, or maybe he wasn't attracted to me. I always thought he was attractive, but I wasn't physically attracted to him. Anyway, by then I was married and had enough problems with heterosexual sex. So it just never happened.

He was handsome. He also seemed to bring up a certain thing in me where I thought he represented the more contemporary scene – as if I was already an old-fashioned person and he seemed to be in touch with something that was new, the rock world, etc. Robert was that much younger than me and that much more fashionable. He wasn't interested in being a bohemian, even though he chose people who were. But they were also attracted to drugs. That was a big part of our relationship. I don't mean we did so much drugs together – he did more when he was away from me, with other people. He'd come back with these stories . . .

MARIANNE FAITHFULL   I first met Robert at the Indica Gallery. He came round to check out the competition. I fell in love with him there and then, and invited him round to my flat in Lennox Gardens. I think I was only seventeen when I met him. I was so beautiful. I'd learned it was very cool to not say much. When I was with John I would let him talk, and I'd listen to them talk. That's how I learned about art, just listening to them. I learned that they all meant to take over the world, they had serious plans.

And I learned about Andy Warhol through Robert, a very big thing to learn about so early. One of the lovely bits of being married to John was that Christopher Gibbs and Robert would come around, and Dave Courts. It was a great little group. Robert was utterly charmed by John, thought he was fabulous. So we started to see a lot of Robert. But when I left John and went to Mick, Robert didn't miss a beat. He always stayed fond of John, but he was so able to accommodate this new situation.

JOHN DUNBAR   I had never heard of him before I met him. I was just out of fine arts at Cambridge, and Marianne was having a baby, and I thought I'd better do something. My previous ambition was I thought I'd travel around for a few years. I think he came round to the gallery in 1966, when I'd just opened it.

To us Robert seemed like the 'businessman', not to the rest of the art world. To us he was an established figure. We were kids, I was twenty or twenty-one. Robert had been doing the biz in New York, etc., was this rich gallery guy.

This guy Chris Case who worked for Robert had given us the gallery's mailing list. Robert was, kind of, you know, really interested in the fact that we were doing all this barmy stuff by unknown people, the kind of thing which he really liked. But on the other hand he had a big rent, you know – it was a much more pukka gallery. As I say, I just did mine on – we borrowed a couple of grand off Peter Asher and just sort of went ahead. It was nineteen quid a week, I remember.

We just liked each other, I guess. And I had glamorous friends, and I was young and pretty, and I was doing this gallery, which got all famous.

BRYAN ROBERTSON I thought Indica was a silly place where people used to go and smoke a lot of pot and drank a lot of cheap, bad red wine and look at absolute rubbish on the walls – so-called 'kinetic' art, and druggy drawings and druggy paintings and druggy sculptures, and I thought it was all nonsense. So Indica is no good as a comparison. And Dunbar was part and parcel of all that. Probably charming, probably very intelligent and probably meant well, and for all I know there might have been a few good things in Indica, but a lot of it was nonsense. And it did have this silly atmosphere, this silly sort of identity in the sense that the people who frequented Indica, and some critics and various sorts of promoters, and the kind of people that they took up and blazed away in a wave of excitement about, didn't seem to me to be very good. David Medalla was quite a sexy young character, but I thought he was monumentally ungifted. Clever, quick-witted, arty, knew the language, knew the patter, but totally ungifted. So that to me it was not what is now called 'cutting edge', like Robert Fraser, at all.

MICK JAGGER So here is Robert, a dapper art dealer with this nice shop, lots of good suits and a flat in Mount Street, where we used to hang out. We all knew he was gay but he didn't flaunt the boyfriends too much. There were lots and lots of boyfriends, but we didn't see them – as I said, it was an old-fashioned thing. No real relationships. He was homosexual but not at all camp – you'd never have known he was gay really. He was theatrical but not camp. But he was the one who invented Spanish Tony, Tony Sanchez. He's a ghastly person. Why did he invent him? He did provide drugs, but there was more than one drug dealer around. He was a particularly difficult drug dealer. Unpleasant person. I don't know what Robert's relationship with Spanish Tony was. Possibly sexual, but that's just a guess.

From Up and Down with the Rolling Stones *by Tony Sanchez*
Marianne was often at Robert's flat with her husband, John Dunbar, but
more often with Brian or Keith or Mick. Once she asked me if I could get
hold of half an ounce of grass for her. Then when she came to my flat in
Kilburn to score, we turned on together. I noticed tears were running
down her perfect face.

'I'm so alone, Tony,' she said. 'I can feel myself slipping away from John.
We seem to drift apart all the time. I don't know where I'm going any
more.'

I put my arm around her tiny shoulders; she put her head on my chest.
And we made love.

JIM DINE I loved Spanish Tony – such a funny guy, he was so funny. He'd
make deliveries to me, I'd call him up and buy some hash off him and he would
bring it round. I remember once at Christmas he came round and had some
Christmas drinks with us just to deliver the stuff. He played with my kids and
he was just great,

CHRISTOPHER GIBBS There was Greek Tony and Spanish Tony. Spanish
Tony was picked up, I think, in some pinball arcade or somewhere – introduced
to some important punters and the rest is history – *Up and Down with the
Rolling Stones* . . .

Spanish Tony was very attractive physically, but he had a Neanderthal streak
which I never found terribly appealing. Robert always went for, always liked, that
hint of the Stone Age about people. The noble savage, you know. It was a pattern
– there were a series of (in Robert's eyes) gorgeous brutes, whom he inflicted on
his friends. Robert would tweak them up to be particularly monstrous. Robert
with people I like that – he was not looking for the 'gold' in them . . .

From Up and Down with the Rolling Stones *by TONY SANCHEZ*
Robert was becoming bored with marijuana. He smoked half a dozen
joints or more a day, but they didn't seem to have much effect any more.
He started to eat hash cakes, to put hash in his coffee, but no matter what
he did the buzz didn't seem to be there any more. When an American
friend called Bill Willis told him about the wonders of cocaine, he was
intrigued. Willis managed to get hold of a little coke, which Robert sniffed
into his nose through a rolled pound note. Afterwards he would talk for
hours to anyone who would listen about the sensational uplift the drug
had given him.

'It was like filling my body with liquid fire,' he said.

BILL WILLIS I discovered cocaine in Italy, turned Robert on to that and then he turned the Rolling Stones and the Beatles on to it. Nobody was taking coke in those days.

Then I had a regular supply of absolutely pure cocaine. Once I was staying in Mount Street with Robert and we'd had so much coke. He went off to his gallery and I decided I would redecorate the apartment. I moved all the sculpture and furniture round the way I liked it, then I passed out.

PAUL McCARTNEY Once or twice with Robert I said, 'What's that you're doing? Coke?' I felt very lucky, because he introduced it to me a year before most people were doing it. That was '66, very early. The film industry went mad on it a few years after that.

I did a little bit with Robert, had my little phial, and the Beatles were warning me. I said, 'Don't worry. Johnny Cash wrote a song about it.' It didn't seem too bad. I started to find, though, that I had a big problem with numbness in my throat. Some people quite like that, but I'd occasionally think I was dying. I thought, 'I'm paying for this pleasure. I've got to get sensible here. This is not clever. I'm not actually enjoying this.' With pot I could sit back and enjoy it and find some pleasure in it. But with coke, the first couple of months were fine, but then I started to think, 'No, this is not too wonderful. I'm not in love with this.' So I got in and out of coke very quickly, was able to rise above it.

BRYAN ROBERTSON Robert believed in pleasure. Nice weekends away, nice dinner parties, good food and drink, all of that, yes . . . I think he was a sort of Gatsbyish last of the great spenders. I think he really did like deciding on impulse over dinner to take the midnight plane to Los Angeles, and book in at the Garden of Allah or God knows what. And do this all on whim. That whim and sudden excitement. I think there was a good deal of that sort of nonsense.

BROOKE HAYWARD Robert and Dennis met at the time when miniskirts came in, when everything exploded, England came on to the scene with the Beatles and the Edwardian dressing came in. Around '65–6, not much earlier than that, Robert came to California and he created a sensation. That's all I remember. It was the first time serious cocaine was brought in on that level and Robert brought it.

DENNIS HOPPER One day he just showed up at my door, when Brooke and I had the house with all the Pop Art in it. Probably he came to see Irving Blum, who brought him to the house. Robert stayed with us for a couple of weeks.

We then went down to Mexico. I convinced him that Mexico's primitive art was the equivalent of what Africa had been to Picasso, that the influence of African art on Modigliani and Picasso was the same kind of influence that was affecting artists here, but coming out of Mexico. So I took him down to Tijuana and he bought a lot of stuff. And we used to go to the beach with Terry Southern and hang out at Robert Walker's, with Jane Fonda and Roger Vadim next door.

I had a great time with Robert. Our tastes were very, very similar. It was just amazing. I'd never met anybody with such similar tastes. And he was so eager to learn, wanted to see new stuff so badly, so curious. It was very exciting for me to be with him. I know it was the same for him. We were visionaries, exploring.

BROOKE HAYWARD I remember one trip I was allowed to go on, to Mexico. It was a very short trip across the border. I don't remember why we went. Anyway, it took several days and during the course of that time Dennis and Robert were experimenting with lots of cocaine, which in those days was not a serious problem. It was a very clean drug. The drug of kings, it was called. Anyway on this trip Robert had some kind of weird speed and we all got crazy, completely raving mad, and were unable to go to sleep for about three days. I was very angry about it, because I had three children and really another life. I felt terribly betrayed by it. I don't remember where we were in Mexico or how he slipped me this pill. It's the only lost time in my life, three days lost. I was not thrilled.

The drug scene was beginning but it hadn't hit the mescalin stage, and certainly hadn't hit the cocaine stage. Robert had a lot to do with that, in my opinion. He was a very seductive character. That's all I really remember.

MARIANNE FAITHFULL We were at a very elegant party at Christian Marquand's house for a celebration on getting the money to make *Candy*. There was Christian and Terry Southern, Anita, Keith, me, and maybe Mick was there. It was a big flat in Kensington with many rooms, all empty – *Last Tango in Paris* style. Fireplaces in every room, but no furniture. Robert was very attentive and looked very alluring, very handsome, very devilish, in one of those gorgeous suits. He took out a little packet of crystally stuff and put out six lines on the marble fireplace, rolled up a $100 bill and said, 'Here, try this.'

I didn't know the etiquette. I'd never had coke before. But it looked gorgeous. So I said, 'What do you do?' And he said, 'You put the bill here and then you snort it.' I wish I could do his accent. If Michael Cooper were alive, he could do Robert perfectly. Anyway, I snorted, took the whole lot. Robert didn't know whether to be angry or impressed. Then he just waited to see what would happen. Well, the party was great and it went on for a long time. But over the next twenty years I still never knew anything about drug etiquette, he never informed me. He went round telling everyone about that moment, though: 'Do you know what she did? She took all six lines. What can you do with a person like that, I ask you?' That kind of thing. A young girl corrupted by Robert Fraser!

Dear Carol Schapiro

Frank O'Hara wrote to me saying that you would come to see us when you arrived in London. I believe that you did come in once when I wasn't here, but I hope very much that you will call me some time very soon, as I am looking forward very much to meeting you.

CAROL SCHAPIRO (Robert Fraser's assistant) I didn't know anything about Robert at that time. I knew the gallery, that's all. I went to see him with my letter and he was very impressed, and that was that. He signed me up. But it was some lunch, though. We went next door to this fancy French restaurant and I don't think Robert sat down for more than ten minutes during the entire time we were there. Someone would come in from the gallery: 'There's a phone call.' He'd get up, say, 'Order anything you like.' Then he'd come back and a few minutes later he'd be off again, another phone call. It took me a while to realize what he wanted from me.

'Like' is not a word I'd use about Robert. Interesting, perhaps. Almost everything that came out of him was a surprise. Entirely changeable. I was a bit afraid of him. He never seemed entirely logical and it was a struggle to be with him. But he was open and friendly and kind and warm. It's just that he was never consistent. He seemed nervous or worried about one thing or another.

4–25 JANUARY 1966: BRIDGET RILEY/HAROLD COHEN

BRIDGET RILEY Robert had so much to offer. He *did* have great potential, he *did* have gifts, he *could* have made a contribution. As it was, he was just a flash, a promise not fulfilled. Which was tragic.

Robert was fundamentally an outsider. He really didn't help his artists. Not only did we have difficulties getting what he owed us, he also arranged almost nothing for anybody, any sort of contacts, any sort of exhibition. Robert was absolutely a dilettante, the perfect example.

BERNARD COHEN His kind of dilettanteism was, I think, from a kind of refined hooray-Henry type background. There was that kind of frivolity when the pop world mixes with the art world, and that was very much his gallery: Rolling Stones, Marianne Faithfull, rock concerts . . . My brother was the odd person out; the shining examples of what I'm talking about were Peter Blake, Derek Boshier, Richard Hamilton and Paolozzi, who showed with Jim Dine there. There was this kind of mixture of pop and art. Of course the pop side did bring a razzmatazz and media side to it. Robert obviously enjoyed that.

ED RUSCHA You could tell right from the begining Robert wasn't a straight businessman. You could tell there was a bit of craziness there. That's putting it mildly, isn't it? He wasn't berserk, but he wasn't a business-orientated man. I felt he was the kind of person who was able to communicate with artists. A lot of artists are not able to do that, they can't share the ideas. Robert was special in that respect. There was a crazy edge to him. There was a special communication between him and the artist that I didn't see with other dealers. Robert wanted to break ground with his gallery and I don't think he had profit in mind. I don't think he was that sharp a businessman. It wasn't his interest. Most gallery owners want sales, results, and I don't think that's where he was at at all. He wanted the fun and games of it, means to the end, to be in the hoopla.

26 JANUARY–19 FEBRUARY 1966: LOS ANGELES NOW
8 artists from the Los Angeles area: Ed Ruscha, Dennis Hopper, Larry Bell, Wallace Berman, Jess Collins, Bruce Conner, Lyn Foulkes, Craig Kaufmann

CHRISTOPHER FINCH My favourite show would be the LA show. Nobody else in England would have dreamt of going to California and getting a bunch of young artists and bringing it back. It was just a beautiful show. A ground-breaking show. That kind of thing he did wonderfully.

ED RUSCHA I first met Robert here in California. He came by my place with Dennis. He bought some little works of mine, which he sold to John Lennon and some other people. I was just floored that someone from so far away would come and buy my work. It woke me up right away. The Californian artists were treated almost like equals in England – not like Martians from outer space – but at the same time, not part of the establishment art world.

DENNIS HOPPER Being in England when Robert had the LA show at 69 Duke Street, England, was the most exciting time I'd ever seen, or have seen since. There was such a revolution going on. The whole fashion world was on fire. Now people are emulating what was done, there's no new spark. But then it was all new. Abstract Expressionism was still new. The Pop/Poptical thing was just exploding. All art was new. It's something I felt at the time I was there and I knew I was never going to experience it again. London was dictating fashion, music, everything to the world. It was incredible, amazing.

Pauline Fordham was a dear friend then. I haven't seen her since. I had a mad fling with her then and she gave me a tie made out of the British flag. She was a really hot designer.

PAULINE FORDHAM Robert was having an exhibition of Dennis's work. I went before the opening and preview to see it, and I saw all these marvellous polystyrene cactuses, twelve foot high, great desert boulders – everything desert and rocky and barren. Very effective. Beautiful in fact. But I have never been able to understand why Robert put me with Dennis.

I didn't know Dennis at all at that time. He wasn't much known then. But this strange paranoid, neurotic guy arrived. I couldn't understand why Robert didn't have him stay at his flat. Out of the blue I got this phone call: 'Hi, Robert here. Listen, I'm sending Dennis Hopper over. Hope you can put him up for a few days.' Then a few minutes later Dennis arrived, covered in camera equipment in tan leather cases, straps, thongs, etc. – masses of it – which never left him. He slept, ate, went out with it – whether we went out to dinner or a nightclub. I'd say, 'I don't think you really need to take all this rather wonderful camera equipment with you.' He'd reply, 'Yes, my wife, who I've just married, gave it to me, and if I lose anything, she'll kill me.' It was quite bizarre to see this smallish man covered in equipment.

He was in my sitting room, which has two long windows at the front, in Knaresborough Place, just off the Cromwell Road in Earl's Court, what used to be the old air terminal there. I'd broken up with Derek about six months before and was just getting myself together. That was horrific. I was in deep shock. So I was just getting myself together when Robert sent Dennis over. That really shook me out of myself.

He'd look out of the window: 'Come here a minute. See those two guys over there?' – it would be two guys in grey suits, macs – 'FBI. They're following my every move.' I thought, 'I've got a nutcase on my hands here. I don't need this.'

After about a week I rang Robert: 'You'd better have your friend back to stay with you, dear, because I can't cope.' I didn't then know about people like that, with complex brain matter. I don't know what happened after that. I'd been blown to smithereens by this guy. Robert did laugh about it. I thought, 'You knew exactly what you were doing when you gave him to me to look after . . .'

BILL WILLIS   I had plenty of money in those days. I'd heard of acid and was dying to try it. I had a great friend in the Living Theatre, Rufus Collins (who also became a great friend of Robert's). I'd known him years before in New York. The Living Theatre came to Rome and these kids had what they called sugar cubes. I'd give them $20 for one sugar cube: nothing on it . . . Then one day some girl sold me 500 trips. Oh, my dear, now it's coming back!

I gave a party in Rome. Linda Christian was there. Paul Getty, etc. Robert was staying with me, and Rufus, and we dropped acid. It was wild. The colours, the light. Suddenly Robert disappeared. We were really out of our minds. I thought, 'God, he's gone off in the night. Where the hell can he be?' He was tripping more than we were. He didn't know where he was. I said, 'We've got to find him.' I was incapable of driving, someone else drove, and we got in my car. Turn right, turn left, turn right, and so on, and there's Robert under a tree. How I knew exactly where to find him I don't know. He was sitting under a tree in the middle of a Roman square. He didn't know who he was, where he was. We took him back to my apartment. Very psychic.

Robert and I almost had the same brainwave. I knew what he was up to, he knew what I was all about. That's why we were such good friends. And why we had such idiotic fights, which in retrospect I regret terribly. You had only those intense feelings for a dear friend. I've never been that close to anyone again.

CHRISTOPHER GIBBS The hallucinogens came in about '66. I was taking acid about 1966 and smoking dope quite a lot earlier but Robert probably moved into it rather before everyone else (and rather *more* than everyone else).

The first acid trip I remember was round at Robert's. He might have taken it once before then. There were a lot of hip Americans there – Sid Caesar, Dennis Hopper, Bruce Conner, Kenneth Anger, who was certainly there when I took my second trip. Bill Willis was there, and Michael Cooper, who had just appeared on the scene. For all of us it was pretty nearly our first time. It was a great levelling thing, making a new camaraderie. There was a bit of 'Doors of Perception' in it, certainly, but it was mostly good-timing.

I took to acid like a duck to water. What fun. I took it in a Jermyn Street Turkish bath, 10 p.m., left immediately – completely out of my head. I had a very good time with it.

ANITA PALLENBERG Robert introduced me to acid. He was the first person I know of who had LSD in London. I was just used to hash, but Brian and I one night at his place took this trip, went home and started to hallucinate.

PAULINE FORDHAM Mainly everybody smoked hash and grass. Drank a lot on high days and holidays. Mandrax combined with drink produced quite a delirious state. But there were no hard drugs at all. Not even acid. When acid did arrive, I didn't get into it for a long time, and had to be coerced to take an acid trip at Christopher Gibbs's house in Cheyne Walk. Mark and Jenny Rylance were there, Chrissie Shrimpton, etc. The first time was fantastic, but it's never like that again. You're connected with rebirth and life after death. Brilliant.

JIM DINE Robert took us to a reception for Sammy Davis Jnr at the Claremont Club or something and there was some Hollywood producer there. Robert said, 'How's Dennis?' And this guy said, 'Robert, Dennis is not on this earth any more. He's taken so much acid.'

21 FEBRUARY–19 MARCH 1966: JANN HAWORTH
First one-man show of life-size dolls and other objects by California-born artist now resident in this country.

THE STRANGE WORLD OF JANN HAWORTH
Jann Haworth is a pretty, petite, 23-year-old Californian who looks as wholesome as an orange juice advertisement.

But Jann also makes life-size dolls which are as chilling as something out of a Dr Frankenstein laboratory.

For almost three years Jann has been the wife of Peter Blake, one of Britain's leading Pop artists, and this month she is having her first exhibition at the Robert Fraser Gallery in the West End. (Evening Standard)

JANN HAWORTH Robert showed my work and so many came to see the shows. Why? He was such a wonderful front man, in terms of elegance, certainty, not speaking very much, not trying to sell, like many dealers do.

Robert responded to the art primarily. It didn't matter if you were gay or not, male or female. So he was an odd customer in that respect. Not a typical Englishman, although he had all the accoutrements: the expensive clothes, the good education, the banking family, the mother.

TONY SHAFRAZI The gallery at the front was one big sheet of glass and a glass door, so as you looked into this rectangular space from the street you just saw all this glass. I remember one opening where Robert told me, 'Don't be late for the event!' I arrived a little bit breathless, jumping out of a cab, running to the door, and the other side of this massive glass wall jam-packed with star-studded people. Between them were Bunny-type girls in high heels and stockings and bunny tails serving drinks, all in pink and white outfits.

All kinds of people were there and suddenly they're all looking at the door, towards me. I thought there must be somebody behind me. No, there's nobody there; so I half-froze as I went to open the door. And suddenly I noticed someone pulling back the doors, sweeping and bowing, welcoming me in. Look at this person, it's Marlon Brando! I believe there were two sisters who were with him, beautiful Indian or Oriental young ladies, one either side. So although they were letting me in, they were all just looking at him.

Robert introduced us, we talked a little bit, then I disappeared into the crowd. It was one of the most extraordinary events I remember. Mick Jagger was there with Marianne Faithfull, very sweet and young. I don't know whether they had just met – well, it was obviously a new relationship – and they were having a mock fight. Then he poured champagne down her dress, soaking her dress, and she was screaming and giggling, having a champagne fight. Things were flying all over the place.

Robert later had Marlon's belt. Brando had given it to him. I felt this was something not only affectionate, but there was also a sexually loaded implication there.

PAULINE FORDHAM The shows were all excellent. People of the sixties could identify with that gallery. It was the only one you felt a sense of identity with. Robert was part of the sixties. The only other one like that was Kasmin. All the others were staid, old, traditional, no life, no energy shows. The openings were all bow ties, straight cocktails. Robert was the first to waken things up. His shows weren't like that at all – very lively, more like a happening. Film stars who were in town dropped in. Everybody came who wanted to part of the scene.

CHRISTOPHER FINCH All these shows worked on different levels. As art shows, as occasions. In those days in London it was really just Robert and Kasmin doing the hip stuff. But I thought Robert's the most exciting gallery in London. I'd just hang out there all the time, either at Duke Street or at Mount Street. Then, after a while, I was welcomed into the inner circle. I was living in Marylebone at the time. This was a very exciting period – the whole swinging London thing. Robert was an amazing catalyst figure. He had this wonderful eye and pretty much plugged in to the fashion world, or at least to the people in it.

About once a week I'd get a phone call around midnight and Robert would say, 'Come over to the flat.' I'd go over to Mount Street and there was Tony Curtis, or Bill Burroughs, or Tom Wolfe. This extraordinary mixture of people and a spontaneous kind of party.

ANITA PALLENBERG For me Robert is the one who opened up everything – in Mount Street anyway. For a while he had it all together in his flat. People were talking, dreaming, fantasizing, and things began to come true for others. It was a very exciting, buzzing period. Ideas were being exchanged, films being talked about. I think Donald Cammell was often there, talking about his scripts about pop stars being kidnapped, which turned into *Performance*. Robert would have these wonderful evenings with Bruce Conner, Kenneth Anger, Andy Warhol, films that were unseen in England. It all started off at Robert's as far as I'm concerned. He was feeding Brian, and then later Keith and Mick, with his bit, and they were feeding him their bit. They were on equal terms. They were all young, handsome, successful, with a sexual connotation under it all.

MARIANNE FAITHFULL If all wires were going to one place, they would be going to Robert, or to Michael Cooper's in Flood Street, which was also Robert, because he had backed Michael. If those were the brain centres in your body, your nervous system would be Robert. He was where you went to tell what was happening, or where you went to find out what was happening. Better than having or even being a copy of *Time Out*. Robert was a serious conductor of lightning.

NIGEL WAYMOUTH David Litvinoff said to me one day, 'Guess what, I've just given your record collection to *Robert Fraser*!' He just wanted to impress him, I suppose. It was a pretty nice one. So it was, 'Thanks, David. That's really good.' It meant I had to keep ringing this Robert Fraser up. I tried hard to get it back. He was very reluctant to let me have it, but by the end of it we knew each other. He was very cool about it.

At that time I had a shop, Granny Takes a Trip. It was a boutique. All the pop star thing. Robert used to come in. The first time I saw him he was wearing a polka-dot suit. But very, very tasty. Instead of stripes it was tiny pin dots. Very, very smart. He was quite a dandy.

J. PAUL GETTY The sixties did seem glamorous at the time to me. Very. Particularly so perhaps because I wasn't living here. I was living in Rome. I'd arrived in Rome just at the height of the *Dolce Vita* thing, when Rome was the most fashionable city in the world. Fellini had made his great film and that was *the* place to be. Then in a couple of years it turned out to be London where everyone wanted to be. So you noticed it from Rome particularly.

Certainly it was a glamorous time. How could it be otherwise, when people were walking up and down the King's Road in snakeskin boots from the Chelsea Cobbler and long coats – I remember a dyed suede coat I had in about eight different colours, like Joseph's coat of many colours – from Granny Takes a Trip?

London was where you could buy the in clothes and where all the beautiful girls were. London was always, probably still is, the place to find beautiful girls. That was the first time hairdressers were fashionable. I can't imagine any previous generation inviting a hairdresser to their dinner parties.

ALASTAIR LONDONDERRY We saw Robert quite often. We would go to the cinema, or he'd come and stay at Wynyard or something like that. There are all sorts of memories that I have, having drinks, meeting Bill Willis, and through Bill Willis one met Linda Christian and people like that. And meeting Kenneth Anger through him, you know. After *Fireworks* and *Scorpio Rising* I was a solid Anger groupie. And then to my amazement I went round to have a drink with Robert once and I was sitting on the sofa with Nicola and I think Brian Jones was there and people like that. And I wasn't aware of the fact that sitting at my feet talking to someone else was none other than Kenneth Anger – *the* Kenneth Anger – yes, the fucking Kenneth Anger.

KENNETH ANGER I met Robert in the fifties in London. Robert had a wonderful sense of humour and a lot of the time it was laughs and fun. He always had an air of danger about him. He certainly had some friends from the East End. He was fascinated by the Krays, and I think he knew them. He liked flirting with danger and found these people colourful and interesting. He covered the spectrum of types.

Robert always had charisma. I loved the way he turned what might have been considered a mild handicap into something that he used in a good way, which was his stammer. It's charming the way he could get your attention by it. It was something that came and went. Months would go by and it wasn't even there, but occasionally it would come out.

He always gave me encouragement for my films. He arranged screenings for me. I've always depended on a certain amount of patronage, because my art costs more than it brings back. I've had grants over the years – from NY Arts Council, Ford Foundation, National Endowment, etc.

J. PAUL GETTY I bought a copy of Kenneth Anger's *Scorpio Rising* from Robert and took it back to Italy with me. Brigitte Bardot was married to Gunther Sachs and I took the film out there one afternoon, thinking that, as a film-maker, Brigitte would be interested in it. She'd been married to Vadim, I thought it was the kind of film she'd be really interested in. So I showed the film. They were horrified. They thought it was the most pornographic thing they'd ever seen. Brigitte was so embarrassed and horrified. Even then it seemed mild enough to me. But they were really horrified by it. Gunther – I think he wanted to have me soundly thrashed.

KENNETH ANGER I wouldn't say I miss the sixties. I remember good times. But life goes on. I do kind of miss the creative chaos of those years. LSD was great until it became a menace. I wouldn't say LSD influenced my film-making, but there was a cosmic quality that came from it. I miss those first trips, when the wallpaper used to dance, when shapes did the hula.

ALASTAIR LONDONDERRY When you were turned on in the sixties it *was* funny. You did used to roar with laughter. And one used to go to Rome and get stoned in Rome and everything. Those sides of the sixties were very, very funny indeed. But I think there was a very bad side to it.

The Pop Art was wonderful and so was the pop music of the sixties. And Robert was quintessentially one of the leaders of the culture in the sixties. I think he spearheaded that movement and it's valid, very valid. I used to go to the gallery many, many times. I met Antonioni there once and Anger used to go there quite often. And Jann Haworth – when she had that exhibition, I can't remember what it was, but anyway, Robert was on a trip at the time. The pictures and everyone there assumed diabolical shapes. Stoned out of his mind and paranoid, he kept moving everything round – much to the artists annoyance. Yes, those times were great fun.

BRYAN ROBERTSON What gave me pause, and this is something that could sound terribly pompous and I just hope it won't, is that at Whitechapel I was trying my level best to, as it were, 'educate' the English, who, I felt, were frightfully ignorant and had really missed out on modern art in the early decades of the century. So that by the time I put on a Mondrian exhibition, or Malevich or other people, they were really historic events because it was the first time anybody had seen these things. And I was so aware of the appalling ignorance of the English, and of the very tenuous nature of the foothold that modern art had got in England. People were just beginning to look seriously and not just poke their fingers at it and jeer.

Then when Robert gave his parties, to which the divine Julie Christie came and the terribly nice Terence Stamp, and all the rest of it, Mick Jagger and so on came, they inevitably ended up with photographs of these occasions in either *Vogue* or what was then *Queen* magazine. And why not? They were perfectly harmless occasions. Anything that Robert cared to do was harmless. He was a sophisticated man. He didn't corrupt anybody. But they drank a certain amount and they certainly smoked a bit of pot. Well, the whole rest of the world was too – in universities, in schools, everywhere. So it wasn't anything untoward. There were no great orgies or depravities. But the gallery ended up with that kind of tag to it. Plus the fact that he seemed to particularly enjoy Pop Art, in one form or another. He was emphasizing the slightly more frivolous side of art, which was Pop Art, and I had reservations about that.

The parties, the social life that he lived at the gallery, also pulled out into that sort of area of swinging London – shopping bags with Union Jacks and so on, all fine. But it gave out a slightly louche and silly aura.

ANITA PALLENBERG It was a time of dreams and fantasies. Some people made them come true, others just stayed with the fantasy. But it was all there. Whether the drugs had anything to do with it, I don't know. Everybody was young. But there were also Terry Southern and William Burroughs, and other older people. It was definitely a feeling of a kind of renaissance. There were Jane and Michael Rainey, there were all the love affairs. Robert's was a place where everything was going on: fights, arguments, me and Brian fighting. Not that I see Robert as the instigator, but he liked to be the devil's advocate, always taking the opposite opinion, sneaking in his wicked little ideas. He was totally anti-establishment, which was great as well.

BILL WILLIS The sixties was an era of social liberation. Social barriers were falling – very creative. You had the Beatles, the Rolling Stones, the way-out movies of Michael Cooper, and Robert was on the pulse of all that. I was living in Rome, but suddenly I'd go to London and visit Robert, and it was so swinging. Rome, by contrast, was so incredibly provincial.

Life in Rome was like a champagne cork popping all the time. I was lucky to be young and to be there at that time, but it very quickly became self-conscious. It was very spontaneous for about a year. But it wasn't swinging London.

The sixties in England saw the breakdown of class barriers. You'd have the son of a duke sitting next to the Beatles, or Michael Cooper, who was East End Jewish. Robert was interested in creative people. It had nothing to do with class. That was very exciting.

I went one time with Robert and Mick Jagger to Wilton, the Herbert family's incredible country house. Henry Herbert took us round the entire house, pointing out the Holbeins, the Rembrandts. Here we were with fabulous van Dyck paintings everywhere, and we're in jeans and T-shirts. Incredibly high, of course.

NIGEL WAYMOUTH In those days there were camps. There was Chelsea, more bohemian and arty, a bit aristocratic, whatever. Then there was the other crowd – what has become Notting Hill Gate, I suppose, but they were more political, more agitprop, people like Miles and Indica, etc. Out with the banners, flying the flag. We all read *International Times*, smoked joints, took trips, so there was a connection between the groups. All sorts of things were happening which were great fun, both then and later on, like Mark Palmer going off on his carts. We didn't go to people's country houses, we joined the gypsies for the weekend. It was very funny. Of course they were parked on somebody's fabulous estate. It was all very prankish. It was either rotten or great fun, so who cares? Behave badly and have fun. It was very like Lord Snooty in the *Beano*, this strange mix of people running around. It was kind of mad. But you couldn't stay on that merry-go-round together.

There was still the old English class thing then. It's much easier now, more meritocratic. But that time was the great shake-up. You had bright young people from all backgrounds who needed still to shake loose a few things. But it was the beginning of the end in that sense. The establishment was still very much the establishment, whereas now . . . it's all changed. That's when it started.

I was a grammer school boy. I'd opened Granny's but having lived all over the place, I wasn't entrenched in my background and I didn't care. I was freer of that than most people. I had friends on either side, so to speak.

Robert was very patrician. Very sophisticated, very worldly, hip, cool. In that sense he was different. But he didn't go off shooting and all of that. He was wild. Groovy Bob!

PAUL McCARTNEY A lot of mixed people were on the scene, a kind of aristocracy in which I'd put Robert as part of. He had his friends among the Ormsby-Gores and the Londonderrys. I didn't get into that much. Mick and the Stones more. I got on OK with them, but they didn't turn out to be my crowd.

We often did drugs together, that was the scene. We'd occasionally have some acid trips out at my house at Cavendish Avenue. That was the secure place to do it. The thing I didn't like about acid was it lasted too long. It always wore me out. But they were great people to be around, a wacky crowd. My main problem was just the stamina you had to have. I never attempted to work on acid, I couldn't. What's the point of trying, love?

J. PAUL GETTY You've heard about the famous Tara Browne twenty-first birthday party, I suppose. I have nothing exciting to tell you about it, it was just a marvellous confused memory. Because we were all out of our minds on various substances. But it was a highlight of the glamour side of that era. We stayed all over Ireland I think. Talitha and I stayed with the Guinnesses at Leixlip, as did Robert. The Rolling Stones were there as guests and played as well, doing gigs in between those of an Irish band. There were some very extraordinary characters there. Eugène Jolas was there, the art dealer who was Magritte's dealer. He was very, very strange. I think it was the only time Jolas had done anything like taking a trip. I remember him the next day saying, 'Oh, my dear, it was so theatrical!'

PATRICK CAULFIELD It's very difficult to swing if you haven't got any money. I was a student during most of that time. Every summer I would work in a factory somewhere. You know, as well as being a student, I had to work in a Pepsi-Cola factory in north Acton in the summer holidays, and things like that. So it wasn't at all swinging. But in retrospect if one thinks about it, the nearest I came to it was in Robert's company, whenever we did something. And particularly his private views, where he used to have all these famous people. Like you'd see Marlon Brando on a staircase! And you'd be chatting up a woman and find it's Marianne Faithfull. So he definitely brought me near to that. I was still an outsider, though, as my fellow students were. We were mostly terribly down to earth and far from swinging.

But I'll tell you, not only did he show me the swinging sixties, he showed me *la dolce vita* as well, because – do you want a story about that? Well, this is one time when I became close to him through a situation rather than anything else. I had an opening – I had a show in Milan which Robert had organized with this other dealer. And he was going to collect me in a chauffeur-driven car to take me to the airport. I lived in Holland Park and he came late. I got in the car, we drove to the airport and missed the plane we were meant to get. And we were going on the afternoon of the opening in Milan. Openings were about the same time as they are here, early evening some time. And so we got on this plane. I wasn't sitting next to Robert, he was across the aisle. And I noticed he was getting sort of frantic in his behaviour, his legs were going up and down. It was only in retrospect I realized he was on drugs and maybe he'd had some or didn't have any or – it's on an aeroplane.

However, worse than that, half-way across the Channel the aeroplane had to turn round because there was something wrong with it. So we ended up back in Heathrow, which I hate anyway, going through the same waiting process, with Robert totally, like, somewhere else. And then we got the next plane. Of course, I realized when we were flying to Milan we were in the air while the private view was going on. There was no way we could get to the private view.

The next morning Robert said, 'How about going to Rome? Do you want to come to Rome?' And I said, 'Yes', because I didn't speak any Italian and I'd suddenly found myself in Milan not knowing what to do. I felt, 'Well, he's like a man of the world.' I felt at a loss without him, you know, not knowing what to do.

And we spent the first night in Rome without sleep at the house of a film star who was one of the brothers in a famous film of that time – *The something Brothers*, it was called. They weren't actually brothers, they were actors playing brothers. But anyway, this particular actor of the three became a popular success and he had this house which must have been right in the middle of Rome.

It was like the Forum, you know, you could see the ruins. It was like . . . like looking out of the window on a Rousseau landscape. And I can remember going into a hallway and it was circular, with a marble floor. And on one side of the room there was a plinth with a motorbike on it – a shining motorbike. And he had this vast staircase going up and apparently his mother lived at the top. It was so Italian.

And the guy was really charming. He was so nice. Everybody was on drugs, but this guy looked after me, giving me drinks and stuff. He was not at all pretentious or anything. He was a lovely guy. But we sat all the night doing nothing, sitting round talking (I can't remember what language) and then the early morning, just before dawn, we all got into motor cars and we drove down to where the seaside is.

And I remember us walking in the dawn mist along the beach in single file. In fact, myself and some young sort of gigolo character who had slightly gone over the top, some fat guy who was something to do with opera, you know, and I think a woman, all very extraordinary people walking in the mist to what appeared to be a native hut on the beach – all made of bamboo and reeds and stuff. But when you went into it, it had tiled bathrooms and everything in it – absolute luxury. That was the actor's seaside place. So we spent the next day, me getting sunburnt, not thinking and drinking as much as I could, and them all on drugs, and then driving back long a tortuous route – I think Robert drove. It was the most frightening drive in my life. I mean that was the *la dolce vita* as they say. You could see it.

It would appear glamorous from the outside, but it wasn't glamorous at all. It was rather painful, the whole experience. We didn't sleep, couldn't talk to anybody, got burnt by the sun, you know, a totally unexpected climate. I can't remember what time of year it was, certainly early in the year. So I ended up going back, leaving Robert. I went back to Milan. I got on the aeroplane. I looked like a beetroot! My face is flushed usually anyway, but the sun – I really got burnt.

So the whole thing was a bit disastrous, except that the dealer in Milan is a charming character and he bought some things off me and made me happy in the end. But it was all like a dream actually. I mean, it was the most decadent situation I've ever felt close to. Although nothing really definite happened. Nothing happened, we just sort of sat around – like zombies.

KASMIN That was a time when young people had more money, were more vociferous. But it was not for me a moment of great liberation – that was all in the fifties. I was from the Beat generation. In the height of this season I had already been married five or six years, with a house and two children. Robert was a faking-out, drug-taking homo. Very, very different base to work from. So, however much you're hip, you are still lining up your kids for school and doing family things. You might go wild and get turned on at times, but in the background is the wife, the child, the mortgage, etc. The difference between Robert and me was that I was always considered the soul of probity, and he was bohemian, financially irregular, shall I say.

22 MARCH–16 APRIL 1966: 'WORKS IN PROGRESS'
Richard Hamilton, Bridget Riley, Harold Cohen, Peter Blake

RICHARD HAMILTON The only way I can date that occasion of showing with

Robert was that I left teaching in Newcastle in 1966. Robert Fraser said, 'Give up teaching and I will guarantee that you have the same income that you're getting from teaching, plus a few things that you're selling.' So I said, 'That sounds like a reasonable deal,' and I gave up my job.

A few months later I got a cheque that bounced, so it didn't seem ideal at that time, as a relationship.

BRIDGET RILEY He didn't understand other people's needs. He didn't understand. I think it was quite genuine. He literally had no idea of how other people lived. He didn't *want* to know, but he actually didn't know. And this made him, well . . . out of touch. Deeply and profoundly out of touch with people.

I do remember on one occasion when he had in fact paid me a certain amount and he was trying, I think, in his own way, to pay me a little bit more. But he came to tell me that he couldn't actually do so, and he kept a taxi outside while he went a very long and tortuous way about explaining just how hard it was for him to put his hand in his pocket and pay.

RICHARD HAMILTON But on the other hand I found that Robert was absolutely right, and I bless him for having persuaded me to get out of the teaching racket and into the thing that I really ought to have been doing for the previous twenty years.

robert fraser gallery ltd

69 Duke Street

Grosvenor

London W1

I am proposing a short-term loan of £10,000 repayable in full by June 1st, 1966, in order to finance the sales guarantee for exhibition of 15 recent oils and about 10 gouaches of Jean Dubuffet. This exhibition will be held from April 20th – May 20th, 1966 . . . It is hoped that part of this sum be used in order to obtain at a price not including commission to this gallery of an important Dubuffet for my mother's personal collection . . .

In my opinion, shared I might add with many experts I could name, the prices of Dubuffet's paintings at present in comparison with the absolute certainty of appreciation in the next 5 years, makes acquisition of his work a very excellent long-term investment at this time.

Robert Fraser Galleries : BANK MEMO
The following are my thoughts on Robert Fraser's memo on the proposed Dubuffet Exhibition in April/May 1966.

1. At the present time the Gallery has a very substantial overdraft with its bankers.

2. During his lifetime W. L. F. advanced £32,000 for the purpose of buying with a view to eventual sale specific pictures. One picture was sold just before his death and £18,000 repaid. The other picture(s) have, I believe, been sold, but instead of repaying the outstanding loan further pictures have been purchased, so that the present position is:

> Bank overdraft unknown (believed to be substantial)
> Loan from Mrs Fraser £14,000
> Less legacy set off   £5,000   9,000

3. Mrs Fraser has a natural desire to help Robert and furthermore I believe she respects his artistic judgement . . .

My main concern is for Mrs Fraser to avoid an escalating (a popular word now) involvement in the Gallery.

20 APRIL–28 MAY 1966: JEAN DUBUFFET, 'UTENSILES UTOPIQUES'

KASPAR KOENIG His mother was an incredibly overpowering figure. I think she helped him out too, financially. I discovered a small, beautiful painting by Magritte, just clouds in a black box, big as a postcard, and Robert sold it to his mother. Basically he was always in debt to her, so really she supported him. It was all – getting money for nothing, you know. The chauffeur would come, very formal with a Rolls-Royce and a uniform, and collect some painting. He probably thought, what is this decrepit piece of shit?

MRS MORRIS Cynthia had a wonderful Magritte. I think Robert pursuaded her to let him sell it or swap it for this really grim thing. Looked like sort of corregated cardboard. Robert kept saying, 'It's more valuable than the Magritte.' I knew he was cheating her. Seemed obvious to me. It was a horrible thing, by somebody very famous. I didn't pay much attention to art.

CHRISTOPHER GIBBS I used to buy things from him, write out cheques for them, and he'd buy things from me. And I'd sue him after six months because he never paid for them. That sort of relationship. Then I wouldn't speak to him for three months, then forget I wasn't speaking to him and we'd go off and do something together.

MICK JAGGER I liked Robert very much, but he was obviously a tremendous sharpie, someone you had to be a bit careful with, moneywise and otherwise. But he was a great taste person. Nobody in England was involved in the kind of art he was trying to promote. There were very few modern dealers of quality. Robert was bringing in a new kind of visual sensibility.

MARIANNE FAITHFULL There was all this money, but it was Mick's. Robert never had any. I certainly didn't. So it was Mick's money and I was trying to spread some of it around through my friends. We did a lot of that, but not enough.

I remember one funny time Stash had somehow got hold of one of his father's paintings and Robert had got hold of it too, it belonged to them both, and they wanted to sell it to Mick, and I wanted Mick to buy it. Partly because I was on Robert's side automatically, against Mick, against everybody. So I talked to Mick and said, 'Now look, you *have* to buy this painting, it's the find of a lifetime.' And it really was. I didn't know enough about Balthus then. If I'd understood all the sexual stuff, I could have really talked him into it. But Robert hadn't prepped me properly either. He'd go, 'Now just go and do this, da-da-dah, and I'll see you at eight, I hope it'll be done by then.' But he didn't give you anything to go on.

MICK JAGGER There was a slight aura of raffishness about him. He wasn't a straight dealer. As far as I was concerned Robert was this interesting taste-maker, but he was obviously always on the make and it was a bit worrying. He was obviously a hustler. I don't think he ripped people off, but the paintings did seem very expensive when you didn't have the money. But they're even more expensive now. Robert wasn't a very good businessman.

Anyway, it was a good hustle for everyone. If Robert was going to hit me up for money, that was the number – £1,000. If it was now it would be £10,000. Still not a huge amount of money.

MARIANNE FAITHFULL Of course Mick was very resistant. In the male macho league, he thought he was being taken for a ride by Robert and Stash.

Anyway, I had the very unedifying experience of watching Mick Jagger say no to this painting. Robert couldn't believe it. There was a moment when he realized Mick would never be good for selling paintings to. He wasn't a Paul McCartney in that respect.

PAUL McCARTNEY In my garden at Cavendish Avenue, which was a 100-year-old house I'd bought, Robert was a frequent visitor. One day he got hold of a Magritte he thought I'd love. Being Robert, he would just get it and bring it. I was out in the garden with some friends. I think I was filming Mary Hopkin with a film crew, just getting her to sing live in the garden, with bees and flies buzzing around, high summer. We were in the long grass, very beautiful, very country-like. We were out in the garden and Robert didn't want to interrupt, so when we went back in the big door from the garden to the living room, there on the table he'd just propped up this little Magritte. It was of a green apple. That became the basis of the Apple logo. Across the painting Magritte had written in that beautiful handwriting of his '*Au Revoir*'. And Robert had split.

I thought that was the coolest thing anyone's ever done with me. When I saw it, I just thought: 'Robert.' Nobody else could have done that. Of course we'd settle the bill later. He wouldn't hit me with a bill.

KEITH RICHARDS You'd get a phone call from Robert: 'I say, loan me a couple of grand. This painting that I was supposed to have sold – they've taken it but they've not paid me.' He didn't mind putting the touch on you. Sure, yeah. Always got the money back. He was never a sponger. 'Could you tide me over? I could go to my mother, but I hate to do that.' 'Oh, don't go to Mother. Here.' My other feeling was that he nurtured the Beatles, specially Paul. He liked John very much, but I always thought there was a slight sense of manipulation.

He saw the obvious possibilities of being associated with the Beatles at the time. The Stones? Everybody kinda knew. We were just sort of friends. I've got the feeling he pulled a few things with the Beatles, deal-wise, that he wouldn't have done with us, and didn't try with us. He'd try and sell me things. 'This is a wonderful thing.' 'Yeah,' I'd say.

MICK JAGGER I think Robert saw the Beatles as a hustle. Everyone did. They were the richest people in that age group. Very silly with their money, they didn't seem to care. They did very good things, like *Sgt Pepper,* and did attract good people. But people did target them as a hustle. Robert saw them as a gravy train when he knew that I was not. First of all, I was too suspicious. Second, I didn't have the cash. I was to get the cash, but I didn't have it then. Which is unfortunate, because I could have ended up owning all these Magrittes and things.

PAUL McCARTNEY Robert wasn't good with money. I lent him bits of money that I didn't see back. The way I looked at it, he'd actually made me so much money with some of the paintings he'd helped me get that it didn't matter. We didn't have to dot the i's and cross the t's. I figured I'd won financially. Not that it was a competition, but he certainly made me a lot more money than he lost me. But he did have a bad reputation with money.

SUSAN LOPPERT Robert was an extraordinary character who did extraordinary things in his time but he was also a *monster*! First impression: I was taken aback by this elegant dandy with the stutter. And how thin he was – so thin! He was like a skeleton, with long tapering fingers, like his mother. So skinny, and he wore these very dandified, waisted suits and hand-made shirts. I thought he was an extraordinary dandy, more than anything else. There was something rather frightening about him, something maybe to do with the stutter.

I was about twenty years old and very proper, having worked before this on the *Paris Review*. I went for my interview to the gallery, because he'd told me, 'We're hanging a show that day. Come here!' So I arrived and they were busy doing things, or should I say everyone else was – he was busy instructing people. Not in shirt sleeves, because even when he had his jacket off it was always these beautiful shirts. Throughout this time he didn't actually say anything to me other than, 'Sit down over there.' I just sat there and watched.

Then after about two hours, or maybe only an hour, in which he hadn't actually said anything to me at all, he said, 'Right, will you come back on Monday at 9 a.m.?' So I realized I'd been employed. It was bizarre. It was only when I arrived on Monday at 9.00 and Carol Schapiro said, 'Can you type? You'll earn £15 a week, which after tax is £12,' and so on, that I knew what I was supposed to be doing.

In fact my interview there was while they were hanging Bridget Riley's show, her second one. It was with fragments – all black and white. She tells a wonderful story about this in an interview – showing Robert's imagination.

JUNE 1966: BRIDGET RILEY

BRIDGET RILEY I had a large group of studies, very small drawings, using blacks, whites, greys and pencil notes, and there were about forty or fifty of these which Robert wanted to show. They were very tiny things and framed, close-framed, in Perspex, so that one saw only the actual image. We had worked all day on putting these up and we were in despair, both of us, because it didn't look at all right.

I went home, and about two hours later Robert rang up and said, 'Don't worry, I've had an idea. I think it's going to be all right.' The opening was the next day and I asked him, begged him, to tell me what his idea was, but he wouldn't.

And when I went to the gallery first thing in the morning I was amazed. He had painted the entire place black – walls, ceiling, all the woodwork, everything was completely black. And so these little light, pale studies, very fragile pieces of paper, shone, and were set off in an amazing way. And the whole place looked absolutely beautiful.

SUSAN LOPPERT I think he was a man of great sensitivity when it came to art and possibly to people, but very little perception. I think his knowledge of art was very unlettered. Robert was not an intellectual at all but he had this instinctive understanding. His mother said somewhere, 'He saw a Vuillard when he was six and he just *knew*.' But he was inarticulate, not only because of his stutter but also because of his inability to explain. His strongests words of approbation when I was working for him were, 'It's very strong.' He couldn't talk about art like Kasmin or John Dunbar. He couldn't talk to artists about their work. If they were really close, they'd talk about getting stoned or Indian music or something.

JANN HAWORTH But that, to me, is what characterized that time, nobody inquired about anything, about anybody, and it was just this sort of very stand-offish thing, and if you put together more than fifteen or twenty sentences in terms of a conversation you were intellectualizing and being a kind of university swat, you know. And it was really like that. A funny, funny thing. And it seems so strange to me now and I can't think why I put up with it. It was really odd, you know. Everyone was so busy being cool – but it was also incredibly lazy and unfriendly.

PAUL McCARTNEY Robert could play the academic game quite easily, he was very knowledgeable, but I think he found it a bit boring. It wasn't our scene, being academic. I've heard him hold his own with academics, but that wasn't the buzz. The buzz was more of a mixture, a cross-over with musicians, etc.

He turned me on to quite a few things, quite a few artists. We went down once on an impulse to see Takis, the great sculptor who did things with tank aerials with little lights on the end. That sort of thing was great. We'd just turn up at someone's studio, smoke a bit of pot, sit around and just chat art.

NIGEL WAYMOUTH You'd go round to Robert's of an evening and you'd get stoned, but there wasn't an awful lot said. You weren't allowed to be nervous. A lot of that chatter was nervousness or shyness. Sometimes you'd get a bit restless, a bit bored, but: can I be bothered to move? The joint would cool you out. It was a great time. People would just be sitting there listening to music, passing the joint. You just felt comfortable being quiet. Conversation was *dead*, man!

SUSAN LOPPERT And then the other thing (apart from his strange stutter) was this extraordinary American jargon that he picked up when he was living there. You know, to hear Robert saying to Terry Southern on the phone, 'Hi, Tell, we're g-g-gruoving!' It was just so bizarre and incongruous.

ALASTAIR LONDONDERRY Certainly that Groovy Bob phase set him apart from the Old Etonian Bob, no question of that. You'd sometimes be talking to him about something and he'd give some funny answer, you'd think to yourself, 'What *is* he talking about?'

SUSAN LOPPERT Then you'd go to Mount Street and there'd be people sitting around all this awful smell of incense and grass. I can't stand the smell myself. You could never get a drink, nobody drank anything, and they'd be sitting around uttering these pseudo-profundities which were *rubbish*! Unless you were part of it, you were completely out of it. I'll never forget one time – he had ceramics at one point, one of Robert's phases of collecting things, he would be continually changing his furniture around – these people were sitting around on his floor and one said, 'Like, get a hold of that red pot, man.' And everyone said, 'Yeah, man, yeah.' I've never forgotten that.

ALASTAIR LONDONDERRY Oh yes. That was when we used to get stoned, in the sixties. It's so long ago, a different ethos. And he always at one point when we were stoned after a couple of joints or something – we'd have gone through a couple of boxes of mints or something, you know. And, 'Wow, wow, man. I wonder what it would be like to turn on in outer space!' Nico and I would just collapse. Even if we were as stoned as he was . . . It's so long ago – one of the things I used to like getting stoned for was it just made one laugh or giggle. And that remark. I always knew at one point in the early hours that he'd be bound to make that remark. And quite often I used to lead him into it, you know. Used to make a few pretentious remarks – 'Wow, man. Look at that painting. Isn't it groovy?' and that sort of thing. And then he'd come out with it, 'Wow, what would it be like to turn on in outer space?' Dear Robert.

KAY GIMPEL One day I came in from the street and said to my brother-in-law, 'That young brat Robert Fraser is really bloody rude! I've known him for so many years and he just looked right through me!' Pete looked at me and said, 'Don't you realize? He's stoned out of his mind and doesn't even see you, so don't take it personally.' Then I saw him again at the Biennale in Venice. And again I think he was probably stoned. If people are either very drunk or very drugged they do act very strangely.

JOHN DUNBAR My artist Julio had some stuff in the Venice Biennale. I drove down in a Mini Marianne had been given – didn't have a licence or anything – and got to Venice and there were all these weird parties at palazzos and embassies, so it was a big bash after all. I ran into Robert and he had a suitcase full of drugs, all sorts of ace drugs! It was, 'Wow! Hi, Robert!' It was a pretty lame scene in those days: embassies, British Council, etc. So we were really pleased to find each other there. He was like the Merchant of Venice! So we talked and talked about various things, and got to know each other very well, and remained friends. We got to know Venice by night when all the punters were asleep. Got sick of the Biennale, drove back and heard on the radio that my bloke had won! I benefited, but got into trouble for selling stuff too cheap after that. They should have been triple the price. I was so pleased to sell *anything*!

JULY 1966: ANDY WARHOL

Dear Leo [Castelli],

Just to say thank you for your hospitality and help in New York.

I spoke to Ileana who said she was leaving today.

I hope you will be able to make necessary arrangements about the Warhol show and let me know soon; the dates I fixed provisionally were May 23–June 18th.

I look forward to seeing you again in March.

With best regards,

Robert Fraser

LEO CASTELLI I didn't do much with Robert, but we had a rapport so we did see each other, even if there wasn't any special project involved. The drugs obviously had an influence on his activities; he could have done much better. But he was London-based and it was difficult to achieve things there. Being the person he was he could be very successful carrying out things whenever he wanted to. He had great energy, incredibly good manners, a real friendly presence.

We didn't do much business together, but whenever there was something he wanted to do, I was more than happy to do it for him. He would come and go and he would talk about things – it was an ongoing relationship. He would casually say, 'Well, what about this? What about that?' He wouldn't come especially to ask me about something. If he had an idea, he would mention it, and if I could help, I was happy to do it.

PAUL McCARTNEY Robert was a good friend of Andy Warhol's and when Andy came over he said, 'Can we hire a projector and show one of Andy's films?' Paul Morrissey really made the movies – he was quite a good friend too.

PAUL MORRISSEY I was with Andy at the Cannes Film festival in 1967. We connected with Robert in London right away – he was really nice.

We had the print of *Chelsea Girls* with us when we got to London. We'd taken it to Cannes to show at the Film Festival, and there were so many reels and it was so expensive that we'd taken it in our luggage. Andy had paid for seven or eight people to go. Some were in the film, some were friends of others. There was a whole bunch of us: Nico and Eric, Gerard, Susan Bottomley and someone else. But they never screened it. They had announced it, it was part of the programme, but they hadn't given it a date. They didn't know how to screen the film. They needed two projectors and two screens, and I had to try and show them how to do it. Then they were afraid there'd be some scandal because of ten seconds of male nudity, which they'd heard about but never seen. They never screened it. They refused to show it. The first time ever that an invited film was never screened.

And then we left and took it to Paris and showed it at the Cinémathèque, and then took it to London, all in our suitcases. And we met Robert and we must have shown it in Robert's apartment. He was renting his apartment from Kenneth Tynan and I was very impressed by that. It was pretty empty, that apartment – we went over there a number of times. Robert would just call up Paul McCartney or John Lennon. A lot of people came. Paul McCartney lent us one of the projectors.

STASH KLOSSOWSKI Robert called and asked me to bring Paul's 16mm sound projector, because *Chelsea Girls* needed two projectors used simultaneously. So I took it over, arrived at 23 Mount Street and found about fifty or more people crammed in, lying all over the floor, all the Warhol entourage. We showed the movie and someone complained about the noise and the police came.

Robert had this amazingly arrogant attitude towards the police which stopped them coming in. They tried. They were pointing to people passed out on the floor, saying, 'Is he all right?', but Robert just ignored this and ordered or pushed them back out on to the landing.

PAUL McCARTNEY There wasn't that much action in the Empire State Building. And we just sat around with a bunch of friends, and Andy was very enigmatic, didn't say more than two words: 'Nice room. Thank you.' Then we ended up going to the Baghdad House, which was the only place we knew of in London where you could smoke hash downstairs. We sat around this long table and ordered up various little couscous things. I never really talked to Andy though. But it was great fun and I thanked Robert for engineering those moments.

PAUL MORRISSEY The English up until then had been very insular. It was just that period where Europe was getting more international and more open. I think English people generally don't tell you what they feel, which is a wonderful thing. Now you get all these English actors who are coming on all emotional on the surface, which is the way you get attention from the reviewers, well . . . Robert was very sophisticated and sharp. And he did make a big change. He did have that finishing-school accent, a very artificial aloofness, which really I think is wonderful. I enjoy it. We seldom see it in America and I find it refreshing.

PAUL McCARTNEY There were many good times in Robert's flat. Through my Beatle connections I'd hire a 16mm projector for the evening – I remember Ringo showing *Jason and the Argonauts* endlessly – and I started off with *Wizard of Oz*. Robert got into this, wow, and he'd get some art movies. We got a lot of Bruce Conners, showed a lot of that. It was a very exciting period.

BILL WILLIS On Mount Street he had this very big room. One thing in it was this Yves Klein sculpture, and then he bought a couple of chaise longues from me that I had made in Rome, and we just sat on cushions on the floor and projected these films. The first one I saw of Michael Cooper's had Stravinsky's *Sacre du Printemps* as music, with all these amazing images. Absolutely mind-boggling. I'll never forget it. Plus we were on acid. You see an intensity of colour like you've never seen before. By then we were so into acid, dropping acid three times a week.

JOHN DUNBAR Robert and I used to go to John Lennon's house in Weybridge quite a bit to take acid. John Lennon had already been to my place and bought some Takis stuff. He wasn't a 'wander about the art gallery' kind of guy. But once he met Robert I'm sure he would have been around there a couple of times.

Once Robert came on this mad trip to Ireland. It started off at Weybridge and we were snorting coke from a pestle and mortar, and from Spanish Tony came this Technicolor dream . . . So we all got in a motor and went to . . . I can't remember it clearly, you understand, we were taking acid for a week or more and we ended up on this island off Ireland that was for sale. I think John bought it.

SUSAN LOPPERT Dunbar had his gallery, Indica, and used to come in. They were all so beyond anything else! Robert was seven years older than me, but it was like a chasm, a gulf, you can't imagine. I mean, I'd been a student too, but it was this extraordinary time of everything opening up! Everything was for the first time. They all still belonged to the generation where everything had been closed, but although Mick Jagger is the same age as I am, and Marianne Faithfull and so on, they were like creatures from another planet. You couldn't believe it!

22 JULY–10 SEPTEMBER 1966: 'NEW IDIOMS'
Including Clive Barker, Derek Boshier, Richard Hamilton, Ellsworth Kelly, Roy Lichtenstein, Craig Kauffman, Eduardo Paolozzi, Claes Oldenburg, Colin Self, Bridget Riley, Andy Warhol

CLIVE BARKER His gallery was famous as soon as it opened as it showed remarkable things. He had marvellous shows of Dubuffet and a lot of Surrealists. I mean, it was a marvellous gallery. I can't think of any show that Robert had that was ordinary or middle of the road or not terribly interesting. They were *all* marvellous shows. You saw things there that you could never see anywhere else, with anybody else. You saw Jim Dine and Andy Warhol there before you saw them anywhere else. And he'd go to America and bring things back and people would laugh and say, 'God, what the hell are you up to?' And of course they were marvellous things. He had a marvellous eye. He had a fantastic eye. Before he got involved in all the pop thing, he had marvellous people anyway. And for me he was a great dealer. Probably the best dealer we've seen for many, many years. They are very few and far between, good dealers. When I first knew him he had a good eye and money as well . . .

I think he seemed very aloof when I first met him, very arrogant. But then after a while I realized why. His upbringing and whatever. But when he was great, he was absolutely marvellous.

I met Robert when I had this show. I was going down the stairs and coming up was Robert with Marlon Brando. And Robert said, 'And here he is now' to Brando. He said, 'This is Clive Barker.' I put my hand out and Brando said, 'I'm Marlon Brando.' He was at his peak then. He'd signed his belt, on the inside, 'To Robert Fraser.'

We went across the road to a pizza place – they were quite new then – where Brando said very little. I hate pizza. Robert chatted. But it was nice. I knew Robert owed me money. That was one way of getting out of paying you: he introduced you to someone like Brando. You'd chat for a bit, then say, 'Sorry, got to go,' and Robert would say, 'OK, talk to you in the week.' And you'd left *again* without getting the money.

In the mid-sixties Robert would say to me, 'I'll give you that money when I see you.' But he didn't realize that I needed it that day, to live on. He didn't understand. It was inconceivable to him that I could need £100. I'd go down there and he still wouldn't pay me, and yet he'd have a white Rolls-Royce with a chauffeur sitting outside waiting to take him wherever he wanted to go. And be talking about buying big pictures. It was sometimes dispiriting to realize he'd probably spend that night the money he owed you. But when he was lovely, he was lovely. He was so generous.

But he could be very touchy about things. I mean, we got on very well but we didn't go out together or anything. I mean, I did go to places with him but I came home afterwards, because what I was interested in was working. I didn't want to go to nightclubs or whatever. I wasn't interested in drugs. I'm not homosexual. So I wasn't interested in the two things that were interesting to him, you know. The only reason we got on was that he liked my work. Robert went to clubs and things. Later on he would talk about picking up boys, but he knew I wasn't interested in that.

STASH KLOSSOWSKI All I can tell you about sex and Robert in those days was that Tina Aumond fell madly in love with him. When I was staying at Mount Street, she would drag him to bed in the back bedroom. He'd give me one of these helpless looks but allow himself to be dragged off to bed. In the mornings he'd complain, 'I can't make it with chicks.' But he couldn't say no and kick her out, he just allowed it to happen. That's the only sex I remember him having there at 23 Mount Street.

MARIANNE FAITHFULL I've always felt that if Robert hadn't been gay, if it hadn't all been so weird, he and I would have fallen in love. And we sort of did. It was an extremely deep relationship in which he had a lot of power. I probably did too, but I didn't know it. I worshipped him, that's all; literally worshipped him.

I used to ask him, 'What kind of woman would you like, if you weren't gay? Tell me exactly.' Must have driven him crackers. Eventually he said what he really wanted was a beautiful Hindu princess, completely trained to obey her man, i.e. Robert, who would do anything he said without question and just serve him for the rest of her life. I must have thought then, 'Better turn your mind to other things.'

ALASTAIR LONDONDERRY Women did find him attractive, no question about that. But – what's the expression, 'kick against the pricks' or something? – they kicked, but I'm afraid that was all they could do. I've no idea where his homosexuality came from. His parents were Christian Scientists, but I don't think they shoved it down his throat or things like that, surely. His father was a very broad-minded man.

MARIANNE FAITHFULL It was a summer evening in 1966, the summer of love in fact, and Robert and I were very close. I had only just started going out with Mick. I'd gone round to see Robert – I went out a lot on my own – and I never questioned my feelings about Robert, I just did whatever I felt, and I felt like going to see him, so I did.

Anyway we smoked a joint and it became very sexual – that's what happened. And it was the most amazing experience. We kissed and we were just about to make love when Mick walked in. We'd left the door open – it was a very hot night – so no ringing of doorbells. We'd just finished kissing and were lying on the sofa, among the cushions – all very Indian, very beautiful. He looked amazing and I looked amazing, and we could both see that. I think I was nineteen. I smoked this joint and was absolutely immobilized, except that my mind and my senses were working.

There was this beautiful man beside me. After we kissed, we both had to pause and look at each other and think about this: so what do we feel we should do now? We had just started to move back together when Mick walked in.

Mick was wearing a beautiful Mr Fish silk jacket which had a face painted on the back, or something incredible, I really can't remember what, but one of those wonderful silk jackets – perhaps a Michael Rainey jacket. It was a bit too tight – he wore things very tight – and when he saw what was going on with Robert and me, with me sprawled out on this huge sofa – a transcendent moment really – he freaked. He used his muscles to rip this jacket. We were both stoned and we just couldn't believe it. We watched this tantrum. It was like watching the Incredible Hulk – rip, rip! As he flexed his considerable muscles, the whole beautiful little frivolous thing just tore and tore and tore. With an amazing noise too. At the end of it he said, 'See? Michael Rainey makes such shit.' Then he said to me, 'All right, Marianne? Coming?' I got up and left.

KEITH RICHARDS No, Robert was beautifully gay. He loved women. It's not that usual. He wasn't your obvious London queen. He just stated preference that way. It was still illegal, so you had to be circumspect. But it wasn't just that. I knew a lot of gays who were openly queeny, poofy, all the limp wrist, etc. But Robert didn't show out that way. Always incredibly well dressed. Except at home, when he would affect the Moroccan. He'd say, 'Come to my place for lunch, I've got some new records.' So you'd get up for it, pop round to Robert's pad, the mint tea, nice pipe and some great new sounds. From anywhere, Morocco or Memphis.

You'd see Robert go from this wonderful Savile Row suit to his jellaba and his little Turkish slippers. He enjoyed finding out about other strata of life. He also enjoyed paying you back, knowledge about this or that, rugs, etc. He could get very intense when it came to something he was interested in.

If it was a rug, it's the carpet dealer and the buyer. So he's haggling. Oh, Robert, that's over the top. But look at the *quality*! I wouldn't show this to just anybody. I'd *only* sell it to you. Very oriental way of selling. You have to feel it for days and walk away, no way, and then come back. Like carrying on a little kasbah.

STASH KLOSSOWSKI Robert was terribly efficient. I went with him to Sardinia in the summer of '66 with Michael Rainey also. Everyone was always on a trip and Robert was also very stoned, but he made sure we left the house on time. He was like an agent: now you have to leave. He got a cab and organized all that sort of thing.

When I got back from Sardinia later on, wearing the weird gear I always wore in those days, customs examined my French passport, questioned me, asked me to show my money, etc. But that day they interrogated me and we had a violent confrontation. They said, 'Can you get anyone to vouch for you?' I told them to ring Robert and he got on the phone and in this adult manner told them off. Then it was, 'Yes, sir. Yes, sir.' So I was finally let into the country. They said I didn't have enough money, etc., etc. They didn't like long-haired people and didn't want to let us in. Robert managed to tear them to pieces.

KEITH RICHARDS Robert didn't have to play the Old Etonian too much. But with all Etonians, it's always there. Robert knew how to use it. If it was necessary, it would be: 'Hey, Robert, you know, pull the grand Etonian. Do your bit: I say, and all this.' Otherwise, not at all, not when you were sitting around. It was part of the persona, part of his upbringing. He know how to use it when he needed. After all, he was a captain in the East African Rifles. You've got to remember this too, that my man was a military man in Africa. He definitely had the sense of leadership, no question. How to turn a bunch of undecided guys in a room into making decisions. That's leadership too.

STASH KLOSSOWSKI It was at the end of the summer of '66 that Robert announced that famous phrase 'that inconclusive summer'! Inconclusive though it was, it was an extraordinary period. I took some memorable acid trips. Not at the drop of a hat, I made some definite preparations, and it was always a highly profitable and spiritual experience. That entire period is laced with a very strong spiritual feeling.

BILL WILLIS By 1966 I was spending everything I had a week on coke. I left London in '66. The drug taking was all getting just so wild. I realized if I stayed I would either be in my grave or in a madhouse within six months. I had a strong sense of survival. I remember Gibbs leaving one day, saying, 'Take care of yourself, Bill. No one else will.' That was right.

SUSAN LOPPERT He went away to Morocco soon after I'd started there. I was their skivvy really, Carol Schapiro's and Robert's. Here I was with my two degrees, thinking, 'Really . . . honestly . . .' I was just doing the typing. Anyway, Robert wrote us a couple of letters. I realized he must have been stoned at the time. He wrote telling us how pleased he was, sitting there in Morocco, that he had us working in the gallery, Love Robert, and all of that.

CHRISTOPHER GIBBS We took a house together one Christmas in Marrakesh – Keith Richards, Robert and I – from this very louche hairdresser (who was murdered some years ago in rather a grisly fashion). And he had this house, now all built over, not very big, a run-down house with a huge garden with lots of palm trees and peacocks gone wild and bright narcissi coming up through the weeds everywhere.

I can't remember too much about it, you know. It was a . . . well, chaotic oblivion. I expect there was a muddle about the rent and I expect either the gardener or the cook or something was in bed with Robert instead of gardening or cooking or polishing our shoes. It was nice. It was rather a wet Christmas. We had a lot of majoune, which I think I had brought down from Tangier. My friend Achmed there had made a whole pot of jam with it – which made the whole of Christmas rather dream-like.

BILL WILLIS I came to Morocco alone in '66. I then went back to Tangier and one day up drives this Bentley with black-glass windows, and out poured Robert Fraser, Keith Richards, Anita Pallenberg, Marianne Faithfull and Mick Jagger, and Keith's chauffeur, some thug he had. The steering wheel of the Bentley had this plastic knob attached and this chauffeur would drive it as if it was some thirties getaway car. My dear, that black glass just drove me *wild*.

I was staying in some very cheap hotel in Tangier, and they, of course, were staying in the Minza. They were driving down to Marrakesh, so we rented another car and I went with them. As soon as I got into the car I passed out, we'd had so much to smoke, and I didn't wake up until we drove into Marrakesh – an eight-hour drive.

Brian Jones was on that trip also, he was with Anita in those days. We stayed in the Sadi Hotel in Marrakesh, rented a whole floor. They'd picked up Brion Gysin in Tangier too. We had the Sadi Hotel serving us dinner at 3 a.m. That's when Anita split from Brian and went off with Keith. And we left poor Brian Jones to pay all the bills.

ANITA PALLENBERG Keith, Robert and I would go off on our own, wandering around the kasbah and on the beach. One day, there were these two men walking along the beach in their suits. Strange beach boys, you know, in their suits looking like the Blues Brothers. It was the Kray twins – we were amazed to see them there! In those days, Tangier was a place where everyone went to get away – gang members, all that kind of stuff – and it all looked very sinister. In those days you'd hear about the axeman and all the people they'd nailed and done. And what were they doing in Tangier? You'd immediately imagined it was something horrific . . .

Robert obviously knew them. He went up to them and said, 'What are you doing here?' They said, 'Oh, we're on holiday.'

Me and Keith were sniggering away. 'Holiday!' We didn't ask Robert how he knew them. We were too cool to ask that! Sixties nonchalance, you know . . .

KEITH RICHARDS Robert had such wide interests. He was an art dealer, that was his business, his main thing, but he was just as much interested in music or literature or carpets. Haggling was our other great thing. To go down to the souk in Marrakesh or Fez and say, 'Let's fuck the old bugger about.' Go round to Achmed's, round the corner from the old Minza Hotel in Tangiers, where Achmed would fill you full of hash and sell you things at exorbitant prices with this little old transistor radio blaring out Radio Cairo . . . You'd sit there all day discussing a rug or a hanging. It was called the Bazaar Petit Port Said. Achmed was the best hash maker in Tangiers at the time. You didn't mind even – you'd give up haggling, say, 'Here's the money.' It was worth it just to sit in the shop and smoke. 'Oh, you come back tomorrow . . .' One of the best salesmen I ever knew. Even Robert and I gave up haggling in the end. But Robert would say, 'I say Achmed, old boy, that's a bit steep.' Meanwhile, Marianne's crashed out on some divan . . . Robert and I enjoyed being transported. You could be Sinbad the Sailor, *The Thousand and One Nights*. We loved all that shit.

SUSAN LOPPERT And when he got back he brought me a beautiful necklace, which I've still got, of Moroccan coins and two heavy silver bracelets. But he couldn't bring himself to give them personally. He'd leave them late at night so you'd find them in the morning. I think Robert was very lonely. I think part of the problem was that he never had a relationship, at least not in my time. There were always people around whom he liked, Spanish Tony for example. I don't know who Spanish Tony was, or what, but he was always around. And people like his Moroccan valet, Mohammed. They were big, good-looking guys whom you felt looked after him somehow. You know, Mohammed was clearly also his lover, but kept at servant level. And I think it was part of this whole English thing . . . Moroccan boys and having to go abroad, it's all part of this English upper-class thing of needing somewhere where people are uninhibited. You'd walk along in the flat in Mount Street and Mohammed would be sitting on the lavatory with the door open and his pants down, reading the newspaper.

Robert would just take no notice of it. But he could also treat Mohammed absolutely like a servant – 'Get that done!' His driver. He had the unthinking upper-class way of treating people who were of another class, the servant class.

CHRISTOPHER GIBBS Mohammed – I remember Mohammed. Handsome, smiling, not very clever, a quite sweet-natured boy who, I think, had either been a waiter at the bar on the beach or had been spotted playing football on the beach and brought back to London – and rocketed to stardom . . .

KEITH RICHARDS Mohammed was servant and boyfriend, double duty. Confidant, servant and lover, definitely. Robert could find them. If you were with Robert, there were no bums in the room. If there were, they didn't stay long. Mohammed was treated like a servant and he played the role to perfection. When Robert got into his Moroccan or Middle Eastern thing, there'd be Mohammed with the mint tea. But you were conscious it was a great double act as well. 'Mohammed, get out of bed, get up.' Then he'd become the servant.

BRUCE CONNER I'd been in London three times and each time I'd seen Robert Fraser. The second time was on the way to Berlin to join a panel and show films with other American independent film-makers at the Congress Halle. I stopped in London for four to five days. I was staying at Robert's apartment and didn't quite know how to deal with that, because he had a manservant. I didn't know what you'd do with a manservant, but he would talk about, 'Shall I draw water for you?' I'd say, 'Gosh, I can do things like that for myself.' And I kept trying to relate to this guy, which didn't work at all.

CHRISTOPHER FINCH Mohammed was indeed charming, though I wouldn't have trusted him as far as I could throw him. Intelligent. Very devoted to Robert. And Robert was very affectionate to him on a master–servant basis. He'd do the driving – Robert was a terrible driver. He'd give Mohammed his credit cards and he'd go off and buy clothes. He'd hang out at the gallery and because I'd spent time in Morocco I'd sit and chat with him. He was a kind of uprated Jeeves, the houseboy who took care of all the problems.

CAROL SCHAPIRO Robert used to go back and forth to Morocco a lot, of course, and he'd always have handsome Mohammed around who would do what one wanted him to do. The driving, or help for a show. But then later he'd be at Robert's apartment. As for the relationship, Mohammed was such an independent guy he did pretty much what he wanted to do.

I remember spending a night in bed with Mohammed in Robert's canopied four-poster bed. The two of us were brain dead on hash. We had been racing around London in the gallery van. I think Robert was away, I don't know how it happened, but we wound up in his bed, absolutely smashed, with the TV especially adjusted so that it flashed and pulsated like a light show.

But that was the sixties. All this freedom, breaking away from the restrictions of the fifties. Young people were literally bursting. London was it, was the trendsetter. I came back to New York about Xmas and didn't think I was wearing anything special, but going down Fifth Avenue everyone turned to look at me. I realized how staid and stifling New York was.

BRYAN ROBERTSON At that time – don't forget that what we take for granted now, you couldn't take for granted then – the so-called sex revolution, this emancipation, this change in attitude to sex, only existed in art schools and in some circles. It didn't obtain for the rest of the country. In London the new freedom, the new tolerance, the new attitude only existed in some circles. It's very important that people know that. People think, oh, the swinging sixties, you know the sexual revolution or whatever it's called, how wonderful it must have been.

If you were a young girl growing up in the rather slummy suburbs of Bradford or Liverpool or Manchester, in an ordinary working-class family, if you suddenly found at eighteen or nineteen that you were pregnant, you would be in big trouble. A big, big disgrace. If you were a young fellow growing up in the same sort of family and you suddenly found at the age of sixteen or so that you quite liked wearing an earring or quite liked rinsing your hair, or you quite liked the other fellows rather more than you did the girls, you were in very big trouble. The freedom was in art schools and areas of general permissiveness. Art parties, yes. Some London parties and dinner parties, well, yes, OK. The London art world, well, yes, quite a bit. Outside that, forget it! Terrible condemnation; and that's what informed police work at that time, and their attitude to everything, because the police generally came from ordinary middle-class suburban families, with suburban middle-class values. What's more, I'm fairly sure it's still true today.

So what I'm talking about is the social thing, the old, ghastly thing that will grip England for ever, I'm talking about a class thing.

13 SEPTEMBER–15 OCTOBER 1966: JIM DINE, 'LONDON 1966'

JIM DINE Robert sent me a telegram that said: REGINA VERSUS VAGINA. LOVE ROBERT. So I knew there was a problem. And then it was in *The New York Times* the next day. I thought it was ridiculous.

OWNER OF GALLERY RECEIVES SUMMONS FOR 'OBSCENE' ART
London – The London art gallery that exhibited pictures by the American pop artist Jim Dine has been served with a summons under the Vagrancy Act of 1838.

The act defines as a 'rogue and vagrant' a person exposing his person or exposing in any public place any obscene print or picture or any obscene exhibition. It also covers fortune telling, and persons exposing wounds to gather alms. (The New York Times, *17 October 1966*)

The Police visited the gallery this morning and seized the greater part of the show of drawings and watercolours by Jim Dine, and collage collaborations by Jim Dine and Eduardo Paolozzi.

They also seized catalogues, which include a preface by the respected art critic Father Cyril Barrett, SJ.

It is regretted, therefore, that it will be impossible to present the show as advertised – at any rate for the time being. If charges are brought they will be vigorously defended; we hope also that as many people as possible will make known their reactions to this seizure, in order that the intolerable situation whereby members of the police force are permitted to be arbiters of what may or may not be seen in an art gallery, be put to an end; remembering too that the Obscene Publications Act, under which these works were confiscated, states that their removal is necessitated by the fact that these pictures are 'likely to deprave or corrupt anyone likely to see them'. Twenty-one drawings by Dine, some of them showing various parts of the human body, were seized by police and are to be referred to the Director of Public Prosecutions. (Gallery handout)

BRYAN ROBERTSON The whole thing to me was so absolutely ridiculous. I had been commissioned for a year by Stuart Mason, the very vigorous and imaginative education officer for Leicestershire, to buy works of art – contemporary works of art – for a very, very brilliant collection. That is to say it was an unpatronizing-to-children collection. It was a work of first-class contemporary works of art, designed to hang in schoolrooms and school corridors and everywhere so that children could grow up quite unselfconsciously at ease with contemporary art – it wouldn't present any problems.

I agreed with some enthusiasm to buy for them, and did so. And one of the works I bought was this collage, which seemed to me totally innocuous – there might have been a genital or two in it, heaven knows. Mostly they were red hearts and a rather charming bits of collage, brilliant colour. It was a very inventive use of collage, which is why I rather warmed to it, as an example of what children could do with bits and pieces of different materials. And there was certainly nothing offensive in it. There was nothing more offensive than you see sometimes chalked up or scrawled up in a school playground. And I bought it and of course then the exhibition was closed.

JIM DINE POP DRAWINGS: A DENIAL

Leicestershire Education Committee has not brought one of the Pop Art pictures by American Jim Dine which were seized by police at a Mayfair gallery.

The Robert Fraser Gallery in Duke Street, London, where Dine's drawings were on exhibition, told the Leicester Mercury *that one of them had been bought by the well-known art critic, Mr Bryan Robertson, for the committee.*

But a spokesman for the Education Department said that Mr Robertson did not buy pictures for the committee – he advised them what to buy and they had not bought one of the controversial works. (Leicester Mercury, 23 September 1966)

BRYAN ROBERTSON I had to go to some deep dungeon, where they were held by the CID or Scotland Yard, whatever it was, to have another look at all the works. I wanted to make quite sure that I could describe everything very accurately in court, because I'd agreed from the beginning to appear on behalf of the work, and on behalf of Robert also.

And when I chatted up the man in charge of the works, inside the fortress, I said, 'Who on earth could possibly have been offended by these? Somebody must have complained.' And he said, 'Oh yes, indeed, there was rather a complaint launched.' And I said, 'Well, who was it?' He said, 'It was a Mr Major from Tunbridge Wells.' So I could hardly contain myself. It sounded like a farce.

I went away and bided my time, and then appeared with Roland Penrose and various people, to appear if necessary on behalf of Robert. And in the corridor of the court, just outside the courtroom, there was a group of officials at the other end – policemen, and Scotland Yard people – and in the middle of them all was an extremely louche-looking young man, with flowing black greasy hair, impenetrable shades – enormous black glasses – very, very pale and rather depraved-looking, and wearing rather farouche clothes. And I thought, 'Dear God, Robert's blown it! He's brought one of his friends along for support and now the fat's in the fire!' And I said to somebody, 'Who is that fellow down at the other end with the other lot?' And they said, 'That's Mr Major from Tunbridge Wells.'

It turned out that he was a representative of the Lord's Day Observance Society. And I think the Lord's Day Observance Society was used by the CID to go around and snoop and make trouble, I really do.

ART GALLERY MAN DENIES HOLDING INDECENT SHOW

An exhibition of pictures by the artist Jim Dine, on show at the Robert

Fraser Gallery, Duke Street, Mayfair, was not obscene within the definition of the Obscene Publications Act 1959, but was crudely offensive and disgusting, alleged Mr John Matthew, proscecuting for the Director of Public Prosecutions at Marlborough Street this afternoon . . .

Det Sgt Beale, who executed a search warrent and seized 21 pictures at the gallery, told the magistrate, Mr John Aubrey Fletcher, that some of the pictures could be seen from the street. Twelve compositions on one wall depicted the male genital organ and three on the opposite wall showed the female organ.

The officer alleged that when he told Fraser that he was objecting to them, but admitted he was not an artist, Fraser replied, 'I am certainly not bothered by the opinion of a tuppenny-halfpenny policeman.' (Evening Standard)

PICTURES INDECENT RULES COURT

The sergeant said he started to make a sketch of the picture with the obscene word on it because this composition did not appear in the catalogue. Fraser gave him a photograph of it, saying, 'At least let us have it accurate.'

When the sergeant asked if he had photographs of five other paintings not in the catalogue, Fraser said, 'No.'

He was told again that the matter would have to be reported to the Director of Public Prosecutions. Fraser said, 'Yes, all right. Run away and do it.'

JIM DINE SHOW RULED INDECENT

London – A British magistrate found the works of American artist Jim Dine indecent today and fined the Robert Fraser Gallery for holding an exhibition of Mr Dine's work.

The gallery was fined 20 guineas (58 dollars) and ordered to pay 20 guineas in costs. Fourteen days were allowed for an appeal.

There will almost certainly be an appeal. This is something of a test case. Mr Dine's work is in the permenant collections of the Museum of Modern Art, New York, the Tate Gallery, London, and others. (Herald Tribune, 28 November 1966)

MAGISTRATE SEES 21 PICTURES –
THEN FINES ART GALLERY MAN

Mr Fraser, aged 29, of Mount St, Mayfair, told the court, 'These pictures have got humour. The one thing that stands out among them is their *humour and their optimism.'* He said he had decided not to appeal.

In New York, artist Jim Dine said, *'I would have no qualms about show-ing those works to my three boys.'* (Daily Sketch)

BRUCE DOUGLAS-MANN Letter to Robert from Douglas-Mann and Co., solicitors

I am sorry that we did not succeed but I think that we nevertheless achieved some successes, both in illustrating the absurdities of the law and in obtaining from the representatives of the Director of Public Prosecutions' Office an assurance that, if it were alleged that the pictures were obscene, proceedings would be brought under the 1959 Act (under which expert evidence is admissible) and not under the Vagrancy Act.

It was the exhibition which was held to be indecent, not any individual picture. The prosecution agreed that if the pictures had been displayed individually, and probably if they had been displayed so that they were not visible from the street, no offence would have been committed *in the eyes of the prosecution.* I think it is very probable, however, that the magistrate would have been quite willing to hold each picture obscene in itself and, if a private individual were to prosecute, there is no certainty under which act proceedings would be brought. You would therefore be wise to be discreet so far as these pictures are concerned or any similar exhibition.

SUSAN LOPPERT The nub of the matter was that the pictures were visible from the street through large plate-glass windows and might entice people who wouldn't otherwise penetrate an art gallery. The hypocrisy was that, had the pictures been exhibited in the basement (with me sidling up to people and inviting them down to look at our dirty pictures), all would have been well.

BRYAN ROBERTSON I think that it was a put-up job. The whole thing was preposterous. And for the very solid reason that I went on one Saturday morning to see the show before I actually made a purchase. I arrived just too late, the gallery had closed, Robert had gone, and I stood peering from the street through the window and could see nothing – could see nothing. Wasn't a question of time and day and reflections. Not in any climate or light could you possibly see what was actually on the walls. You could see they were small framed objects and bits of colour. But not even with my very strong spectacles on – and I've got perfect vision – could you make out what they were up to.

I think it was a put-up job and really they were after Robert for drugs, quite simply. Not serious drugs. They were smoking a lot of pot, there were boyfriends coming in and out – that sort of thing. Although I don't think

Robert was particularly noisy. He was rather an elegant character. His parties were rather proper affairs. And I think the whole thing was ridiculous. One of those silly little criminal vendettas that went on in the sixties.

OCTOBER 1966: RICHARD HAMILTON

RICHARD HAMILTON I liked Robert very much, liked the style of his gallery. I thought it suited me much more than other galleries I'd been with. And I had great affection for Robert as a person who made very good shows and who seemed to love what he was doing. So I enjoyed the shows I did with him. I think I was doing quite well with Robert. He sold to people like Ted Power . . . to various people. Ted Power was there for the opening day as I came in, and he came up with Robert from downstairs and said, 'I've bought half the show. I thought I'd better leave something for other people.' Which I thought was very nice of him.

Dear Arne [Ekstron],

I am extremely interested in the idea of arranging a Richard Hamilton show with you, and what I have in mind is an exhibition of the six Guggenheim reliefs with related drawings, the subject of our latest show, plus the series of works involving retouched photographs.

I am enclosing herewith coloured transparencies of the Guggenheim and some of the related works. The exhibition was great *succès d'estime* but I made practically no effort to sell as I felt it was more important that the show be seen in New York, and had the reliefs been sold it would of course have been more difficult to arrange their being shown in a commercial gallery.

I have been a little upset by what I feel has been a slight coolness towards me in recent months, and am terribly anxious that our good relations be restored. I know it's been very unprofessional of me not to settle the matter of the Lindner payment much earlier, but it was delayed for a long time and then I simply forgot – no excuse is offered but I hope this isolated piece of bad management won't be allowed to come between us as I have always wanted to collaborate with you on something and now feel that here is the opportunity which could be of enormous benefit to us both: I am convinced that Hamilton is an artist whose star is firmly on the ascendant, and were you to consider permanent representation for him in the States I can think of no more able or more prestigious gallery with which to form an association.

RICHARD HAMILTON But there was something amiss, I thought, because Robert seemed to be spending much more money on everything – like drinks, catering, parties – so things were going a little downhill. It seemed as though there might be strange circumstances which were causing him to spend. I got the impression afterwards it might have been the case of being hung for a sheep as a lamb. So he was really letting rip.

Messrs Coutts & Co.
440, Strand, London WC2

Dear Sirs,

In respect of the account for Robert Fraser Gallery Ltd 'Artists A/C', we have mistakenly written checks against this account (4897153; check numbers C151 08257 through 08264) and would appreciate your debiting instead our other account, Robert Fraser Gallery Ltd. (4897102).

The Marquis of Londonderry
Old Grove House
Hampstead Grove
London N W3

Dear Al [Alastair Londonderry],

Enclosed is a statement relating to the sale of the Dali drawing at Christie's. The cheque was sent to us in August while you were away, so I forgot about letting you know that it had come through and that we had deposited it in our account.

Letter from ROBERT ELKON
Dear Bob,

I am getting very annoyed with your cavalier attitude. I have written to you time and again and have not received a single reply, nor have you sent me a check of $900 which you promised would be forthcoming almost two months ago. Will you please read over my past letters and write to me as soon as possible.

Dear Bob,

It might save wear and tear on your nervous system if you were to pay a little more attention to my letters to you. I think I explained to you that I would be buying the Balthus for myself and would give you the money for it when I can. As you had that group of Balthus drawings for about a year and a half yourself, I really don't see why you should keep on nagging about the sum of $900, which I can hardly believe is that desperately urgent. I repeat: I haven't forgotten, so I suggest you just calm down.

Letter from ROBERT ELKON

Dear Bob,

I could take your letter amiss; however, it would be foolish and immature for us to bicker over such small and unimportant issues. I am sorry if you think I have been nagging you but the fact is that I could have sold that last drawing too and since you bought it for yourself I felt that you might have paid me before this. $900 is not a great amount for you or for me but you, being in the same business as I, must realize that small amounts have a tendency to accumulate and can be most helpful when they come . . . so let us forget our mutual 'gripes'.

CAROL SCHAPIRO He was getting into really bad financial straits at that point. I left, but he kept Susan on. She'd been working under me. She was cheaper. To me, Robert seemed to be increasingly nervous. And physically manifesting it – pacing, waving his arms around.

Susan felt Robert's paranoia was down to narcotics. In retrospect I would agree. We didn't really discuss him. He was crazy, unpredictable. You never knew when he was going to show up, no matter what he said.

Towards the end of the time I was at the gallery, he'd call up before he came in and say, 'Is there anyone outside watching the front door?' I'd go and peer around outside, go back: 'No, nobody's watching.' I wasn't aware of angry clients ringing up, perhaps Susan was. Everything that went on in the gallery was Robert in a personal relationship with whoever it was, a client, an artist, etc.

Dear Delphine [Seyrig],

This is just a line to let you know that the Lichtenstein has been sent and will be delivered to you by

    Jonemann & Co

    52–54 rue Ricquet

    Paris XIX   BOT 9560

who will, I hope, let you know before delivering it.

Also enclosed is our invoice; you may pay in any currency convenient to you.

It was lovely to see you in August and I'll let you know when I come to Paris. I had a marvellous time in Morocco and went on an extraordinary voyage to the Sahara with Brion Gysin – I'll tell you all about it when I see you.

SUSAN LOPPERT Robert had done all the networking [to get Delphine Seyrig to buy a Lichtenstein painting] but by the time she came to the gallery to collect it, you know, he just wasn't there . . . He never used to show up until midday or whatever, and sometimes he wouldn't remember what he'd said or done or anything like that. Of course, I was very naïve – we weren't into the whole drug culture then – and it took me a long time to realize that he wasn't peculiar (I mean, he was peculiar) but that he was drugged.

JOHN DUNBAR Robert was sort of the older generation and hadn't caught the first 'drug wave', but he immediately dived into it. It was an extremely exclusive kind of club and one felt one was on the cutting edge. You know, so many new things were happening. It just obviously was somewhere that people hadn't got to yet. It was so unknown that you weren't an outlaw if you did it. The police didn't know anything about it. I remember the little bottles of coke that if you spilt a bit would just float down like bits of paper, glittering as they went . . .

Smack was very much an arty scene – very much. I mean, how I was introduced to it was from the Americans. All the jazz and poetry and beads and all that. The ones who were into it heard that England, you know, it was the promised land. You could get it from a doctor, just from going in and asking for it . . . I mean, not quite that easy, but almost. In New York needles were illegal – it was all this eye-droppery business – so England was just amazing. So they came here. And you know, William Burroughs and all this lot, they were all here.

He certainly got his habit pretty quick. I kind of warned him about it – do be careful, because it's not like smoking dope, it's real easy to get stuck. And by the time he'd got a lot of connections – these were the days when you got it off a doctor and, you know, people would sell you a bit of their script for a pound a grain. In other words, it was sort of like 10p for a pill half of which would do you fine if you weren't into it. Literally, it was more or less free.

And he was sort of – I mean, I remember saying, 'No thank you' to some more and he was going [posh voice], 'Oh, you're so paranoid, John!' about getting a habit sort of thing. Or I'd say, 'Look, I've had it for three days on the trot, it's enough,' that sort of thing, and like within a month or two he was really, really bang into it. You know, shooting, and a habit.

KEITH RICHARDS He was obviously into it way before I did it. With Robert it was always crème de la crème, it was pure, manufactured by the British government for the British junkie. Except you didn't register, cos that hindered your movements. You'd have to register wherever you went. Plenty of junkies exaggerated the size of their habits, double, and sell off the other half. And it was pure stuff. Another thing I learned from Robert: never, unless you've really got to, buy anything on the streets.

The bizarre idea in England was that if you registered as a heroin addict, whether you wanted it or not, you were forced to take the same amount in pure cocaine. On the firm belief that you'd be more useful as a member of society instead of lying about smacked out. That would bring you up, the perfect speedball. So we were living in the place where the perfect speedball was available. Junkies would sell off the cocaine and a bit of their smack. It was easy to get, the best stuff in the world. It was never cut, none of that lowlife thing about it. Robert was your gentleman junkie. Very nineteenth-century gentleman: 'Wonderful stuff, don't you think?' Sherlock Holmes comes to mind. That was the atmosphere. The attitude was the same. Or Baudelaire-ish. That was after a little while, when we realized what he had been doing in the back room, with this blue needle.

BILL WILLIS We had our first snort of smack together in his Mount Street apartment. I must say I have never felt so euphoric. I thought I knew all the answers to all the problems of life. Then we did it again three days later and I didn't feel a thing. So the immediate tendency is to take more. I said, 'No, this is how it all starts, I'll just remember that first experience.'

CAROL SCHAPIRO I didn't realize he was shooting up from time to time in the gallery, but Susan knew. I didn't see any traces of it.

SUSAN LOPPERT I'd come and work at Mount Street while he was redoing the flat. I had a key to Mount Street and I'd let myself in. He'd be in his pyjamas and one of the worst things I ever saw was when he inadvertently lifted his pyjama leg – I saw all the pockmarks from the needles. We were intimate in that way and, although I never saw him naked, I saw everything else. I often found syringes and things like that.

ALASTAIR LONDONDERRY Most people who snort cocaine or shoot or snort heroin, one of the first signs of their addiction is their restlessness. And leaving the room the whole time, coming in and out of the room. It was always a sure sign. But I never noticed it and I never – I mean, he did once tell me. The only reference he made to heroin addiction, he said, 'You know, taking heroin is like putting an overcoat on when you've been freezing cold. You put this overcoat on and are immediately warm.' That was the only reference. I mean, I never discussed it with him. *Never* discussed shooting heroin or snorting it, or snorting cocaine.

LEO CASTELLI What happens in cases like Robert is financial problems, certainly. Then the fact he was a drug addict did contribute to excessive expense and therefore less money for the gallery, and less attention to it.

But he was very, very good. He was a superb dealer. It was a pity that he had this weakness. That his undoing.

22 NOVEMBER 1966–15 JANUARY 1967: CLAES OLDENBURG

CLAES OLDENBURG In NY in the early sixties, everything was very creative and intense. That lasted for a couple of years. I went off to LA because I wanted to start again. Then I went to Europe in '64. I came back to NY in '65, and by then everything had become institutionalized. Warhol had taken up all of the original elements from the scene and made them into his own scene, and that got a lot of publicity. So things had already begun to decay at that point, had become celebrity/publicity-driven. London hadn't quite reached that stage. In '66 it was a very creative time there, in terms of clothes, music, even art. It was mostly music and lifestyle. You had the feeling that it was still very accessible. Everybody mixed and there wasn't a lot of distance between people. They hadn't set up camps, etc.

Robert wasn't living in a world I was living in. He was too fast-lane to what I was doing. I would see him from time to time, but never had much real communication with him. He was always off somewhere. If you met him for dinner, he may or may not show up, etc. He was leading a hectic life.

Anyway, we'd put together this show very carefully. It looked very good. He had rented a place for me across the street, a studio, and that made it easy to keep in touch with the gallery. My stuff is always very difficult to install – arrives all in a heap and there are lots of different ways to put it up. So it was important for me to keep in touch with it and I was there for quite a long time, at least a month, setting it up. That's the only show I did with Robert.

In that sixties period he was certainly very open to whatever you wanted to do. Obviously I had to take charge with what was going to happen with this exhibition. I more or less hung it, with Susan's assistance. Robert was in and out, that's all. He had a very good eye for things though. Probably I was so self-absorbed during that period, I didn't notice much about other people.

. . . He had this show and sold a number of pieces, and somehow didn't forward the money to my parent gallery, which was Sidney Janis. I think Sidney sued him eventually. Robert's point of view was that it was a great time, we met a lot of people, we had a great show and what do those things matter? From his point of view it didn't matter, because even when he went bankrupt he was still very rich. So it all ended on a sour note.

After Stockholm the work came to London, the first time it had been shown here, and it was very successful.

That was my first encounter with London. I'd come over briefly in the summer, then back later for the show. I did a lot of drawings in London – the first impression was very strong. I stayed there for quite a while and did a lot of work there, across the street from the gallery, and that reverberated when I got back to NY.

This was also the time when Lennon met Yoko Ono. When I arrived in London I went to Trafalgar Square and the lions had strings hanging out of their months – that had been a performance by Yoko, organized by Mario Amaya. I'd known her in NY, but she was part of the scene that autumn.

We didn't do a happening in London, although we talked about it a lot. Robert would have arranged it. We looked for spaces for it, but somehow there wasn't enough time to put it together. Then we talked about doing something the following year. Robert and I talked about it, but nothing happened.

That was a very creative time for me. It was great. I was very happy to be there. I don't remember going to any other galleries than Robert's. I just focused on that. But that was probably the best time to come to London. It was all fresh, at least from our point of view. It did feel to me that my show was a high point, a nice feeling. There wasn't a great deal of media attention.

The role of the Rolling Stones was to be the bad kids on the block, early punks if you like, and the Beatles were the good guys, and they played their roles very well. They came to the opening. Mick Jagger said awfully nasty things to everybody, and Paul McCartney was very nice, charming.

Some of the work I did in London did become part of the exhibition. There was a big piece of chocolate, for example. And drawings.

Robert really had an eye for draughtsmanship. Very few dealers have. He was obviously a very involved dealer and that's why he was nice to work with. He really was interested in art and that made it a pleasure, even if he did have all these outside interferences. I felt that what I was showing would be very much appreciated by him and that was more important than any sales. I don't even remember the sales or who bought anything. That all went through Sidney. That was the spirit of the time.

I don't remember that we talked a lot about the financial side. That happened after I left. When Sidney didn't get the payments, there was correspondence and then, I believe, there was some kind of settlement. I wasn't really part of that. And probably Robert wasn't either – it was probably in the hands of his lawyers. That didn't spoil anything at the time, it came afterwards, like a hangover.

Robert was exasperating. You'd expect him to be somewhere and he wasn't there, or he'd put things off, speak sarcastically about things. We were not physically compatible. You have this large ponderous bear trying to put up his work and then this mercurial figure beside. I think we got along, but I wasn't travelling as fast as he was.

He was probably operating on two different levels. But how could you resist doing that, under the circumstances? This has always been the problem of art in relation to the popular scene. I see art as one stream, popular music as another stream. I don't see them knitted together. If you have an interest in both, it's not necessarily shallow.

I think at the end of the earlier period, he really was broken down. I remember when I went to say goodbye to him, when I left London in '66, he was completely collapsed.

Robert in his gallery, photographed by Ian MacMillan.

PAUL MORRISSEY Robert's a good example of a well-educated, well-brought-up human being buying in to the permissive sixties. An Englishman who bought in to all that garbage of the sixties.

It wasn't the beginning, it was the *end* of modern civilization, that whole period from the second half of the sixties. I don't think we'll ever recover from the horrors that started then.

PAUL McCARTNEY Then there came the time when young Robert got busted . . .

Robert, Debrah Dixon, Anita Pallenberg, Donald Cammell and friends in France.

Robert and Terry Southern in California, photographed by Dennis Hopper.

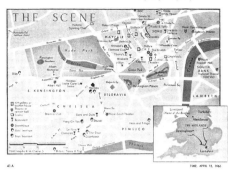

Time Swinging London edition, 1966.

Map of Swinging London including Robert's gallery.

LEFT TO RIGHT: Gerard Malanga, Andy Warhol, Robert Fraser, Michael Cooper.

Robert with Dennis Hopper and friends in Mount Street, 1966.

Dear Mr. Fraser,

     I understand from The Guardian that the seizure of the Dine pictures is to be contested.

     If the enclosed postal orders enable it to be contested a little more vigorously I shall have been repaid.

     Yours,

     Fred Westwood

The Jim Dine show, *London 1966*.

OPPOSITE: The Claes Oldenburg show.

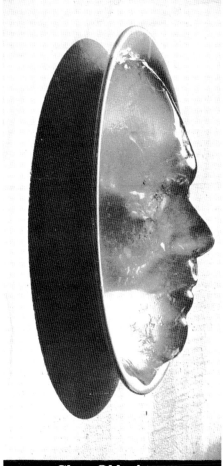

Claes Oldenburg

22 November–31 December 1966
Robert Fraser Gallery
69 Duke Street London W 1

7 Swingeing London

1967

In February 1967 *the* News of the
World *wrongly quoted Mick Jagger as
saying that he had frequently taken
drugs. He initiated a libel action against
them. It is widely believed that the
newspaper then suggested the police visit
Keith Richards's house, Redlands, the
following weekend, knowing that drugs
would be found and Jagger's case then
weakened.*

*For many people this seemed timely.
London might suddenly be the centre of
the action, but there were plenty who
preferred it the way it had been before.
Having the chance to punish some of the
leading representatives of this new
world (of which Robert was seen to be
a part) was an opportunity not to be
missed.*

Detail from *Swingeing London '67 II* by Richard Hamilton.

162

JIM DINE The sixties scene didn't seem normal to me. I came from Ohio and I was dazzled by it, and dazzled by Robert – for a minute. Then I leave, come back to live there, all ready to make an exhibition at this gallery, and he said, 'I've become a *shmecker*' [Jewish word for sniffing]. I said, 'What?' He said, 'You know, man. Heroin, man. I've been busted and I'm going to jail.' And then he was gone.

RICHARD HAMILTON Why did I call it 'Swingeing London'? Among the pieces I used for the collage, there was a phrase that struck me very forcibly, a remark made by the judge in the case, who said, 'There are times when a swingeing sentence should be administered' – something like that, anyway – and only a few months earlier Robert had been very well represented in the *Time* piece, which was called 'Swinging London'. So it was a pun on swinging London and the swingeing sentence. ∎

CHRISTOPHER GIBBS You know about the bust, etc. That was to a degree brought upon them by themselves. Obnoxious behaviour at one time or another. It was all in the stars, it was the plan. So there's no point looking for villains.

I was staying at Redlands at that time. We had a walk on the beach on that morning. We then drove over in the afternoon to try and see Edward James's house. We were having a nice quiet supper in the evening (I think Mohammed was cooking the dinner), which was then rudely interrupted by rather a lot of people from the West Sussex Constabulary . . .

PC DON RAMBRIDGE There's not many of us left that went down on that notorious day. But I do remember Bob Fraser very well, and what happened that day.

Stan Cudmore was the DS in charge at that time, the CID link. He wasn't our Divisional DS, he was a Headquarters man, but he had the link with the press. It was the *News of the World* story that put us on the boys, backed up with some other information from a reliable source – Stan was a very careful man and not particularly pro-journalist – and so about thirty of us were on the raid that night. It was just a knock on the door, we went in, quite an orderly situation, no hassle.

As I recall it, when we got there the procedure was that we were all instructed to grab someone and then follow him through, go through the whole of his system – go through their clothes, go to where he was sleeping or whatever – take on one person. I was allocated Robert. I picked him up at a fairly early stage.

He took me back to where his coat was and in his coat he had a little bottle of white pills, quite a lot of them, and he told me they were prescribed for him for a problem he had. Drug taking was in its infancy then, not a lot of it going on. It was very much a new thing in the police world. It was one of my earlier drug raids certainly.

Robert was a very affable guy, good as gold, very pleasant individual. So we went there and he was very cooperative, telling me the pills were for a stomach problem, prescribed by his doctor. I accepted what he said. He seemed an articulate, intelligent individual. I showed them to my boss, who said, 'Oh, God, they could be.' But we accepted what Robert told us. However, I took a dozen and let him have the rest back. And of course the lab analysis showed them to be pure heroin. And we'd given him the rest back!

I didn't feel he was arrogant. I dealt with him personally all the way through on my own – no other person involved – and he wasn't arrogant. He obviously lied to me, but everybody does that, it's part of the job. He was cooperative, told me where his jacket was. He could have been obstructive, could have stayed silent. But he didn't. I think he was hoping to get away with it, but of course the lab results stopped that. After that, there was no denial, no lying, just a plea of guilty.

I knew Keith Richards and his family, and they're very nice people. They in effect were caretakers of the property. At that time Keith was not the predominant drug taker, although he turned out to be later. Then it was more Mick, I think. It was always the boys against the police sort of thing. But Keith in particular was not an objectionable bloke and his parents were super people – very pro-police.

Redlands gave us a bit of a shock. From the outside it's a beautiful house – Olde Worlde, half-beamed. Then you go inside and it's decorated in mauves and blacks, all the beams painted like that. It turned out to be a typical ravers' place. It really hurt looking at the inside.

All that about Marianne Faithfull and the Mars Bar was all a load of rubbish. She was sitting there wrapped in a rug, nothing on underneath it, and that was about it. She wasn't anything to look at anyway – she was obviously a drop-out type.

We were all fairly inexperienced about drugs then and no one recognized those pills as heroin, not even Stan Cudmore, who probably knew more than anyone about drugs. Even today heroin pills are rare. It doesn't usually come in that form. These ones were very, very small. I think Bob had three dozen all together, and we took just twelve.

I think he told us where his jacket was, even knowing the pills were there, but he realized we'd find them anyway. We were very determined and drugs then was the most serious thing in the world.

There was an American there, called the Acid King, but we didn't find anything on him.

As far as I remember LSD didn't come into that night, it was really just cannabis. They had joss sticks around, smell of incense everywhere. To hide the cannabis smell, of course.

They all had long hair and the way-out language. Alien to our way of life of course. At that time Keith Richard was bright bloke, spoke well with a good accent. As a group I don't think they were that bad.

So we went in there and we did it right. We had to do it right because it was a high-profile job. We didn't even arrest Bob then, just reported him. I don't think any of them were arrested that night. I think all we found otherwise was cannabis.

KEITH RICHARDS The weird twist is that we were all on acid. Just coming down off an acid trip. When you're on acid you take things in a different way. My house in England was nearly 1,000 years old, little windows. There's a great thundering at the door and we're all just relaxing in front of a big roaring fire. We'd been out all day doing nuts things, God knows what. And driving – 'Keith can drive, he's a good driver' – and I'm seeing bursts, angels flying around. There was Christopher Gibbs, Marianne and me. George Harrison had only just left. I think they were waiting for him to leave. It was some tip-off from a chauffeur, a newspaper, shabby stuff.

Knock at the door. And we looked through the window. 'There's all these little people, wearing the same clothes!' We took it with a sense of bemusement: 'Oh, do come in.' Then they read the warrant. 'Yes, that's fine, OK, please do look around.' Robert tried to get rid of some. I didn't have any in my possession. The others had brought the stuff. That's what I got done for, allowing people to use controlled substances. 'What if I don't know what that stuff is?' That was my end of the story.

Robert was still high on acid, trying to talk to the Chief Inspector of the Sussex CID, you know. 'My good chap . . .' Robert conducted himself in his usual gentlemanly fashion. 'I say, old boy, can't we have a little chat?' This is to the CID. He treated the cops: 'Well, look here, if you *must* take them all. You shall be hearing from my solicitor, etc.' Robert had some stashed away, so he wasn't worried about going cold turkey. When he came down to the house, he had fifty jacks, I'm sure.

But it did put a damper on the evening. Although there was Marianne and the fur rug. She'd just taken a shower and come down to see what the commotion was, wrapped in this rug, which kept slipping off at all the right – or wrong – moments, depending how you looked at it. There were a few other peripheral people around, Nikki, a certain Mr X, a Canadian guy, and they let him go, but he was the dealer. He had angel dust with him and all this other stuff. It was a conspiracy, a small shabby plot, between the *News of the World* and the chauffeur and the cops. Why didn't they do this other guy, who had everything? I didn't mind. The less found the better.

CHRISTOPHER GIBBS I can't remember who arrived when or what . . . Some of us were more out of it than others – I not particularly. I can't really remember what happened next – whether we stayed the night or whether we went up to London or what happened.

Mick just had some perfectly ordinary upper. We were just normal hop heads who were equally well happy with a glass of red wine or a joint. We were very surprised at Robert having heroin. A little bit shocked . . .

MARIANNE FAITHFULL He was busted with twenty-four jacks of British Pharmaceutical in a beautiful little box. But none of us knew that. Maybe Anita – no, but she wasn't there. You could have knocked me down with a feather – hard drugs!

MICK JAGGER I was naïvely shocked when he was busted at Redlands that he was taking heroin. He didn't talk about drugs. Drugs were the core of his life. Here was a very intelligent person with a great eye, who'd done interesting things, but he was so into drugs, obsessed with them. It was a shame. It obviously ruined his whole life. We were very tight then, me and Robert. The bust obviously brought us closer together. Was it a plan to make an example of us or was it just a bit of bad luck? I was on the bad-luck side. Because there wasn't any real hard evidence it was anything else. There was a tremendous amount of drug taking going on. So what? It was a big drug bust. There were a lot of theories. Robert and I used to talk about it. How could we find out what was behind it? But we never did find out. I don't think there was a conspiracy, but this touches Robert a lot. I could go on about this a lot.

From Up and Down with the Rolling Stones *by Tony Sanchez*
It was after midnight on Sunday when I was awakened by the persistent ring of the telephone. Robert was at the other end and he sounded distraught.

'We got raided, Tony,' he said. 'And what do you think they found on me?'

My heart sank, because in those days possession of heroin meant a virtually certain sentence of imprisonment.

'Come over to the flat, Tony,' he pleaded. 'I've got to talk to you.'

He told me the whole story when I arrived. At the end I asked him, 'What else did they find down there?'

'I couldn't care less about them,' he said bitterly. 'It's their bloody fault that I'm in all this trouble. I'd never have been searched if they hadn't been so stupid.'

In those days I had friends who claimed to be able to buy off any kind of prosecution. Certainly I knew a couple of policeman myself who were not averse to accepting the occasional discreet present in return for turning a blind eye to some of my more nefarious activities.

I talked to one of my friends about Robert's situation and he told me it was not impossible that the confiscated heroin could be discreetly swapped for harmless glucose, if the price was right.

When I told Robert the good news he wept with relief. 'Christ, Tony, if you pull this off I'll never, ever be able to repay you,' he told me.

I was told by my friends that the cost of perverting the course of justice for Robert, Keith and Mick would be £6,000.

Within hours Robert had made a few phone calls and a messenger arrived at his house with a black leather attaché case. Robert opened the case to show me the money neatly packed away inside.

I could hardly believe my eyes. Though I was used to seeing large sums of money paid over in casinos this was, at that time, sufficient to buy a reasonable family house. However, it would be a small price to pay if the action against Robert and the Stones really could be bought off.

I handed the money over in a pub in Kilburn late on Tuesday night and it looked as though everything was working out. Not one word of the raid had appeared in any newspaper; no summonses had been issued; it was as though the raid had never happened.

OLIVER MUSKER Spanish Tony said he could pay off the police and Mick and Robert gave him a considerable amount of money – I was told £7,000 – and I asked Robert if he'd paid off the police (I remember this conversation). He said, 'How can one ever know, but he did have a new Alfa Romeo when I came out of jail' (meaning Spanish Tony). Often in these cases people just keep the money. It's far more likely.

KEITH RICHARDS Spanish Tony had always had that Alfa Romeo. It was a shabby one, not good enough for the money. Also, he's smarter than to suddenly flash a brand-new car. Nothing surprises me about Scotland Yard. The great myth about that lot is that they're incorruptible. That's the myth. Those guys were all on the take.

From Up and Down with the Rolling Stones *by Tony Sanchez*
I basked for a few days in Robert's gratitude until the following Sunday, when he interrupted my revelry with an angry phone call.

'The News of the World *has got every single detail,' he exploded. 'They've got my name and the time the raid happened and who was there. It's almost as though they had a reporter sitting in the middle of the room taking notes. They even say that a "quantity of substances" were taken away.'*

It seemed extraordinary that the newspaper had first had Mick's libel action against them wrecked by the raid and had then managed to hide their sensational, exclusive information about it from the rest of Fleet Street for a whole week. I worried then because no one was going to risk taking a bribe when the operation was so obviously being carried out hand in hand with a newspaper.

CHRISTOPHER FINCH Robert was very much hanging out with Bill Burroughs at that time. Bill was living in London and over at Robert's all the time. These times I was invited to Mount Street at least half the time Bill was there. He knew Robert well. He was a walking pharmacopoeia. So I assume Robert was using drugs in a very sophisticated way.

We'd planned to go to Amsterdam together to see a show of Jim's. I think this happened the week after he was busted with the Stones down at Keith Richards's place. I think a raid had been rumoured but hadn't hit the papers yet. I'd been out of town, of course, and somebody told me about it when I got back. So Robert's behaviour was understandable.

I came back in the middle of the week and the next day, which was the day before we were due to leave, I got a phone call from the galley, from Susan Loppert, saying, 'Oh, Chris, your tickets for Amsterdam are here. You'd better pick them up.' So I picked them up and Robert called and said, 'I'll send a car over for you tomorrow.' The next day a fancy car rolls up with a chauffeur and we go off to Mount Street to pick up Robert and go to the airport.

Robert was especially nervous, even more so than usual, and hardly able to look at me. We got to the airport. We were flying first class to Amsterdam. Robert still extremely nervous – out of his seat, striding up and down the aisle, just couldn't sit still for a minute. We got to Amsterdam airport and we were approaching Customs. There were three or four lines, and suddenly Robert said, 'Oh, there's a *bureau de change*, I must go and change the money. Hold my briefcase for me.' I only had a small overnight bag because it was just a three-day trip and I joined one of the lines. I'm looking round, I don't see any sign of Robert. Literally just as I was confronting the Customs clerk, just as I was putting down his briefcase and my bag, I saw Robert, on the other side of Customs. He'd obviously gone through on one of the other lines and was waiting at the exit. He took his briefcase very sheepishly, and I immediately realized that Robert was fairly heavily drugged and what was in his briefcase. Fortunately it stuck me as funny, until I realized the possible consequences. Then I was absolutely furious. By the time I got to the exit Robert had already hailed a taxi, so I couldn't say anything and sat there fuming on the drive into Amsterdam. We had connecting rooms at the Amsterpol and I opened up the briefcase. There were several little aluminium canisters of coke in there. I was really furious. But somehow he handled the whole thing so charmingly. When I confronted him, he grabbed one of the canisters and ran off into the bathroom. When he came back in he was apologetic but giggling at the same time. But somehow after an hour we were friends again and had a wonderful weekend.

I'd known he was using hard drugs, but that weekend might have been the first time I knew he was using heroin. We went to many parties that weekend. At one of them there was a very good-looking Dutch boy who had heroin and he and Robert went off and then came back. So I wasn't actually an eyewitness to Robert taking it. I was told it was heroin. I certainly knew he was using cocaine, but that might have been the first time I realized he was on heroin as well.

After coming back from that Amsterdam weekend I probably called Susan, who filled me in. My wife had heard something about it. I certainly didn't know about it when I got on the plane to Amsterdam. The story was in the papers that weekend.

DRUG SQUAD RAIDS POP STAR'S PARTY
Charges alleging illegal possession or use of drugs may be made as a result of a police raid on a pop star's house-party last week. Several stars, at least three of them nationally known names, were present at the party.

It was held at a secluded country house near the south coast. I under-stand that at least on person present is believed to have been in posses-sion of the drug LSD, a tiny dose of which gives up to sixteen hours of hal-lucination. Drugs in pill form were taken from one pop singer present at the party. These were later sent for analysis at a police forensic laboratory.

Also seized and sent for laboratory tests were the contents of ashtrays and other items, including substances in bottles. These are being exam-ined to discover if they contain marijuana or other drugs.

Acting on a tip-off that one foreign national might abscond abroad, the police have been keeping watch at major sea and airports. The raid, which was organized from the regional police headquarters, included officers specializing in anti-drug measures. Only a few minutes before squads of police entered the house, which lies at the end of a tree-lined drive, one pop star and his wife drove off and so quite unwittingly escaped the net. Police acted swiftly in organizing the raid – the information on which the application for a search warrant was based was received only a few hours before the party started. (News of the World, *19 February 1967*)

JOHN DUNBAR Robert sometimes mentioned the bust – oh, yeah. But he was always pretty well smacked out at that point, so he didn't really care about the trial. He was very proud of getting rid of the policeman, making him just take two of his pills by saying they were his diabetic pills. He didn't really care about being busted, as long as he had some gear. He was really pleased he'd fooled them into letting him keep the rest of his jacks. He knew he was just bun-dled up into the excitement of busting the Rolling Stones. But he really didn't seem to mind too much.

25 JANUARY–30 MARCH 1967: BARKER, BLAKE, HAMILTON, HAWORTH, SELF

CLIVE BARKER If you were outside the orbit Robert was interested in, you didn't exist. If he wasn't interested in you or your work, it was 'Beam me up,

Scottie', you know. Anything was possible with him unless it was money, and then it was Mission: Impossible! And sometimes, true to what he'd said, the cheque would come, but often it would be the hesitation waltz . . . He did some silly things, you know, like he'd send you a load of roses, whereas I'd rather have had the money.

COLIN SELF I've somewhere got a pile of Robert's gallery stickers with the odd lettering. Also one of his bounced cheques. Looking back, I treated Robert like family when the setbacks came, as if he was my youngest uncle. If you got ripped off, it was like a family rip-off. I always thought Robert was special.

CLIVE BARKER I remember saying once, 'You always knew where you were with Robert – he always let you down.' Robert would send you a cheque. Ring up and say, 'I've just put a cheque in the post to you.' It would arrive ten days later, unsigned. So you'd ring up and get Sue: 'Oh, I'm sorry about that, well –' and you'd say, 'Sue, he's done it again.' 'Oh,' she'd say, 'he's in Amsterdam for two months.' And you knew he'd sent you that cheque, timed to reach you after he'd left for somewhere else. Then he'd come back: 'Oh, didn't I sign that?' I felt sorry for Sue, she was in the middle.

When I was owed money by Robert almost always I had to ring Sue. 'I've got another one of Robert's cheques,' and she knew what I meant. Then he'd come back and be marvellous – sign a cheque for you, take you out. So you forgot what you'd been through for the past six weeks with no money. But with Robert it wasn't only money. For all of us it was, where was our work? If he'd sold it, where was the money? But when he did a show for you or you were in a show, he placed it right, did everything marvellously. If it was a solo show, it looked brilliant. He knew exactly where to place things. You could leave it to him. His shows were marvellous, whether they were little drawings by Dubuffet or great pictures by Hamilton or Magritte. Peter Blake's shows, every one looked a gem, the show overall looked brilliant. Robert just knew how to do it.

PAUL MCCARTNEY Robert used to come round to my house in Cavendish Avenue, which was my bachelor pad in the sixties. It was bit more of a salon really – everyone just came round, anyone stuck for somewhere to stay. And Robert would ring and say, 'Do you want to go out to dinner?' His day revolved around dinner. Once he'd got dinner set, everything else fell into place. So he'd come round and I'd play him all the new stuff we were making. He was interested to hear all the demos, then he'd move to a visual on it, which eventually came true on the *Sgt Pepper* cover. By that time we were firm friends.

So Robert and I would just sit around, chatting late into the night, and I'd come back from America one time with this idea for *Sgt Pepper's Lonely Hearts Club Band*, and the concept was we'd pretend that the Beatles were this band. That would liberate us from our egos, so we'd be able to approach a microphone and think, 'This is not me doing a vocal, this is someone else.' That was very liberating and I think the album echoes that. So Robert would get all this.

Robert represented to me freedom, freedom of speech, of view. Mainly he was the art eye that I most respected. He turned me on to a lot of good art, and he turned me off a lot of not so good art, which was very helpful. Robert was very instrumental in getting the *Sgt Pepper* cover together. He really became the art director on *Sgt Pepper*.

JANN HAWORTH The whole mood of that was quite interesting, because the original part of the commission was based on the fact that Robert absolutely hated the original of the cover by this group called the Fool. He thought it looked like psychedelic Disneyland, which it did. It was a mountain with all these little creatures on it, slightly cartoony. Robert said to the Beatles, 'You just cannot have this cover, it's not good enough. You should get Peter and Jann to do it.'

PAUL McCARTNEY There was a group called the Fool who made clothes for everyone – Simone and Mareika, from Holland, who came over to join the hippie London crowd. They were quite loose, very nice people. They started an art thing called the Fool. They designed clothes for Apple, did murals for us on the Baker Street building. And they were going to do the inside cover of *Sgt Pepper*.

Robert started getting into the visuals and he said, 'I think you should get Peter Blake involved.' Because I came back with this idea of having the Beatles being presented by a Lord Mayor or something with a municipal award – very Northern – and I wanted it to be by a floral clock, which is very British.

JANN HAWORTH The cover that the Fool had done looked quite groovy and I don't think George was too happy about abandoning it. I thought it was fun, quite entertaining, and if you'd heard the music, which I hadn't, probably apt, in terms of the psychedelia. I don't think the final *Sgt Pepper* cover is at all psychedelic. Neither Peter nor I had anything to do with drugs and it was very much a continuum of both his work and mine.

We didn't know until quite late on whether they would actually use our cover or not. We went over to EMI and were shown this cover and the three of us were discussing what might be possible, rather briefly. Then Paul came over to the Chiswick flat one evening and discussed it further and really progressed it.

PAUL McCARTNEY The other part of my concept was to get everyone in the group to mention their heroes. You'd have a portrait of someone and around him would be all the little portraits of Brando, James Dean, an Indian guru, whoever you were into. Or rather the alter ego's heroes. There'd be H. G. Wells and Johnny Weissmuller, Issy Bonn and all those people, and Burroughs would have been a suggestion probably from Robert, and there were a few kind of LA guys that Robert had slipped in. He'd slip in people that we didn't even know but we didn't mind, it was the spirit of the thing. Those ideas developed and combined, so that instead of a mayoral presentation it became that famous cover.

PETER BLAKE They [Paul and Robert] happened to come to the studio one night and were just on a trip, you know, they were seeing things that weren't there – seeing colours and seeing things that simply weren't there and persuading me that I had to do it! You know, saying, 'Look, you've got to, you're not living a full life unless you experience these things.' I don't know how I ever insisted on not doing it, because the pressure to participate was enormous, but I just never did, you know. Which I am not particularly proud of. I mean, I am glad I didn't, but it would have been a great deal easier to. The idea of that amount of responsibility being taken away from you. I never mind getting drunk and I never mind losing that sense, but LSD did frighten me. That was probably a good thing.

JANN HAWORTH A very strange scene met us the first time we went over to the studio. The Beatles were recording, and their 'court' of Marianne Faithfull and all these weird spaced-out people sat around the walls. Peter and I were probably the only people who were stone-cold sober. It was really funny, two very upright people doing this psychedelia.

Paul played us the tape of *Sgt Pepper*, which was still being worked on, and Peter thought the idea of making a Lonely Hearts Club would be interesting, a group of people with the Beatles in front. Early in the sixties Peter had done some things, cutting out Victorian heads, engravings, sticking them down, then doing a circus act in front of that. He maintained at that time that Paolozzi nicked that idea from him, the collage effect of people and things, dissimilar but in the same environment.

The part that's very much my own was that I always hated lettering on things. I loved the idea that lettering could be an integral part, and I was into fairground lettering at the time. So I thought it would be nice to have a real object with lettering on it, instead of lettering the cover. So I thought about the drum, then about the civic lettering that was around at that time. We pointed out to Paul the Hammersmith lettering: You could do it like that.

What I wanted was that very tight, little ice plants, a very tight floral near-to-the-ground thing. I discussed all this on the phone with the florists. Then they turned up with all these dumb plants – hyacinths. And then only a quarter of what we needed to cover the whole thing. After all these instructions. At least when they set it out you could read the word 'Beatles', but it was very much a failure in terms of the original concept.

The other part I felt very strongly about was that when you went from the front, you wanted to have that connecting point of 3-D things that bled into the 2-D things, as we were not doing it as artwork. This bothered Peter a lot later on, because it was so retouched, so messed about, the photograph, it ended up looking like artwork, a collage done on paper, rather than a set that was built.

Madame Tussaud's were very generous, lending us some figures, and then the Beatles were going to be in front of the crowd, and I put some of my figures in, and that blended the 3-D world into the 2-D world.

PAUL McCARTNEY Right up until the end we knew the cover was going to be Michael Cooper/Peter Blake, but we wanted this inside cover to be the Fool's drawing. Robert kept saying, 'I don't think you should use it.' I'd say, 'Well, Robert, it's our album and we're gonna use it.' And the other Beatles were quite adamant too. A week would go by, then Robert would say, 'I *really* don't think you should use it. It's just not well drawn. It's not right. It's bad art.' We said, 'Let us be the judge of that. It's our album cover, not yours. You're just the art director. We don't have to listen to you.' In the end he came round with the cover as it exists now, with the four of us gleaming hopefully out. Give everyone a love vibe. He'd come round, saying, 'I say, I think, this should be the inside cover. It's much better. Works with the front, works with the back.' And he put the package together as it eventually was and persuaded us finally not to use the Fool's artwork. And he was right. I've seen it since and he was really right. With things like that he was pretty right. He had an opinion and stuck to it. He could be a little bit too arrogant – luckily not to me. I would just say, piss off or whatever. I had a little way of deflating him, which was all right. I can see what my kids didn't like about him. It was just Eton overbearing, I'm just superior to you, which is what you're taught at Eton.

JANN HAWORTH They did use ours, of course; but in the end it was totally mucked up, because the plates were wrong. The photograph was beautiful but the reproduction was absolutely lousy. It would be lovely to see it done properly.

PETER BLAKE I have very mixed feelings, because it's sometimes given an over-importance. I mean, I've been painting now for forty-five years – and as

Chrissie, my wife, says when I get upset about it, it was just a record cover. But, on another level, on any kind of list of record-cover designs it's usually the number one. So I'm very proud to have done it, but also very bitter that because of Robert signing away any rights I had to it, we were paid only £200. I think the people who delivered the flowers were paid £250. I've never had any more money from it.

So although it stills sells constantly, and everybody else is still making money from it, we never did. So I'm thrilled to have done it, but bitter about it.

PAUL McCARTNEY At the time, Robert was doing heroin and I was thinking, 'I really shouldn't, but go on, it's Robert, give us a sniff.' Luckily it didn't do much for me. I'd rather have a joint. So Robert said, 'Great, I won't offer it you again. It was expensive. If you didn't like it, no point in giving it to you.' I'd just say when asked to have some, 'No, I don't, thanks.' Robert continued on with it. He was the one who said, 'There's no such thing as heroin addiction, you've just got to have a lot of money. The only problem comes when you can't afford it.' I took that with a pinch of salt. Much as I loved Robert, I didn't listen to his every word.

JOHN DUNBAR There was lots going on at that time. Robert came out to John Lennon's quite a lot that year, up to St George's Hill. We took lots of acid. I think that was the same year as the twenty-four-hour trip – the Technicolor dream. There was just lots going on, it was a busy busy time.

The trial wasn't important enough to talk about. He was pretty casual about it I seem to remember. It was just a nuisance. Nobody thought he'd go to prison – he didn't, not for a minute.

I'll tell you, no way did he slump around going, 'Oh, my God, there's the trial coming up.' It just never got mentioned, except as a story about the bust or the latest talk with the lawyers, you know, that kind of thing. As an entertaining story, not an 'Oh dear, oh dear – it's coming up' at all.

I don't think anybody thought he'd go to prison – for a minute. It was all a bit unlikely. It was just a small possession charge, first offence, so on, Eton boy, just not likely. It's important to get across Robert's insouciance. I think it was a bit like a parking fine, except a bit more interesting because he'd been busted with Mick. That far outweighed any anxieties that might have arisen.

The bust if anything was a bit of a treat, because it made him famous too. He was more part of the Stones than he would have been. He was in the papers – it's being 'in', isn't it? He got to go to court with Mick and everybody, you know. Honestly, it was almost – you know, a good one.

MAYFAIR MAN ACCUSED WITH THE ROLLING STONES
West End art gallery director Robert Hugh Fraser, of Mount Street, Mayfair,
has been summoned to appear with the two Rolling Stones Mick Jagger
and Keith Richards, at Chichester court tomorrow following a raid under
the drugs regulations.

He is the third person to be accused by West Sussex police after the raid
on Richards's country home at Redlands Lane, West Wittering, three
months ago. All three accused will contest the accusations. Mr Fraser runs
an avant-garde gallery where works by contemporary and pop-type artists
are often on view. (Evening Standard, *9 May 1967*)

NICHOLAS FRASER Robert was always carving out new directions. But for
a young man with his background, it was a bit of a surprise. I didn't see Robert
in the late sixties and wasn't conscious of anything in particular. I don't know I
knew Robert was on drugs. I was very shocked when I heard. Robert wouldn't
have told me. I would have seen it in the papers, or my mother would have rung
and said, 'Robert's in trouble.'

SUSAN LOPPERT He always kept himself at a distance. I mean, we didn't
become intimate – he had this kind of reserve always. He avoided anything that
spoke of emotion. I don't think we ever touched each other – never any hugs – and
I think he was a man who *craved* affection more than anyone else. I think he did.

And yet when he went to jail, the day before his trial, because I couldn't actually put my arms round him and say Good Luck or anything, I left this on his desk.
He wrote his additions on the side.

The Founder, Chairman & Secretary of the Robert Fraser for President
Club hope that everything goes well tomorrow.

God	Susan Loppert	*Thank you*
	Founder	
is	Susan Loppert	*Thank you*
	Chairman	
Love	Susan Loppert	*Thank you*
	Secretary	

I always kept it, you see.

NICHOLAS FRASER I went down to the trial, my mother didn't. I went to
the trial at my mother's request, but she didn't want to go, didn't want to be
photographed, etc. I suppose I rang her up and told her what went on. What
passed between Robert and my mother, I don't know. They circled around one

another, but were very interdependent. I don't know whether he was the first Etonian to be a heroin addict, but it was shocking. The establishment was amazed at his getting involved. It must have been a great shock to my mother. She didn't say much – she was pretty buttoned up too.

COMFORT, MONEY, RESPECT . . . DRUGS

Robert Hugh Fraser's background is comfortable, prosperous, respectable, distinguished – just the sort of background the less swinging middle classes of a generation ago would have envied.

His father, Mr Lionel Fraser, white-haired and stately, was a City banker with interests in investment trusts, insurance and industry – and a trustee of the Tate Gallery. His grandfather was butler to Gordon Selfridge, the department-store king. It is an Eton and Belgravia background. His father carried himself as if born to position and wealth. (Daily Sketch)

THE PRIVATE SHAME OF ROBERT FRASER: THE GALLANT OLD ETONIAN WHO WON TOO LATE HIS BATTLE AGAINST DRUGS

Old Etonian Robert Fraser fought two kinds of war. One was when he saw action against the Mau Mau in Kenya and emerged 'with distinction'. The other was his battle against the craving for drugs . . . A battle he won too late.

Barrister Mr William Denny told West Sussex quarter sessions yesterday, 'This was his private shame.'

Last night Fraser, 29, director of an avant-garde Mayfair art gallery, was in jail. He was remanded there to await sentence after admitting having 24 tablets of heroin. Police found them in his trouser pocket when they raided a house at West Wittering, Sussex, on 12 February.

Mr Denny said he was anxious that the court should not be deceived into thinking that Fraser was a spineless individual. He was a person of no little ability, with considerable spirit and courage. After serving with two 'celebrated regiments' in Kenya he worked hard establishing his art gallery.

It might have been because of his hard work that he became prone to temptation put to him, about 12 months ago, by an employee. That person offered tablets as a stimulant. Mr Denny said that Fraser firmly believed he would have the strength to be able to stop using them should he be threatened by addiction. But he was over-confident and wrong.

After a comparatively short time he found he was 'hooked'. As far as Fraser was aware, no one other than the person who supplied the drugs knew of his addiction. Mr Denny said that it was Fraser's own courage which induced him to seek out a doctor who might help to cure him. After traumatic treatment, he relapsed and took heroin again. But once more he had the strength to telephone the doctor and ask for assistance. The court was told that he was now clear of his addiction and, 'There is no reason why he should get back on to heroin again.'

Fraser of Mount Street, Mayfair, was born into prosperity. His father, Lionel Fraser, started as a newspaper delivery boy and worked his way up to become a City banker.

Robert was first sent to a Christian Science school, but later to Eton. When he left school he went immediately to America to join the art scene in New York. Five years ago he achieved his great ambition and opened his own modern art gallery in Duke Street, Mayfair.

Last November he was fined £20 for staging an indecent exhibition. The paintings were the works of American artist Jim Dine. Before yesterday's hearing, Fraser said, 'I am planning a new type of exhibition at my gallery which will be called "Lighting up the World". There will be special effects of lighting playing on various paintings. It comes from an electronic invention pionered by a Greek.'

When asked recently if he was a rebel, he replied, 'I never thought of that. I just do what I like doing.' (Daily Mail, *28 June 1967*)

THE SHAME AND COURAGE OF A FINANCIER'S SON
The story of Robert Hugh Fraser, the financier's son who became 'hooked' on drugs, was one of shame. But it was also one of courage, his counsel, Mr William Denny, told the court . . . It was this courage 'which induced him to seek out a doctor who specialized in assisting people to a cure from the addiction'.

After undergoing traumatic treatment, Fraser relapsed and took heroin once more, said Mr Denny. But it was an example of his courage that he had the strength to telephone the doctor once more and ask for his assistance.

Dr John Quintion Craigmore, of Bolton Gardens, London, said Fraser came to him nine days after the events at West Wittering. The doctor added, 'At the moment I think he is clear of his addiction.' (Evening Standard)

JANN HAWORTH I think during that time he was said to have taken what he described as a traumatic cure for heroin. At that time I became aware of this thing where they used to inject people with something that would make them sick and then they would show them films of themselves injecting themselves and that put them off. I don't know if that was what the cure was. Something like that, I think.

KEITH RICHARDS Robert did take a cure for heroin. Apomorphine. I did also later on with Gram Parsons. It was useless, most painful. It was Bill Burroughs's old nurse, Smith – a lovely old lady, matronly old lady from Devon or Cornwall – who'd help. You'd do it in your own house. She'd arrive and order you about like matrons do and say, 'Take this.' And this stuff would make you react against – harsh treatment. Made you sick as a dog. Robert did it. But then – 'Oh, I'm clean. Must have a hit.' Or afterwards, 'That wore me out, I must relax . . .' But eventually, he cleaned up.

WILLIAM DENNY, QC One couldn't have told the court as a fact that he had dried himself out and let the inference be that he hadn't gone back to it – when it would have been a matter of record that he hadn't, because he went back to the same clinic! Therefore it had to come out if you were going to raise it at all.

All I really remember is the sight of Jagger and him chatting away rather insouciantly for a little while before more important considerations took over . . .

JAGGER SPENDS NIGHT IN CELL
The prison doors clanged last night behind Mick Jagger, lead singer of the Rolling Stones. And ahead stretched a night in a Lewes jail cell for the long-haired pop idol of the teenagers. . . . Jagger travelled the thirty-seven miles to Lewes in a prison van with Fraser and four other men – and it was to teenage screams that he left Chichester. (Daily Express, 28 June 1967)

MARIANNE FAITHFULL Poor old Mick, in his wildest dreams he had never, never thought he would end up in jail, for nothing. And I would never have thought that I'd be visiting him in jail, for nothing. He wasn't prepared to roll over and say, 'This is OK.'

I think Robert thought it unjust, but it was expected. They could lock you up for camping about, dressing pretty and looking as if you were very rich without a care in the world. Robert knew that, Mick didn't.

He wasn't an outlaw. Robert was, Keith was, I was. We were all by inclination outlaws. It was afterwards Mick became an outlaw. It was after he wrote 'Gimme Shelter', all that great stuff. He wasn't anarchic, we were.

We wanted to change the rules. Robert was one of Andy Warhol's best friends. They plotted and planned the changing of the rules.

I never thought the authorities would overreact like that. I thought they were much cleverer than they were. I thought they'd let us walk on our tightrope in our pretty clothes and never be stupid enough to come down on us. It was really stupid.

OLIVER MUSKER When they went to prison, the police said, 'It wasn't really you we wanted, it was that fucker Mick Jagger.' That night in prison Robert said he put a fatherly arm round Mick to comfort him . . .

PC DON RAMBRIDGE We still talk about that raid – a day to remember. Probably because it was one of the first of its type. And Bob Fraser was one of the first to go to prison for it. The chances of anyone going to prison for that today are pretty remote. It was a major cock-up really, because we didn't know what to charge them with. It went off for the legal minds to decide on. But it was all slung out by the Court of Appeal in the end. The defence big guns helped there.

I'm sure Bob Fraser would have found prison mind-bending and really been affected by it. Take a long time to live it down. In those days people got six months for anything, even for burgling a shed. These days there are twenty a day coming to court, but then maybe only two a year. If those boys came up today, they'd probably just get a wigging and be fined £100.

FRASER AND JAGGER HANDCUFFED YESTERDAY
The rather grim scenes of Mick Jagger and Robert Fraser appearing hand-cuffed together at the Chichester court this morning are surely an unneces-sary humiliation. Are the two really considered dangerous criminals liable to make trouble unless they are manacled? The governor of Lewes prison and the police, who are jointly responsible for security arrangements in the movement of prisoners, apparently think so. The Home Office explana-tion is that when a number of prisoners who are security risks are being moved together it is 'desirable for them all to be handcuffed'. To the public, however, it must seem in this case an act of unnecessary harshness.
(Evening Standard)

WILLIAM DENNY, QC The sentence? It could have gone the other way, I thought, if there had been a very lenient-minded judge, but this was a time when they were trying to crack down on the developing heroin thing, and his was the most serious thing as he had heroin. The others merely had nonsense stuff.

DENNIS HOPPER I was here in America at the time of the trial – how scary. The man decided to sentence him but none of the others because he was the son of a lord and they were commoners. That's how it was reported. Grim, very grim. I was shocked, devastated really. I'd never heard of such things. It was awful.

Jagger must swap his frilled shirts and gear suits for three months of prison blue denims. His fellow Stone Keith Richards was jailed for a year, and Mayfair art gallery director Robert Hugh Fraser sentenced to six months – all for drugs offences . . .

Jagger was taken to Brixton prison and Fraser and Richards to
Wormwood Scrubs – and all issued with regulation blue denim trousers
and jackets and black shoes. Their own Carnaby Street cothes were par-
celled up. (Daily Mail)

KEITH RICHARDS They split us up, Mick went to Brixton, I went to the
Scrubs with Robert, in the van, chained together. 'This is good, innit, Robert?'
'Shut up. No talking.' Robert going, 'Shtum, shtum.' Nice trip to London. Nice
day. Until you get to the fucking walls that were sixty feet high and like all day-
light shut out. I get a year and he gets six months or something. Just routine, kid.
I'd been in the tank before but the Scrubs, that's hard time. The big house.
Robert never lost his cool in any of those kind of matters.

Going to jail, for Robert, was probably the same as being inducted in the Army.
Strip, delouse, open your mouth, let's have a look. Give you clothes you can't hang
yourselves with. I'm sure there's another way out. Robert said, 'Try the kitchens or
the library.' He ended up in the kitchens, doing all right. You get more food that
way. I got out within forty-eight hours. He did the hard time. I got out on appeal.

After four years on the road, which was fascinating, to suddenly step outside
of that, at that age, it was an incredible scenario. You had to put it against the
backdrop of London at that time. This is why we got busted. They saw us as a
threat. Robert and I realized: they're fucking serious. Shit, you know. They're
putting us in hard time, in shackles.

But we certainly didn't expect to be hit that hard considering the crime. Even
The Times, Rees-Mogg, said, 'breaking the butterfly on a wheel', talking about
Mick's and my sentence, which also included Robert.

WHO BREAKS A BUTTERFLY ON A WHEEL?
Mr Jagger has been sentenced to imprisonment for three months. He is
appealing against conviction and sentence, and has been granted bail until
the hearing of the appeal later in the year. In the meantime, the sentence
of imprisonment is bound to be widely discussed by the public. And the
circumstances are sufficiently unususal to warrant such discussion in the
public interest.

Mr Jagger was charged with being in possession of four tablets contain-
ing amphetamine sulphate and methyl amphetamine hydrochloride; these
tablets had been bought, perfectly legally, in Italy, and brought back to this
country. They are not a highly dangerous drug, or in proper dosage a dan-
gerous drug at all. They are of the benzedrine type and the Italian manu-
facturers recommend them both as a stimulant and as a remedy for travel
sickness.

In Britain it is an offence to possess these drugs without a doctor's prescription. Mr Jagger's doctor says that he knew and had authorized their use, but he did not give a prescription for them as indeed they had already been purchased. His evidence was not challenged. This was therefore an offence of a technical character, which before this case drew the point to public attention any honest man might have been liable to commit. If after his visit to the Pope, the Archbishop of Canterbury had bought proprietary airsickness pills at Rome airport, and imported the unused pills into Britain on his return, he would have risked committing precisely the same offence. No one who has ever travelled and bought proprietary drugs abroad can be sure that he has not broken the law.

Judge Block directed the jury that the approval of a doctor was not a defence in law to the charge of possessing drugs without a prescription, and the jury convicted. Mr Jagger was not charged with complicity in any other drug offence that occurred in the same house. They were separate cases, and no evidence was produced to suggest that he knew that Mr Fraser had heroin tablets or that the vanishing Mr Sneidermann had cannabis resin. It is indeed no offence to be in the same building or the same company as people possessing or even using drugs, nor could it reasonably be made an offence. The drugs which Mr Jagger had in his possession must therefore be treated on their own, as a separate issue from the other drugs that other people may have had in their possession at the same time. It may be difficult for lay opinion to make this distinction clearly, but obviously justice cannot be done if one man is to be punished for a purely contingent association with someone else's offence.

We have, therefore, a conviction against Mr Jagger purely on the ground that he possessed four Italian pep pills, quite legally bought but not legally imported without a prescription. Four is not a large number. This is not the quantity which a pusher of drugs would have on him, nor even the quantity one would expect in an addict. In any case Mr Jagger's career is obviously one that does involve great personal strain and exhaustion; his doctor says that he approved the occasional use of these drugs, and it seems likely that similar drugs would have been prescribed if there was a need for them. Millions of similar drugs are prescribed in Britain every year, and for a variety of conditions.

One has to ask, therefore, how it is that this technical offence, divorced as it must be from other people's offences, was thought to deserve the penalty of imprisonment. In the courts at large it is most uncommon for imprisonment to be imposed on first offenders where the drugs are not major drugs *of addiction and there is no question of drug traffic. The normal penalty is probation, and the purpose of probation is to encourage the offender to develop his career and to avoid the drug risks in the future. It is surprising therefore that Judge Block should have decided to sentence Mr Jagger to imprisonment, and particularly surprising as Mr Jagger's is about as mild a drug case as can ever have been brought before the courts.*

It would be wrong to speculate on the Judge's reasons, which we do not know. It is, however, possible to consider the public reaction. There are many people who take a primitive view of the matter, what one might call a pre-legal view of the matter. They consider that Mr Jagger has 'got what was coming to him'. They resent the anarchic quality of the Rolling Stones' performances, dislike their songs, dislike their influence on teenagers and broadly suspect them of decadence, a word used by Miss Monica Furlong in the Daily Mail.

As a sociological concern this may be reasonable enough, and at an emotional level it is very understandable, but it has nothing at all to do with the case. One has to ask a different question: has Mr Jagger received the same treatment as he would have received if he had not been a famous figure, with all the criticism and resentment his celebrity have aroused? If a promising undergraduate had come back from a summer visit to Italy with four pep pills in his pocket would it have been thought right to ruin his career by sending him to prison for three months? Would it also have been thought necessary to display him handcuffed to the public?

There are cases in which a single figure becomes the focus for public concern about some aspect of public morality. The Stephen Ward case, with its dubious evidence and questionable verdict, was one of them, and that verdict killed Stephen Ward. There are elements of the same emotions in the reactions to this case. If we are going to make any case a symbol of the conflict between the sound traditional values of Britain and the new hedonism, then we must be sure that the sound traditional values include those of tolerance and equity. It should be the particular quality of British justice to ensure that Mr Jagger is treated exactly the same as anyone else, no better and no worse. There must remain a suspicion in this case that Mr Jagger received a more severe sentence than would have been thought proper for any purely anonymous young man.

(*William Rees-Mogg,* The Times, *1 July 1967*)

NIGEL WAYMOUTH Robert wasn't someone who moaned and groaned about this. He carried the can after the bust and all those pop stars got off, headlines in

The Times, 'Breaking a Butterfly', etc. Having run the most sophisticated gallery in London, incredibly glamorous friends – the Beatles, the Stones, etc. – sitting at his feet. Who adored him. They looked up to him. He was an example. He was Mr Sophistication. He was a little bit older, not much, rather like Gibbs. He was ultra-sophisticated and hip, and had this incredibly glamorous gallery where all the latest American and English Pop Art was being shown. But he was caught with the smack and sent down for it. He did, what, three months? It was tough.

Letter from TERRY SOUTHERN

My dear Bob,

Wormwood Scrubbs! Indeed! This is all really quite too shocking, Bob! (Surely Lattir or Spanish Tone could have done this stint on your behalf!) In my view, sir, you have gone too far this time in your search for the odd and picaresque! Seriously though, I am confident (for reasons I shall explain under separate cover) that this curious and untoward incident shall <u>serve in very good stead</u>, and indeed, may be turned to CAPITAL ADVANTAGE for all concerned!

Meanwhile I wish you would give me an acocunt of YOUR TYPICAL DAY AT SCRUBBS – what manner of garb, repas, etc., etc. In point of fact, I would strongly advise that you keep a journal – or, perhaps better yet, we might collaborate in contriving one when you are again at liberty. We'll make it quite weird.

Well, Bob, it's race-riot time here in the Apple, and people are choosing sides. Otherwise things go on much as before – except for Lar Rivers, who is busy getting various gear in order, and will soon depart for the Dark Continent itself . . . in the company of groovy frog film-maker Pierre Gaisseau. They are Congo-bound, Bob, where they will eat, sleep, etc. avec les sauvages. And this should prove a memorable trip for Lar since he cannot abide strong sunlight, odd smells, or curious repas. 'It may flip me out, man,' he keeps repeating, and under the guise of this anxiety has devoted about 73% of his gear weight allotment to a gigantic sedation-kit. Speaking of this same Lar, we actually tried to telephone you at Scrubbs the other day. We got through all right, but then there was a ruddy balls-up:

'Whot? New York calling?? . . . Frayser? Robert Fayser? Well, ay meahn to saiy, 'ee's a *prisonor* 'ere, ya know!'

'Yes, well, we just wanted to, uh, you know, talk to him.'

'Whot, talk to Frayser? Whot's it all about then?!'

'Well, we just wanted to, uh, you know, say hello.'

'Whot, saiy 'ello to Frayser?? Oh 'ee's not got the priviledges for that, ay'm afrayed!'

'Pardon?'

'Whot?' (pause, impatiently) Well, ay meahn to saiy, 'ee is a prisoner 'ere – and 'ee's *not* got the priviledge!'

Well, anyway you can bet we gave this chap (I think it was the warden) short shrift for his impertinence. But to no avail.

What about receiving parcels, etc.?

Please give me your news

Best love from all

Letter from PAUL McCARTNEY and JANE ASHER

Dear Robert,

What a drag . . . you know what I mean.

Brother Nick rang and asked about the bread. All will be well, I'll be back in London on Sunday, and on Monday I'll sort it out.

Everybody was amazed by the whole scene, as you've guessed, and rally is the word.

Thursday was one of those days . . . bank raid shooting, Jayne Mansfield dead . . . etc . . . and I tore a ligament in sympathy, so I am hobbling round the Wirral.

Jane sends her love, love, and is baking a file cake. I send mine. The handcuff pictures in the papers are incredible, and 'aroused public sympathy'. Mind you, a tennis player from the Upton Tennis Club (where balls are known as spheres) was overheard saying that he would have given the blighters ten years if he'd been the judge . . . What??? . . .

See you soon . . . nothing to say really.

Sincerely best wishes

Paul McCartney

Jane Asher

THE OFFICIAL ELVIS PRESLEY FAN CLUB OF GREAT BRITAIN

Letter from CYNTHIA FRASER

Darling Robert,

I was so happy to see you yesterday and had I thought I would have to wait all the week, I would have written to you.

In spite of the 'closed' visit, it was so good for me to find you looking fit and keeping your courage up. Darling, you have so many friends supporting you, and as I said I am proud of you for the way you are taking things and I know you can only be rewarded for this – for taking things quietly like a man of character and being courageous. We admire you for it and I know it is going to help you. So carry on this way for the next 12 days.

I think we, and all sensible people, would agree that you have committed no crime, but the law is geared to save people from harming themselves, in some cases at least it tries to, and although in your case you had proved that you were not continuing to harm yourself, you got caught up into a legally awkward situation. I am so glad and grateful to know from you that all you want is for the RF gallery to continue to stand for all that is best and highest in your concept of its purpose. That is what I want to see too – I will do everything I can to support you in this – as I have always wanted to do the best. This is just a short time in your life, judging from your calm and good spirits today, I'm sure you will be able to turn the time in some way to something valuable – you will 'entertain an angel'. I know this has been proved many times by others and you can be just another. You can learn more about yourself, and you can be sure that your family and all you friends have nothing but loving thoughts for you at this time.

I will come again at the end of the week. Thursday or Friday if Ruth and I go to Standon, as we might, for the w/end.

I will post your books tomorrow.

Much, much love, darling Robert

Mummy (Mouche sends you tail-wags)

HOW THE DRUG ADDICT'S TORTURED MIND WORKS

> *King Heroin is my shepherd, I shall always want,*
> *He maketh me to lie down in the gutters*
> *He leadeth me beside the troubled waters,*
> *He destroyeth my soul . . .*

The words above are simple and sad. Some may find them offensive, others laughable. But few could fail to be moved by the feelings of desperation and utter hopelessness that is written so clearly between the lines.

They begin one of the most pathetic pieces of verse ever put to paper – 'The junkie's 23rd psalm'. The author is an unknown drug addict whose tortured mind drove him to corrupt one of the best-loved passages in the Bible to make the world understand. (Newspaper article included with Cynthia Fraser's letter)

Letter from STASH KLOSSOWSKI

Dearest Robert,

The frantic waves of yesterdays echo in roman parting clouds of NOW, with pretty waves 'morrowing'.

I had meant to write at length but . . .

Letter from JIM DINE
Dear R.

Susan tells me you're working in the tailor's shops. How about bringing back peg pants? I see about a 14½˝ cuff with open web seams and reversed pockets. I saw M Cooper and he said you're in good spirits and bursting with new projects for the gallery, can't wait to see you later. We've been doing many funny things. The best was seeing the group called 'Cream' at Saville Theatre in the big deal box. It was a pretty scene. I have many ideas for projects. We must talk. Have joined Tennis Club we must play when you get out.

I would rather talk than write.

Nancy & I send our love

See you next week xxxxx

JIM DINE When I went to see him in prison, it was really funny. He was working in the kitchen and he had on a white kitchen jacket, no shirt underneath, cut to the waist. He'd fashioned it into erotic come-on clothing. He never had a better time than in prison – boyfriends, everything. He used to meet a Catholic boy in chapel and they'd have some action there.

But I was freaked, visiting him in jail. My kids were real little and I sat down and said, 'You must never steal a towel from a hotel even, you don't ever want to have this experience.' And Wormwood Scrubs was creepy, a Dickensian jail. But he really had a great time there.

Cynthia said something clever: 'It's the first time since he was ten years old I knew where he was at night.'

OLIVER MUSKER Robert's mother said going to prison was the best thing that ever happened to him. She told me that when we were trekking. She was under the impression it was the only thing that got him off smack. There were no drugs in prison then, but on the other hand there was no NA either. You couldn't shock her, she was a Christian Scientist.

CHRISTOPHER GIBBS When he was in prison, Nina Midvani gave him the *Bhagavad-gita* to read and that was important to him. And he'd got plenty of time to read. He was very unhappy – he knew he was coming out to an incredible mess, and the help his family would give him would be conditional and limited. I don't know how many times his family sorted Robert out financially – over and over. Till they couldn't do it any more.

He did take prison in his stride, but he wasn't enough of a philosopher to not find it a painful and wounding time. He never said much about it. I went to visit him once, with Nico Londonderry. Nico was rather surprised Robert didn't have more to say for himself. After she'd taken the trouble to go all the way down there.

SUSAN LOPPERT During Robert's absence in jail, the gallery was placed in receivership but left to me to run. My salary was increased to £15 weekly in recognition of my increased responsibility.

Letter from SUSAN LOPPERT

Dear Mr Hulton,

I don't know how much you know of the recent events in London and of Robert's temporary enforced absence from the gallery. It was because of this that our bankers have appointed a receiver, Mr G. R. A. Wixley, of the firm of Alliot, Vernon, Smith and Co., to protect the gallery financially and to ensure that we can continue operating for as long as Robert is away. The letter from Alliot, Vernon, Smith and Co. to you is merely to inform that settlement of our outstanding debt with the Modern Museum will be their responsibility on our behalf, in other words you will definitely receive payment, though not immediately.

We are very much hoping that Robert will be back within the next month, when he will be in touch with you.

G. R. A. WIXLEY I can't remember whether he had already been committed to prison before I was appointed or not. I didn't see him that often, my principal was Coutts Bank. The bank clearly would have been influenced by his imprisonment.

The receiver is appointed by a secured creditor such as a bank. If the amount owing to the bank can't be found immediately, the bank can appoint a receiver, who then has virtually all the powers of the board of directors and his task is quite simple: to turn into cash enough to pay preferential creditors, specialist creditors like tax, VAT and so on. Unpaid salaries of the last month . . . he's got to be able to pay them. He's got to have enough money to pay his own fees of course and he must have left enough to settle the claims of the bank, the secured creditor. Having gone in on those terms, the things you can turn into cash in a small business like that are the works of art, which you can sell. But the number of people who want to buy modern works of art is very limited. I remember selling at least one to the Tate Gallery.

I would imagine that Robert gave me an indication of what he felt we should get for this stock. If not I may have had an independent assessment of the values, because clearly I wouldn't be able to form an opinion myself. So I remember it because of the difficulty of disposing of modern art and also for the fact that Robert was in prison for at least a part if not the whole of the time in which

I was acting. I did visit him in prison at least once, perhaps more often. I found him a very agreeable, pleasant young man. I think he was over the drugs by this time.

The chief thing I remember was that the works of art were not readily re-saleable. There was a very limited market. To me, as I'm not an expert, they looked rather odd. There was a thing looking like a very big, not quite a balloon, but that type of thing, and it was called *The Washbasin*; I remember as it had on the bottom two things representing taps. Slightly like the sort of thing children take into the sea.

JIM DINE It was a mess. I tried to tell Wixley, the receiver, that this stuff was not worth anything to the bank, that they should wait and try to sell it through the proper channels, rather than putting it in auction or just selling it for nothing in the market. I was concerned that my work would just go for nothing.

G. R. A. WIXLEY I probably got enough money to discharge the bank, and if you do get enough money to discharge the bank, you depart and the board of directors comes back. But of course what it finds is not very much in the way of assets, but it still has all the unsecured liabilities.

In the event you get what you can get, and one of the dangers of a receiver-ship is that there is a risk that the receiver will sell quickly at low prices to get the money, leaving little over for the consequent creditors.

I can remember the thing I sold to the Tate Gallery looked to a layman very much like a series of colour stripes on a board and another thing, from what I remember, looked like a pile of tyres. I know I'm right about the striped effect – arranged on whatever it was; three stripes. To me, it was extraordinary that the Tate Gallery thought it was a thing they wanted to buy, but they did.

RICHARD HAMILTON When Robert went to jail I was upset. The gallery was empty, poor Robert was in jail, it was an awful mess. And so unjust. The British legal system seemed to me to have treated him particularly badly. I thought it would be a good idea to make a show, a demonstration of sympathy, by getting all the artists – those who had worked with Robert, together with other distinguished artists in London – to make a show. I organized this and put it together. It was quite a successful show. Altogether a worthwhile project.

5 JULY–8 AUGUST 1967: TRIBUTE TO ROBERT FRASER
The Robert Fraser Gallery will re-open
on Wednesday 5th July
with an exhibition of works lent by
Clive Barker, Peter Blake, Derek Boshier, Patrick Caulfield, Bernard Cohen,

Harold Cohen, Robyn Denny, Jim Dine, Richard Hamilton, Jann Haworth, David Hockney, Howard Hodgkin, Gordon House, John Hoyland, Allen Jones, Philip King, R. B. Kitaj, Mark Lancaster, Claes Oldenburg, Patrick Proctor, Bridget Riley, Ed Ruscha, Colin Self, Joe Tilson, William Turnbull

Half in sympathy, half in anger, a group of 19 young artists have got togeth-er to put on an exhibition at the Robert Fraser Gallery, Duke Street to open on 5 July . . .

They amount to a galaxy of all the young avant-garde talent in Britain today. 'We felt that some gesture was necessary in view of the severity of Robert Fraser's sentence,' said Richard Hamilton, who was largely respon-sible for getting the exhibition together. 'The gallery has got into a lot of difficulty, I believe, over the last four months, partly through Fraser's own foolishness but also from the adverse publicity. Creditors are on his tail and he cannot do much until he is back. We are not going to have any kind of statement sympathizing with his habits. A number of artists have suf-fered materially at his hands over the last year or so. Some of the exhibitors have sworn never to show in the place again. We do hope, how-ever, that as a result of our making this expression of sympathy, he will show more responsibility to his artists when he comes back.' . . .

The exhibition should be, almost by accident, the most exciting to be on in the summer months. (Evening Standard)

PRAISING FRASER'S FRIENDS

London – None are so loyal and quick to kindness as artists if there is a suspicion of unjustice or injustice. Since the matter is sub judice, *I shall make no comment on the trial of gallery keeper Robert Fraser on a drugs charge.*

I have, however, nothing but praise for his gallery artists, their friends, his gallery employees and their friends, who have mounted an excellent exhibition in the enlarged Robert Fraser Gallery, 69 Duke Street, Grosvenor Square, which demonstrates in the most practical manner that all is not selfishness and self-seeking in the art world, despite appearances to the contrary. This is not to say that I am any fonder than I was before of Andy Warhol's Soup Boxes in painted wood, or Claes Oldenburg's nonsensical construction of vinyl, kapok and wood, French Fries with Ketchup, *but it's good to find the sort of camaraderie between gallery owner and artist which this show implies.* (The New York Times, *10 July 1967*)

RICHARD HAMILTON There was only one omission. One might have expected Paolozzi to be there, as he'd had shows with Robert, but they'd fallen out and when I asked Eduardo he said, 'Not on your life, the bastard.' So he was one who was missing. But Bridget Riley, who'd also had some kind of problem with Robert, did loan a picture for the show.

EDUARDO PAOLOZZI Well, maybe messages got mixed up, I don't know about tribute. But as I said, I'd also been very scarred financially by him. So maybe that might have been a reason. Which the others might have felt was not sufficient ground. But whether the tribute to Robert Fraser did any good, except give the artists another chance to show their things, is another question.

STONES' APPEAL DATE BROUGHT FORWARD
The appeals of the Rolling Stones, Mick Jagger and Keith Richards, and Robert Hugh Fraser, art gallery director, all of whom were sentenced to imprisonment last Thursday on drug charges, are to be heard on 31 July – the last day of the legal year. (The Times)

NICHOLAS FRASER There was an appeal against the sentence in Chichester, and Robert was told by the judge that, far from being in a position to appeal, somebody of his background and education was lucky not to have his sentenced doubled. He was appealing against a six-month sentence. The judge was saying, you know, you might forgive the Rolling Stones, with *their* background, but you couldn't with somebody who came from Eton. So they turned down his appeal.

WILLIAM DENNY, QC What I do recollect clearly is that part which is recorded in one of the newspapers, when I was doing what I could to tear-jerk them into some kind of sympathy for the bloke, who undoubtedly had courage to face up to what had happened and then to dry himself out, slip back and dry himself out again. I can't remember which of the Lord Justices it was now, but he simply intervened to say, 'But heroin is a killer.' Absolutely so – once they've got stuck on that . . . And having regard to the position of the family in the public eye, it would have been difficult to upset the sentence once it had been passed.

DETENTION IN HEROIN CASES IN PUBLIC INTEREST
When the court refused an application by Robert Hugh Fraser, aged 29, for leave to appeal against a six-month sentence for possessing 24 heroin tablets, the Lord Chief Justice said, 'Where heroin is concerned, this court is satisfied that, in the ordinary way if there are no special circumstances, the public interest demands that some form of detention should be imposed.

'Heroin has been termed in argument a killer, and it must be remembered that anyone who takes heroin puts themselves body and soul into the hands of the supplier. They have no moral resistance to any pressure being brought to bear on them.' (The Times)

ART GALLERY MAN LOSES DRUGS CASE APPEAL

Lord Parker said Fraser, a 29-year-old art gallery dealer of Mount Street, Mayfair, came of extremely good family. The son of a merchant banker, he was educated at a famous public school and had served in two renowned regiments.

'But, if anything, those privileges raise greater responsibilities and would tempt the court to give more rather than less by way of sentence than to a person whom I will deem the man in the street,' Lord Parker continued. (The Times, *29 July 1967*)

ALASTAIR LONDONDERRY No, I think the thing is he took the rap. He took the rap for Mick Jagger. If he hadn't been a public school boy and had the advantages that Mick Jagger – profoundly proletarian Mick Jagger – if he had had that background and been a pop star to boot, he'd have got off. No, Robert took the rap. No question about it.

Letter from SUSAN LOPPERT

Dear Robert,

We are all so sorry & dismayed that your appeal proved futile; apparently all that very impressive material from the press about the gallery could not be introduced as an appeal can only be lodged on the basis of evidence already given – which was a great pity. There's just been another tremendous paean of praise from Mario Amaya in this month's ART & ARTISTS in the form of a 'Tribute to a Dealer', which should reach you quite soon: one assumes that the Isle of Wight isn't entirely bereft of HM Mails. Are we to continue to have papers sent to you?

The news of the gallery is that the present show has just ended and we're opening another group exhibition, with the impressive title of The American Scene, on Tuesday. Richard [Hamilton] will be overseeing it all to make sure that it's as aesthetically pleasing as possible! I told you about Jerome Zipkin's visit I think; in fact last month was rather good – even Wixley rubbed his hands in what on anyone else would have been Shylockian fashion, at the + £3500 that had gone into the bank.

Telegram from MICHAEL COOPER

MR ROBERT FRASER WORMWOOD SCRUBS PRISON

MY DEAR ROBERT ALL IS NOT BLACK THAT IS A COLOUR THAT HASN'T EXISTED FOR US ON MANY OCCASIONS MUCH ACTIVITY IN MY NEW LEASE OF LIFE AND MANY OTHERS IN THE HIGHEST REPEAT HIGHEST POSSIBLE CIRCLES TO KEEP THE WORLD AND THE WORD TOGETHER AND SPREAD STOP REMEMBER THEY NAILED JESUS TO THE CROSS STOP NOT ALLOWED TO SEE YOU TILL NEXT MONDAY STOP WE ARE ALL IN WITH YOU EVERY SECOND LOVE MICHAEL

Letter from RICHARD HAMILTON

Dear Robert,

I've just heard about the appeal over the radio. It is absolutely sickening. I'm very sorry – Rita and I were no end depressed by the news, not as much as you I dare say. I really felt that there was a chance that British Justice might show signs of a little sanity? But I suppose it is too much to expect.

Well I will hold out if you can. I am working on the assumption that you intend to keep the gallery going and that when you get back to work things will get on to an even keel. Don't let it get you down. Let me know when I can see you.

We hope you are not too upset, and yours is still the *only* gallery in town. R. X

RICHARD HAMILTON While he was in jail, I got this letter from him which was very touching. It was very moving. It was written on that ruled paper with that HMS crest at the top, and written in very small handwriting so he could get as much as possible on, filling back and front of the sheet, as though you were given one precious sheet of paper a week and had to fill it completely. I don't remember much of what he said, but one thing made me, well, very concerned about him but at the same time very touched, which was he said, 'The only thing I don't miss is sex.'

8 AUGUST–30 SEPTEMBER 1967: 'THE AMERICAN SCENE'

BLATANT ABSURDITIES IN AMERICAN SHOW

Much about the emotional temper of American art and the reasons for its appeal can be gathered from the exhibition 'The American Scene' now at the Robert Fraser Gallery, Duke Street, Mayfair. It continues until 2 September.

The first three pictures on the wall seen on entering the gallery could well serve as symbolic for 'The flower people'. These large studies of flowers are by Andy Warhol, arch priest of the new America. Elsewhere, throughout the two galleries, the half-finished state of the rooms suggests the mood of much of current American art. The world must seem like this to a traveller returning from a trip. (Daily Mail)

EMPTY GALLERIES
'Sheer iconoclasm' someone had scribbled in the visitors' book at the Robert Fraser Gallery, where there is currently an exhibition of works by some of America's leading pop artists – Andy Warhol, Claes Oldenburg, Jim Dine and Roy Lichtenstein among others. Even in August, the quietest time of the year as far as most galleries are concerned, Robert Fraser's manages to retain some of its old verve. Doubts about whether it would continue appear to be quite unfounded. (Evening Standard)

OLIVE COOK When Robert was in prison he wrote to me, which surprised me. He didn't refer to why he was there, but said he'd got lots of time for reading and would I send him a list of books I thought might interest him. I thought that was charming. I was deeply touched. So for the first time in his life he read seriously important writers like Henry James. He liked him very much. The first one I sent was *The Tragic Muse*, the story of a woman who wanted to be a great artist and was a total failure. He like that and wanted more. That's when I went to see him, and found him looking so marvellous.

Removed from drink and drugs, there was a great improvement. His mind was much more lucid and he was full of life. He looked so ill just before he went in. He did admit that he felt much better when I saw him. I felt very drawn to him at that time. Previously our relationship had been on a conventional plan.

He was quite a daredevil. Taking heroin, it wasn't done with any nasty feeling. He just wanted to try it. But the prison sentence wasn't nearly as bad as being sent down from Eton. He wasn't ashamed about being there. After all, he was very unjustly blamed. The others were far more guilty than he was. They caught him and didn't catch the others, they just fixed on Robert. He wasn't the leader. I felt it was unfair.

I went to see him quite a few times and quite often he didn't have work to do. He was reading under a tree. The Scrubs has very good grounds and Robert was very often out in them. And he thought about things so much more.

I knew Robert best when he had to go to prison. Before that I'd never seen him alone, there was always someone else present. But I must say prison did him the world of good. He improved in looks, because he had to work outside. He hated open air. Before he went to prison he was terribly pale, looked as if he never saw a breath of air – and nor did he. But in prison he looked marvellous – he was sunburnt, looked wonderful. And he seemed to grow taller. The food was not exotic, but it was healthy, proper food and that did him the world of good. They were very kind to him in there.

Letter from OLIVE COOK

Dear Robert,

I do hope you haven't read this and that it may help to distract you for an hour or so. Edwin and I have been thinking of you with the utmost sympathy and do greatly hope that in a week's time you will be back in your own surroundings and ready to write a novel about your experiences.

It is good news that your friends are making an effort to keep the gallery going. Very best wishes from us both.

Letter from SUSAN LOPPERT

Dear Robert,

We haven't heard from you in some time – hope this doesn't mean that you in turn haven't received our letters; as nothing as been returned to the gallery I'm hoping this isn't so, though I gather that fewer letters have been allowed in: Clive & the Blakes have had letters returned to them.

Things at the gallery continue as before, a little more sluggishly perhaps, now that the novelty of the notoriety has worn off, as well as the usual August deadness.

Clive is getting set to go off to San Marino with Christopher Finch; Derek is still waiting to hear about the proposed world trip; Jann is preparing madly for her show at Felix Valk, which is due to open on the 12th October; Peter is painting away industriously for the Carnegie show; Richard has just delivered ten each of his Toast Bing Crosby & TIME Self Portrait prints for us to sell; Colin has found a new method of doing dyelines so that they last; Pat is back from the S. of France where apparently he took numerous photos of beach balls & umbrellas. All the above send you their love, as do Christopher Gibbs, Nico, who just dropped in.

The best news of all is from Mohammed, in a series of postcards from Disneyland, Los Angeles, Hawaii (a copy of which is enclosed* – this was the most philosophical of the three). The police arrived looking for him the other day – all those parking tickets . . .

*Darling

How are you keeping with Robert. I miss you and Robert but I have to think of my self too.

Love to you.

Mohammed Jajaj

Letter from JIM DINE

Dear Robert,

Hope this letter gets to you as others have been returned. We have been terribly busy doing the various things to keep one afloat in jolly old England. I am going to be the guest lecturer at the Royal College and went there for lunch two days ago. What a scene. That sort of Oxbridge common room scene furnished in early motel and all those guys' palettes framed on the walls . . . very odd. I'm sure Susan has told you of my many meetings with jolly good Mr Wixley. What a schmuck. I'm breaking my ass to hustle like an art dealer (a strange sensation in itself) and he does everything to frustrate the efforts. Michael and I are trying to get some bread together to purchase some things for you so that you will have a private collection which Wixley cannot touch, if worse comes to worse. No strings attached on the bread, I hope it comes thru.

Michael is quite sweet but, as you know, very difficult to pin down into action on every level. We need your driving Yiddish kopf. Michael White has committed himself to producing two plays I have written. I think it will be done at the Mercury Theatre, on a club basis, in Feb. I am into other projects. Alecto has found some bread and I am making a four foot by three foot etching of Mao and LBJ in drag.

I received a postcard from Larry in Africa and he seems to be the Bronx Dr Livingstone. He might stop thru here in his way back to the US.

I am presently done in by my aunt and uncle from Cincinnati who are here after a whirlwind tour of the battlefronts in Israel. This hawk thing is out of hand. I'm not interested in flower love as it seems something like dandy fashions but in a world without politicians and other stupid people manipulating my friends and family's lives. We'll talk of that when I see you. I really think that the grasping for instant mystical straws by your and my acquaintances is futile but what with your mind and perceptions there must be other dimensions to get into. Dear Robert, we both miss you.

JIM DINE I was having lunch at Alvaro's once, with Michael Cooper and Keith, while Robert was in jail. I took it very seriously that he was in jail – not just because of my work being held up by the receiver. This was a guy I loved who was in jail! And they were making jokes about sending him trips on paper. I said, 'Please don't do that.' They looked at me as if I was crazy. Keith said, 'Oh, man, it'd be great to send him a trip.' I said, 'I don't think it would be great.' But I had this Ohio common sense they didn't have. I was thirty, thirty-one at that time and I knew I did not want my friend to remain in jail.

Letter from Brian Jones, Mick Jagger, Marianne Faithful, Keith Richards and Anita Pallenberg

Dear Robert

How's everything – I hear you are really grooving behind jail. Sorry I haven't written earlier but I spent a month doing a nursing home scene then I spent a freaky month in Spain. We are busy right now laying down tracks for the LPs. I'm planning to leave on Friday for Tripoli, then dig some oases in the Libyan desert. I hope to be there for a couple of weeks. I hope to find a groovy scene there. Well, look forward to seeing you soon. Lots of love. Brian

Dear Robert

We really miss you here but I'm sure that you're making it and there's no reason for us to worry. We went to see Maharishi Yogi this weekend who really showed us some nice things, it would be great to go to India when you return. I'm sure we could have a groovy time. We're just doing our album now. We really think of you a lot, and hope that you're happy. Everything will be so much more beautiful when you come back, there will be so many things to do. I'm sure you've thought of a million things so we'll put them all together. All my love, Mick xx

I'm sure you are well and Tantra is keeping you from all evil spirits. Love Marianne.

Dear Robert,

How are things in? on? the old homestead? range? Michael told me about your letter and I'm glad that it's not getting you down in there we're all grooving for October 2? Love Keith (formerly 7855)

Robert? come home!!!!!!! A.

SUSAN LOPPERT At the end of his sentence – four months, after remission – he arranged for a chauffeur-driven black Daimler to collect him from the Scrubs and return him in style to Mayfair.

PAUL McCARTNEY The thing I remember is his smell, after coming out of jail. He smelled like he'd been in jail. Scrubbed with carbolic soap or something – his clothes smelled. It put me off going to jail in a big way, that you'd smell jail. It was only for a couple of days.

ALASTAIR LONDONDERRY Oddly enough I saw him the day he came out of jail. I went to the hotel where Keith Richards was staying and the Stones were staying. I think it was the Mayfair Hotel. And I remember going to see him there. Keith Richards had a suite there. That's where I saw him. I certainly saw him the day he came out of jail.

I don't know who went – rather like Oscar Wilde – a sort of committee going to meet him or something – I've no idea who. But I do remember seeing him the day he came out. He was fine. No different at all. Then life resumed. He spent six months, didn't he?

SOPHIA STEWART I remember Mummy saying, 'Robert's coming out of prison tonight.' And we said, 'Oh, good, is he coming here?' and her saying, 'Yes,' and then seeing this very – obviously we didn't know at the time – drunk man swaying about, and we were told to leave the room. I think I remember Mummy telling me he was drunk later on. It's quite frightening for a girl to see an adult swaying around. My father wasn't there, it was just my mother and Robert.

Soon after that, there was this lunch with Mum, Robert and Brian Masters, whom Robert didn't like, who had come as our tutor. So it was three of them and us having lunch. And Mum, for some reason, apropos of what I don't know – I don't know what had gone on – was drinking. And she never drank. Robert said something to her, he was laughing, but madness, and I remember her picking up this salad bowl and just hurling it at Robert. He sat completely still. At that point our nanny came in. I remember this maniacal laughter coming from my mother. I think it was a difficult time in her life. So we were led away. I just remember Robert covered in lettuce leaves.

JOHN DUNBAR He *loved* prison – it was no problem – it was a National Health cure for a start, which, you know, he needed, and lots of nice boys . . . and he got healthy – and . . . he came out really *good*. He sort of came to visit me the day after he got out and he was really just sort of full of beans. Full of stories – yeah, man, I did this – almost gloating. Though I suppose he might have been a bit worried about his mum or something.

JIM DINE After he came out of prison, there were less drugs, for a bit . . . We went to a concert at the Albert Hall about six months later and suddenly he said, 'Oh, I laid that guy in prison.' This was someone in the audience. He had a ball in prison. He was an amazing survivor, except he didn't survive.

Robert and friends in Morocco, photographed by Michael Cooper.

ANITA PALLENBERG There was one incident in Tangier (we all went there after he got out of prison – Marianne, Mick, Brian, Michael Cooper) and we were all high on acid. I was wearing feathers and Robert came in and started to embrace me, which I found very strange. It was like a violent, seductive attack. That was the only time I saw anything sexual from him. Robert was very private about his sex life. We were all high on acid and I'm not sure now what really happened. I do remember these feathers on me.

TERRY SOUTHERN When I saw Anita she said, 'Robert raped me' – but she said it gleefully!

Keith Richards and Mohammed, photographed by Michael Cooper.

The Redlands house party on the day of the bust, photographed by Michael Cooper.

200

Sgt Pepper set,
photographed by
Michael Cooper.

The American Scene, photographed by John Webb.

Tribute to Robert Fraser, photographed by John Webb.

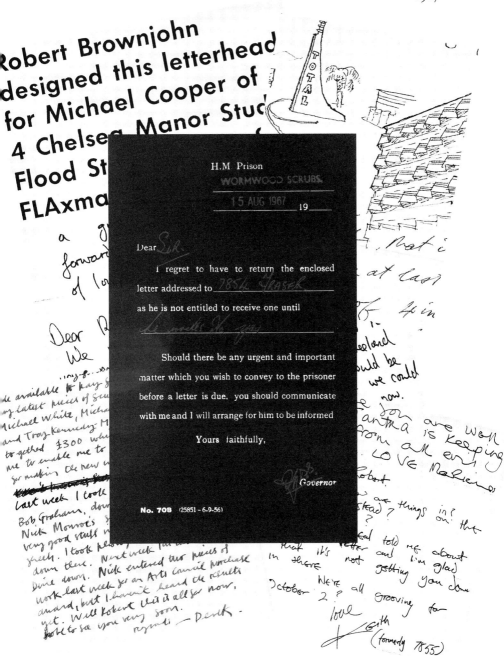

Robert Brownjohn
designed this letterhead
for Michael Cooper of
4 Chelsea Manor Stud
Flood St
FLAxma

H.M Prison

WORMWOOD SCRUBS,

15 AUG 1967 19

Dear Sir,

I regret to have to return the enclosed letter addressed to _____ as he is not entitled to receive one until _____

Should there be any urgent and important matter which you wish to convey to the prisoner before a letter is due, you should communicate with me and I will arrange for him to be informed

Yours faithfully,

Governor

No. 708 (25851 – 6-9-56)

Selection of letters to Robert in prison including letters
from Patrick Caulfield and Derek Boshier and Clive
Barker's lithograph created from his returned letter.

After spending 'the summer of love' in prison having to be businesslike and with the overwhelming clarity that heroin withdrawal brings, Robert might have been expected to adopt a more responsible approach. Everyone who knew him had been outraged by the sentence, but if the artists and those dependent on him had hoped that prison might at least have had this beneficial effect, they were to be sadly mistaken.

Back in London, Robert continued business as usual – that is to say, in a most haphazard fashion – and the party continued, albeit on a sourer note.

Implosion, summer 1968: two frames from a silent movie featuring Robert.

JIM DINE Then the gallery opened again and that was cool for a minute. But then I think Robert just lost interest. Like a child, his attention span was not very long. A lot of people thought that I was less than serious to be his friend.

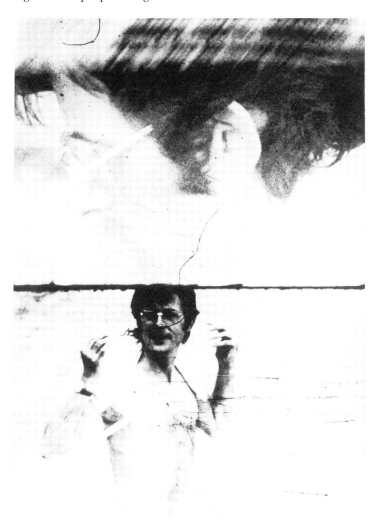

Telegram from KENNETH ANGER SOS NEED SIXTY POUNDS HIRE LIMOU-SINE FILM LUCIFER DESERT DAWNS IF NO DRAG CABLE FUNDS AT ONCE VIA COOKS MAYFAIR TO COOKS CAIRO FOUND CROWLEYS STELE HERE THIS MORN-ING GROOVING ON MAGICK CURRENT ONE TRILLION VOLTS AFTER AUSPI-CIOUS LUCIFER HOUSE BOAT KASHMIR. LOVE IS THE LAW
BROTHER ANGER ■

22 NOVEMBER 1967–11 JANUARY 1968: PATRICK CAULFIELD

It is good to see the Robert Fraser Gallery in action again, reopening with an exhibition of Patrick Caulfield's new paintings (his second there). In Caulfield's work, the subject of each different painting is made just about as distinct as it could be, and the gallery has emphasized this by printing as a catalogue a reproduction of each painting on a separate card each with its poker-faced title: 'Battlements', 'Parish Church', 'Stained Glass Window', etc. (Guy Brett, The Times)

PATRICK CAULFIELD The kind of lifestyle Robert led must have been intrinsically lonely. He was not your dull married man with two children in a semi-detached. But I think he created the situations that made him lonely somehow. He didn't try and join in. I liked Robert in a way I couldn't express to him. I couldn't in any way be affectionate or warm. But then I'd never have got the opportunity. However, I made a terrible mistake. When Robert came out of prison I had a cake made with a file sticking out of it, you know. All in icing. But he didn't think it was funny and he didn't say anything. He just reacted; he was a bit sensitive. I have heard since then that he didn't have a bad time in prison. But it can't have been good though.

17 JANUARY–14 FEBRUARY 1968: CLIVE BARKER

CLIVE BARKER He was probably my best dealer. Not financially. Anything else but financially, he was my best dealer. Robert Fraser was encouraging. He knew he had vision. He knew what you were doing. He saw, when you said something to him that you wanted to do, he saw you could accomplish it. Just do it. He encouraged you in that way.

He had enormous enthusiasm and he encouraged *you* to do things. You'd say, 'Well, I'd *like* to do this, but, you know – it's too big, I can't afford it, whatever.' He'd say, 'Do it,' and you would. You'd get carried along with that. You'd think, 'Course,' you know. And you'd do it and then you'd find you had to pay for it! You know. But – he'd pay for it but it'd take many months, or weeks, or whatever. But I must say there were months that you'd get your money OK. But the thing was, what he had was enthusiasm. And you thought you could do anything, because you had someone that kept telling you as well. You *knew* that what you wanted to do, you could *do* if you had the finances, the backing and all that, whatever. Robert was one of those who kept saying, 'Do it,' you know. 'Just do it. I'll buy it.' I remember saying to him – he said, 'Well, what are you doing?' and I said, 'It may sound rather silly but I'm doing a bucket of raindrops.' And he said, 'I want to come and see it.' And he came out and he said,

'I'll buy it!' And I mean, you know, to look at a bucket with ball bearings in, in 1965 or '4 – I mean, I couldn't sell that to anybody now, but *he* sold it.

20 FEBRUARY–3 MARCH 1968: DEREK BOSHIER

DEREK BOSHIER I had a show in '68 with huge Plexiglass sculptures. I think he did sell one or two of them. Mick Jagger bought one. One went to Leicester City education authorities. But my falling out with him was about that time.

When I brought them in, he was very dismissive, a bit abrupt and rude. Whoever was there at the time said, 'Oh, don't worry, it's just one of his moods.'

His personality had changed. He was more out of it at certain times. People said he'd become more aggressive. Because he had always been so polite early on, gentlemanly. But with the drugs, there was a time when he became irritable, and with himself too. He'd always been so friendly and polite.

STASH KLOSSOWSKI In 1968 I was staying with Keith and Anita at the Boltons – through Robert's agency, I think – a ridiculous kind of place. Keith and I had started to tape all the phone calls, we called it Telephone Blues. Many times a day you'd hear things like, 'Ah, hello? Yeah, Robert here, um . . . all right . . . um . . .' Then he'd get to the point: 'Um, have you seen, ah, Spanish?' 'No, haven't seen him.' 'Well, if you see him, tell him to call, right?' Many times a day.

The Rolling Stones first cover for *Beggar's Banquet*, the one the record company refused, was of the toilets and the songs and titles were written in graffiti on the walls. Robert suggested: 'I need to have added to those walls "Spanish Tony, where are you?"' It's there somewhere; a fitting testament to those times . . .

NIK DOUGLAS When I met Robert, the Duke Street Gallery was in disarray. He introduced me to his mother and I became a trusted friend of the family, trying to steer Robert along interesting, new and positive lines. That was the idea.

I met Robert initially through Olivier Boelen. He was involved with the Living Theatre, a close friend of Rufus Collins. I was in India for a period of time, collecting Tibetan art and tantric art, and I got to know Ajit Mookerjee quite well. I flew back from India through Kabul at Olivier's request to organize a shipment of Indian clothes to Milan. Then Olivier referred me to Robert.

So I showed up in London with this large collection of Tibetan paintings, some bronzes, etc., and a lot of enthusiasm for tantric art in general. As soon as I arrived I called Robert, as Olivier had asked me to do, and he said 'come round'. He was at 23 Mount Street then. Later we moved to 120 Mount Street together and shared it for about three months.

Anyway, I arrived at 23. Robert said, 'Where are you staying? Stay here.' I opened my bags and he took one look and said, 'I really want to get involved in this. Are you trying to sell all this?' I said, 'No, not really, just exhibit.' Then he said, 'Why don't we go into partnership?' So that day we made an agreement where I was paid some money and I had an apartment to live in. He was very taken with Indian art and I had all these things to fill the place with. We sold quite a few things privately to John Lennon and a whole group of them, and we planned to do an exhibition together at the Robert Fraser Gallery.

VISHVJIT PRITHVIJIT SINGH (VISHU) There used to be a man called Ajit Mookerjee, who was head of the craft museum here, and it was the one place in Delhi that had a lot of life in it. He was a maverick and willing to talk to people who were not run of the mill, not part of any establishment, art or otherwise.

I became friendly with Ajit and those around him, and one of them was Ashish Ganju. He was an architect from London, settled in India.

Nik Douglas I knew from the same time. He is a sharp creature. He's got a tremendous amount of drive and energy and a singularity of purpose which allows him to achieve a lot and he's done a lot of ground-breaking work. There's a certain amount of hype, but who doesn't do that?

ASHISH GANJU There was a strange man called Nik Douglas, awful fellow. He walked into my house one day. In those days I was seeing Mookerjee. A group was getting me to design this tantra museum as a talking point. Nik wanted to meet Mookerjee. And he proposed this idea of a film. He wanted all kinds of publicity. So that was it.

NIK DOUGLAS At 120 Mount Street we used to have evenings with Tibetan art up everywhere. Kenneth Anger would hire interesting films on India, etc. We had the Stones and the Beatles there, Marianne Faithfull, a whole group.

In the meantime there was the Kumbh Mela festival in India. Every twelve years there's a big astrological event, a total eclipse or something, and millions of people gather to bathe in the waters, the main place being Rishikesh in the Himalayas. I came back from India and told Robert that this was a Kumbh Mela year and told him all about it and suggested it would be a great idea to make a movie about it. Robert was very excited and so we formed a film company, Shakti Films.

The Stones at that time thought it would be a nice idea to gather ethnic material and were interested in the idea of a film being made in India. Robert and I were co-producers. I ended up becoming the director and basically producing it. The Stones said they'd back it – well, probably it was Mick himself – and they were coming out to India.

Sandy Lieberson put together the deal for the film – he was representing Mick at the time too. So basically Mick provided the money through Sandy, and we went off to India with Kenneth Anger. We hired a very good sound crew – a lot of the emphasis was on sound. The Stones had said, 'Whatever you do, get good sound, we'll need that.' We had four cameras and we had Kenneth Anger – *Scorpio Rising* and all that – to direct this magical film in India, starting at the Kumbh Mela festival in Haridwar, Rishikesh.

KENNETH ANGER 1968 was the year of India. I went along just for a lark, paid my own way. I wanted to see India. Robert was going over to make the film *Tantra*. It was actually made by Nik Douglas, who's written a book of the same name. The film was produced by Mick Jagger, he bankrolled it. I'm sure he has a copy. I found the film rather boring, not particularly good. It's sort of a documentary, with lots of close-ups of painted scrolls. I felt it didn't work too well. But I wasn't involved in the production at all.

SUSAN LOPPERT I remember Robert's first trip to India. On the corner of Duke Street and Oxford Street then there was a Hornes outfitters. And the day before he was going off he said, 'I'd better go and get some clothes,' and he bought the most unlikely things for Robert, a man who was always in these exquisite suits and hand-made shirts. Not quite safari suits – but the *most* unlikely things. I'd never seen him without a tie even. Then I'd get postcards and they were all just like 'Salaam' or 'God is Love' or something like that. I used to think, 'Come on, Robert! What a load of *rubbish*!'

NIK DOUGLAS Six of us flew out to India. Michael Cooper had been in business with Robert, who'd financed a studio that Michael ran. The *Sgt Pepper* cover was done there and various other cutting-edge things. So Michael was with us as principal photographer, along with Les Young, a film-maker, Colin Richards as the sound man. I was co-producer, road man, sub-director, whatever. Also I was the only one who knew India.

ASHISH GANJU Then Robert and Kenneth Anger and Michael Cooper and various others came. There was a small group of about six who arrived in Delhi.

I didn't know what Robert's role in the film was at all. I thought he'd helped to get the finances together. He'd just been released from prison and I thought he was just recuperating. He'd come to India for the first time for recuperation. I was told some money was put up by Mick Jagger, some by John Lennon and some by Robert too. So he was one of the sponsors.

Peculiar things stick in my mind. I remember the day after the arrival of that film crew, I'd arranged for them to stay in Claridge's here and I went to meet them in the morning. I remember Robert holding up a telegram and showing it around, from Mick Jagger, and the message was very mystical – almost a coded message. I don't remember the words, but it was about clouds, heavens – a little poem actually, to wish him well on this expedition. Everyone was completely out of their minds. It was really heavy.

One of the first places we went to film in Delhi was the Observatory. That used to be a favourite place of mine. At that time there were no tall buildings there, or in any place. And then the Observatory wasn't locked. I used to live a ten-minute walk away and I often used to go there at night, walk there, have a quiet smoke. It was wonderful, really deserted. In those days life would stop at ten or eleven o'clock, hardly any traffic – the perfect place to go for a smoke. That's why I took these people there.

I remember Kenneth filming there with his hand-held camera and the way he was moving was very special. He explained, he said he'd trained as a dancer. And his movements were those of a highly trained dancer.

NIK DOUGLAS We hired a bus and we did a magical mystery tour of north India. We took out the seats, had all the equipment on board, then Robert said, 'Where are we going to go?' I said, 'All the places I want to see.' I'd been in India for years and knew my way around. We went to Khajuraho, to Benares. We toured around for about three weeks. Ajit came along with us. There was no schedule. We ended up in the cremation grounds in Bengal. A lot of people got sick, dysentery and things, and left. We did lots of sound recording, about thirty to forty hours' worth, very high quality.

ASHISH GANJU Kenneth was on the bus, sleeping most of the time. We had half the seats taken out and lots of mattresses in the back – it was very comfortable.

Michael Cooper and I were trying to score some hash at one of the places en route while we were in this coach and they played the oldest trick in the book. We went to this place where they sold bang etc. and we couldn't know what quality we were buying. There was a kind of lunatic person sitting there and they said he would give us some to try. We tried it and it was very wonderful, so we quickly bought a huge amount and went away. And of course later on we discovered it was dried cow dung.

Mookerjee was the one who was most uncomfortable – he was not used to this kind of adventure. He was quite old at that time. We were in our late twenties to thirties and he was in his late forties. And he was a government official, a quite senior civil servant, director of the national museum. So he felt out of place with all these people.

VISHU They were all stoned throughout the film. It was a mad period. Everyone was on all sorts of things. Short of injecting yourself, you were doing everything possible to your body. Terrible situation. And in the midst of all that, there you are making the film, getting high on everything from alcohol to – everything. You were completely gone. And you had Kenneth along with you, wearing all kinds of rings, charms to ward off God knows what, control various demons, tattooed all over with magical signs. Along with this nervous creature, Douglas, who was spitting at everybody. He can't speak without spitting, you know. And he was in charge of the film. He would throw tantrums at the slightest thing. He was constantly arguing and fighting with everybody, then blaming everybody else for the situations he landed in. That's what was happening throughout the film.

KENNETH ANGER India was enjoyable but at the same time it was a terrible year – we kept hearing of all these assassinations: like Martin Luther King. That was the year all those things were happening. The Indians would say, 'What's wrong with your country that you're always killing each other?' So we said, 'What about Gandhi's assassination?' Indian has a ghastly history of violence.

NIK DOUGLAS Initially we hired limousines to go up to Rishikesh to the festival, supposedly to connect up with the Beatles and film whatever was going on. We did film there. But on the main night of the festival there was a huge thunderstorm, lightning, and about fifty people were struck by it, killed. That evening Kenneth turned to me and said, 'I can't take this. I'm leaving. I'm taking a camera and going off to Egypt.' So he dropped out.

KENNETH ANGER At one point Nik and Robert had a quarrel over something and Robert said to me, 'You can direct it.' I said, 'We-ell . . .' He was just jockeying around to get at Nik. That's when I named the project *Tantrum*. It was very hot there, and just like the Raj, the Westerners were going to pieces from the heat and stress.

ASHISH GANJU Kenneth was not really into it very much. I think it was his first trip to India. He didn't like the arrangement and I don't think would get on with anyone really. He seemed to be on his own. He didn't seem to be very keen to work with the rest of the crew. In Calcutta Kenneth took our camera and loads of film and just took off on his own and said he was going to make a film on Kali. The rest of us went back to Delhi.

VISHU I can understand the film not being up to the standard of Kenneth Anger, etc. He is a great film-maker, but another individual who's very difficult to deal with. My part then was to make sure I kept Nik under control, a difficult task. He was a mad fellow. If he owed you money and you said, 'Where's the money?' he'd say, 'Please don't trouble me with these mundane things, I'm on a different plane.' And you'd say, 'Get down off your high horse and talk about what you owe me, I want to talk about that.' He was that kind of person. If you said, 'What's the time?' He'd say, 'Time is eternal.' Very difficult to deal with that.

ASHISH GANJU A tremendous amount of the film was shot and put into cans and taken back to London for processing, and then it had to be edited. There is where the problems took place, once editing started. This was supposed to be one of a series of films. But this one film came out and by the time for the second film there was a custody battle over the cans. I saw the film only once, I think, in Robert's flat and it was very blue, and it had been very badly edited.

NIK DOUGLAS We came back to England with all this material and I was still living at Robert's. It was my job to get it edited. I worked with a guy called Nigel somebody, a film editor (he's on the credits), and we produced the film and released it.

Letter to Robert Fraser from PAUL B. M. PANHUYSENS
Dear Sir

Simon Vinkenoog told us about the film 'tantra art', you have made, which he saw at the Arts Lab.

We organise the 31/10/69 in the Municipal Theatre of Eindhoven a mixed media-show, in which the ecstasy is the subject. We will start the evening on your film.

This evening is the second in a series of five events, we organise especially for young people, in the Globe, a theatre en rond, intended for experimental sets. This theatre offers room for about 400 persons.

I will ask you for informations about the 'tantra art' film; can we have this film in time, before October 31? Is there a 16mm copy of the film, is it magnetic or optic sound. At what time can we have the film this evening?

Can you give me this informations, please, so quick as possible and also the date we can get this film.

Many thanks in advance.

TONY SHAFRAZI In '68 the gallery was changing, Robert was collecting Tibetan scrolls. That was a big shock to me. Robert's image had been much more modern, American, Pop, and suddenly there's this shift to the Tibetan stuff. So things were changing, coming out of the grim era, a new language of art, new form of expression. Little by little the climate was beginning to change. His interest in the gallery stated to fade and then he disappeared to do other things.

It was part of a bigger change that happened to everybody, and he was in at the beginning of it, of course. A certain kind of change of time, of events.

COLIN SELF Robert and the hippie thing – you know when the Beatles went all kind of Eastern, Robert was doing that, going to India. I can remember he had lots of tantric objects – those big sea coconuts, big shells. They come from one little island in the Indian Ocean and they drift across to India. Indians thought they were fertility symbols because they literally looked like a lady's buttocks seen from the doggy position. Robert had one of these coconuts, and they used to carve a fanny in and paint it red and pink. He also went in for lingams. I've got one here that he gave me after an Indian trip. He had a lot of tantric stuff – human leg-bone trumpets, bits of jewellery. I think he studied it as well, rather than just being a collector.

TONY SHAFRAZI Then another incident in '68. I'd run over to the gallery, it was early afternoon, gone in through the glass doors. This time there was a guy sitting there. Before I had a chance to talk to Robert, this guy said, 'Kid, do you have a paper?' It was John Chamberlain. I knew he was great sculptor. I didn't have a paper, but he wanted it because just that afternoon Andy Warhol had been shot, and Robert Kennedy was on the cover. On others, Warhol was on the cover. That was spring, maybe April, '68. Such a definitive end to something.

NIK DOUGLAS Then I think there was a family crisis about money, backing for the gallery, etc. Pop Art wasn't really selling, the prices were low and the gallery wasn't really viable. It was being underwritten by his family trust really. They were putting pressure on him. So eventually he said, 'Well, I'll get out of the gallery,' which he did, but some time later. 120 Mount Street came up and originally we were going to turn it into a gallery. It was a very nice large space.

STASH KLOSSOWSKI 120 Mount Street was his other flat, formerly Ken Tynan's. The lease was running out on 23, that's why he moved to 120. That was much larger. The good thing about 23 was it had a lot of light, a great place to have paintings, but the style changed.

MARIANNE FAITHFULL We had a lot of wonderful moments at Mount Street with Keith and Anita, Robert and I. Mick was always out making money and hustling away and Keith and Anita would be hanging out and I would always be with Robert. So there was a lot of sitting on this four-poster bed: seventeenth century, yellow embroidered/painted, with yellow silk hangings – the most exquisite thing. The scenario would always be Keith at the head of the bed, with guitar; Anita looking ravishing glittering and shining and covered in amazing things; Robert in some extraordinary lime-green or pale-pink suit, with his winkle-pickers – and me on the other post. That bed was like the bed of life. We spent hours and hours there, and it was there Keith wrote 'You Got the Silver.' He wrote it for Anita, with me and Robert there at the birth of the song. And I looked at Robert and thought, 'That's how I feel about you.'

5–29 JUNE 1968: NICHOLAS MONRO

NICHOLAS MONRO My first impression of Robert was that he was very laid-back. I only had one show with him, but it was a successful one. Robert didn't ask me anything about my work, just asked if I wanted a show. What went into it was up to me. Which is the way it should be. I think Robert was pleased enough with the show, the sheep sculptures. He had Duchamp with him and said Duchamp had liked my sheep, which was nice for me.

That was my first big show in London. It was nice, but not what you'd call a swell affair. A few friends came. It wasn't a grand opening sort of thing, balloons and champagne. Definitely not. That was one of the nice things about it. I don't really think my show got a lot of attention. It *was* successful, but I don't think there was much coverage of it at all. The work didn't actually sell that day. Robert sent them off to some art fair in Germany and they sold there.

His best aspects as a dealer? Well, laid-back. You could say it was a different kettle of fish from others, where everything was business. I don't think I had financial problems with Robert. I don't think much changed hands. I think I got my percentage on the sheep. But the things that went to the Rolling Stones, I don't think I ever saw money for those. I may have been a bit blasé and laid-back as well.

I didn't see Robert socially, only at openings. But I liked him very much. When I was setting up my show, he came in with John Lennon and I thought, 'Oh, this is good stuff.' I thought Lennon had come to see my show, but Robert was just showing him the gallery, the space. Lennon was a bit disconcerted by the sheep. Also I had a box inside which I'd put a radio which was switched on. I'm sure Robert thought Lennon might buy it and he was saying, 'Look at this! What do you think of that?' I remember Lennon looking very sideways, thinking he was being set up. Not interested at all. The sheep were bad enough.

YOKO ONO I think Robert was a very sensitive, sweet person. We always chatted and he used to come to the town house John and I were in at the time (the one where we were arrested, the town house that Ringo had before us). So Robert would visit us there. We used to have these nice quiet afternoons. Robert was in that circle of people, you know, 'the beautiful people' so to speak, of that time.

When John wanted to do this show, an environmental show that he had in mind, Robert Fraser was very nice about it. I thought that was very brave of him.

1 JULY–3 AUGUST 1968: JOHN LENNON–YOKO ONO, 'YOU ARE HERE'

DEREK TAYLOR When John told me about the idea for this show, he said he wanted to get a lot of collecting boxes of the cripples, people with club feet and calipers on their leg, and guide dogs, dogs with bandaged legs. He wanted to do an exhibition of them in Robert's gallery. There'd be some of his art, some of Yoko's as well. And the balloons of course – we spent many hours blowing them up. I also bought a golf umbrella – it was raining that day. Through all of this I saw Robert Fraser walking round in an administrative role. But not doing any blowing of course.

YOKO ONO Robert's gallery was known for the far-out stuff it was doing at the time, but on a very serious level in the art world. So that was good that he did it. I'd had a show in the Indica Gallery and also at the Lisson Gallery, but I felt that probably Robert Fraser was better suited as a gallery for what John wanted to do. There was always a slight difference between the Indica Gallery and the Robert Fraser Gallery in the sense that Robert's was slightly more event-orientated, on a flashy level. It wasn't my idea, the show, but I think maybe I encouraged John to do it.

DEREK TAYLOR The idea was presented to me under the all-purpose sixties word 'Great', and it may well have been, though I can't be sure any more. I thought it a good enough wheeze at the time and resented those (quite a lot of people in and out of the art world) who thought it daft.

The centrepiece of the show was a large circle of canvas, in the centre of which John had handwritten 'You Are Here' and that is what the event was called. Apple staff and others helped John and Yoko fill 365 small white balloons with helium and they sailed away over the rooftops of London, bearing tags inviting people to write to the couple at Savile Row. Some did; a majority of them were positive and said a sort of 'Good luck to yez both', but a minority were abusive, suggesting, 'You should get a proper job' and so on.

YOKO ONO It was a kind of 'Happening' that we created. The balloons had these little cards hanging from them saying that when you get this, write back – so I think they all wrote back. Some of the responses were terrible actually! But it was mainly up-beat, because this was just a fun thing to do, so there was nothing to be *that* furious about – discovering a balloon with a little tag on it! No, so they didn't get seriously angry or anything like that. Most of them.

It was a very successful show. I would consider it very successful. What John did was very original and interesting. I don't think that that came through that well in the press because they were just writing about the fact of 'John and Yoko', and it was 'balloons' etc., etc. I think they mostly caught the flashier side of it. And of course the press that was interested in writing about it were those that would usually write about the Beatles or famous people – not art people.

YES, I LOVE YOKO, SAYS JOHN LENNON
Beatle John Lennon stood by the side of Japanese artist Yoko Ono last night and said, 'I am in love with her.' . . .

It was at a London 'joke art' exhibition dedicated 'to Yoko from John Lennon' that he confirmed the rumours of his broken marriage.

The 'joke art' exhibition itself provided a surprise for the invited guests who flocked to the Mayfair gallery of Robert Fraser. It consisted of nothing more than charity collecting boxes and hundreds of white gas-filled balloons and lapel buttons labelled 'You are Here'. The balloons were released in the street with a request for anyone finding them to write to John Lennon.

Few people realized that the real object was a 'Happening' – with hidden microphones and cameras recording the reactions of startled guests.
(Daily Mail)

CHRISTOPHER GIBBS I remember Robert and John Lennon standing on the pavement, letting off these balloons, and Robert saying, 'They're good, they're beautiful!' Then Kenneth Anger going along and making them pop – pricking them with sparklers. Being very puckish, he'd been at the Indian hemp – very irritated by this silly exhibition. Robert was furious: 'Why did you bring this crazy druggy creep into my place?' That sort of thing. 'Why do you encourage him? Get him out of here!' They were great friends – but I got blamed . . .

NIGEL WAYMOUTH Robert probably went along with what John was doing at the time. I don't know if Robert was sincere about the peace and love thing. He had such a dark side to him that I can't believe he was totally into that. He wasn't just a 'nice' guy in that sense. He was far too jaded to be taken in by all that.

KENNETH ANGER Robert created a modern art scene in London. Most of the other galleries were so conservative. I don't remember popping helium balloons with sparklers. I did crazy things when I was young. Maybe I'd been smoking something.

YOKO ONO I think you could certainly say that the Robert Fraser Gallery was the driving force of the European avant-garde scene in the art world.

Chris Cerf, Esq.
Random House Inc.
457 Madison Avenue

Dear Mr Cerf,

I have been told by our mutual friend, Jonathan Cott, that you may be interested in publishing a book which has already been laid out in principle by John Lennon. It is a very strange and unique record of an exhibition John held at this gallery last summer. It is a document which includes a photograph of every aspect of the exhibition (the exhibition consisted of various charity boxes and a painting, plain white, with the legend 'You Are Here'), a photostat of the very extraordinary letters which were received at the gallery as a result of the show and of pages from the gallery's visitors' book.

Anyway, this is rather an abrupt paraphrase of what the whole project was. If you wish to hear more please let me know so I can pass the information to John, who is abroad at the moment, to take it up with you.

RICHARD HAMILTON Robert was a big socialite. He was mixed up with swinging London and if he had an openng the likelihood is that the Beatles would be there, or at least Paul and John Lennon. The association between John Lennon and Yoko Ono would have been as a result of this mixture of art society and pop society, because Yoko Ono was a member of Fluxus in New York and was having exhibitions in London of a very avant-guarde kind, making films of people's backsides. And all the art society of London would go along and expose their backsides for her.

It was an interesting time, when everything was very free. And of course Paul, who was the moving light behind any of the sort of executive decisions that were being made by the Beatles, the organizational apparatus would be under Paul's control – he would have gone to Robert and said, 'Who do you think might do a poster for – or record sleeve – for us?' And Peter Blake on the *Sgt Pepper* album cover did this wonderful assemblage of culture heroes, and it was a very significant moment I think, even in the history of cover sleeve designs, for Peter Blake to do that. Because this was *the* image that people remember of the era.

Then they were about to embark on their next project, which is now known as the *White Album*, but it's known as the *White Album* simply because I said, 'I can't follow Peter Blake. I can't fill the cover with anything as exciting as he did. So I'll back out. I'll just make it white.' And this idea was accepted, I think partly because

Yoko Ono would have seen the point. I think she may have been influential. I'm not sure that they quite understood. All I wanted to put on it was a number, to make it an edition of five million, and they should be numbered from one to five million. That seemed to me to be a Fluxus idea. I would have liked to have signed them all if it were possible in a way, to make it a real art object.

Letter from SANFORD LIEBERSON
Dear Robert,

This is to confirm that Goodtimes Enterprises Ltd agree to pay you on behalf of Anita Pallenberg the sum of £30 per week, plus the cost of gas, electricity and water consumed, for the use of your flat during the eight week period commencing September 5th, 1968.

Anita will personally be responsible for settling the telephone bill for the above period, and in addition bear responsibility should any damage or loss occur during the rental period.

CHRISTOPHER GIBBS I think Robert was quite a contributing factor to the *Performance* soup. His gifts for bringing people together certainly had a part in it. With Donald, Anita, me, James – I mean, he was definitely a mover in the whole thing.

ANITA PALLENBERG At one time I needed a flat. Warner Bros wanted to rent me one. We had only the house in the country. Robert said we would rent his flat in Mount Street but then he never really moved out. So all we really rented was Christopher Gibbs's four-poster bed. That was a funny period. It was very difficult for me. Keith and Robert were both so cynical and sarcastic, slagging off the movie every day. I'd come home from filming and they would be slagging off Jagger, slagging off everything. I got quite confused. You know how sharp Robert could be.

SANDY LIEBERSON If Robert was banned from *Performance*, that would be part of his character – mischievous or bitchy. He really like to stir it. That's one of his strongest characteristics, getting people at each other. He enjoyed it a lot.

DONALD CAMMELL I barred Robert Fraser from the set of *Performance* because I felt he would cause too much trouble and Keith was trying to sabotage my movie because he was jealous of Mick with Anita. He didn't want Anita to do the film and wouldn't speak to me for a long time and wouldn't perform on the track of the music; but Anita was having the time of her life. She'd go home to Keith, who'd be terribly jealous when he heard she'd been in bed with

Mick. Michael wanted to come and shoot some 16mm footage because I was using a 16mm camera in the bedroom scene under the sheets with Anita and Mick and their co-star, Michèle Breton. She was fifteen; she'd been staying with Deborah and me in Paris.

Of course, the whole thing would have been a field day for Michael, but I was scared of all the trouble and I was also scared of Robert's machinations and I expected trouble from him because he was so tight with Keith – they were such good friends. I adored Robert, but treachery was an affectionate game with him.

KEITH RICHARDS At the time of *Performance* I was living in Robert's flat in Mount Street. That film was probably the best work Cammell ever did, except for shooting himself. I did kind of like Donald, but I found him a vicious manipulator of people, a selfish bastard. Any redeeming qualities were totally swamped by a very mean streak, which probably in a way came out of an inferiority complex. He was a failed director. He shot himself because he realized who he was.

Donald might have banned Robert from the set. Robert'd be like scoffing basically. While that was going on, I wrote 'Gimme Shelter' and half of 'Let It Bleed'. I just wrote songs. I said, 'I feel a storm a-coming, gimme shelter.'

ANITA PALLENBERG That was the closest I got to Robert, living in his flat, but the heavy drugs didn't help. In that period drugs seemed to be the biggest happening. The bathroom was the most important place. First you'd shoot up, then you'd puke, then you'd feel great. For me, though, it always fizzled out, because next morning I had to go to work. It just didn't seem real. I don't know what opinion Robert had of Donald Cammell and the film, because Keith thought it was rubbish. Although I think Keith liked the finished film, but we never really talked about it. Keith more expressed himself in music.

Apparently it was Spanish Tony that stole a gun on the set, on the last day of shooting. His excuse for coming on the set was to bring me drugs. What else he got up to I don't really know. I'm sure he did report to Robert, that Robert knew about all the things going on. Not that I see Robert as the instigator, but he liked to be devil's advocate, always taking the opposite opinion, sneaking in his wicked little ideas. Really sarcastic. In fact he was totally anti-establishment, which was great as well. Whereas Keith was so cool, never being fazed by anything. Maybe Robert was trying to prick him into a reaction.

KEITH RICHARDS It was an energy thing Robert and I had. We enjoyed each other's company and we'd sit back and observe what was going on and be very cynical and sarcastic. We both have that very dry sense of humour. His remarks, you had to be there, were so to the point. Every remark was a potential song, or a phrase. And the demeanour.

No particular song he inspired – perhaps 'Gimme Shelter'. I'd be sitting in his apartment all day and he'd popping in and out: 'How's it going? Hey, that's nice.' You know. But he did love his music, and maybe that was our other connection. If I came back off tour from the States: 'Got any new records?' I'd pull out the 45s and say, 'Yeah, here.' 'Oh, make me a tape.' I was his sound man in a way. But he was also mine, he would turn me on to music, great Moroccan or Indian stuff. There was an understanding between us. I don't know why he was fascinated by some guitar player from Dartford.

TONY SHAFRAZI It was summertime and I was ready to do the show at the gallery but things were changing with Robert. Eventually he went off. He got involved in the Living Theatre, which was coming through London then. I don't know if he danced with them, he did something with them, began to get involved with exercise and meditation. So the gallery's programme was uncertain for a while.

NOVEMBER 1968: MOSTRA MERCATO D'ARTE CONTEMPORANEA

GILBERT AND GEORGE We knew his first gallery from the start. It was one of the few galleries we were attracted to, because it wasn't anti-figurative. Kasmin was abstract. Marlborough was too old-fashioned. As baby artists, we went to every gallery that there was in London. Not like young artists now, they go to *the* galleries – we went to every one on the list, you know, whether they were showing hunting prints, South Kensington or Bond Street, wherever it was, we went to them and said, 'We would like to make an exhibition at your gallery – are you interested?' And they would say, 'Well, let's see your slides,' or whatever, and we'd say, 'Well, that's not how we do it. If you would like to do a show, then we will make something,' so they all said no of course. And we were very impressed by that. We thought we must be doing something right if they all are saying no. But when we went to Robert and said we would like to do something he said, 'Ye-e-es' (the longest yes ever).

So then we asked him, 'Would you mind showing the *Shit* and *Cunt* for three hours in the afternoon?' And he said, 'Yes', and that for us was amazing. We just showed this pair of portraits, *Shit* and *Cunt*, in a vitrine, which we borrowed from Christopher Place, which had antique shops in it at that time. We went in and asked this lady, 'Would you mind lending us this glass case for two or three hours?' She said, 'Yes, of course.' We then displayed these portraits in the vitrine and invited these people in with a little handwritten message. And amazingly someone [Alan Powers] arranged to film it secretly opposite the gallery – he borrowed a flat opposite for the afternoon – for three hours that afternoon, who came in and out – must have been twenty people. But he showed it for three hours.

Once we were on the way to see him, along Oxford Street, and there was one of those people selling things on the pavement, pictures with a polystyrene frame – what educated people call kitsch – pictures of the Virgin Mary, vulgar pictures. We bought one, signed it and took it in to Robert. He said, 'Great, great.' He liked it.

And then we did another piece with him. We said, 'When you close down for Christmas, why don't we do a slide show on your window? A Christmas show.' And again he said, 'Yes (ye-e-es).' And we made him write Happy Christmas on all the slides. They were just slides of Christmas cake decorations – they were all made of chalk at that time. And we had this whole carousel of slides that you just left on. We just whitewashed the back of the window, cut out the shape of the two slides (horizontal and vertical) and had a projector on a chair in the middle of the gallery. So then it was slide, Christmas greeting, slide, Christmas greeting – each one written by Robert.

We used to pester Robert a little, I remember that. He was interested in us but not totally convinced. But he wasn't dismissive, as all the other galleries were. We were very grateful to Robert Fraser. He was one of the first to show an interest in us. He didn't dismiss us. He went 'Ye-e-e-es . . .'

He was the first one here in England, it's true. After that, when we had lots of shows abroad, then it was easier to show. We were impressed he was able to take an interest. We didn't care how long, as long as he took a little interest in the beginning. It didn't occur to us to ask to do an exhibition. We just wanted to do something, just the little things. We were extremely pleased by Robert. We only needed some little encouragement. And he gave it.

CHRISTOPHER GIBBS Robert by this time had moved to the other Mount Street flat, the Ken Tynan flat. I had a friend who was living upstairs – David Carrit. He was very funny about Kenneth and Robert. I remember Kenneth putting a notice on the door saying, 'Cursed be he who disturbs the sleep of the pharaohs.' And David said, 'I've had *quite* enough of all that roly-poly pudding and pie mumbo-jumbo.' He was very irritated by Robert.

STASH KLOSSOWSKI What I remember of Kenneth Anger and 120 Mount Street is that he had a temple there, all these books, all his stuff. I had my Tibetan room. Then there was some problem between the two of them – I don't remember what it was. I remember very well the razor-blade episode in response to this. Robert showed it to me. Kenneth sent Robert a razor blade with the words 'A cure for your stuttering' . . .

FEBRUARY–MARCH 1969: JANN HAWORTH

JANN HAWORTH Kenneth Anger really freaked me out. He came to the show every day and lit the candles on the Lucifer figure and dusted him. It was horrible. That was the second show.

Libby spat at him at my private view and I thought, 'He's a warlock, he's going to take it out on my child.' I was all motherly at this point. But he said, 'No-no, baby's spit is sacred.'

He came over and wanted me to do a jacket for *Lucifer Rising*, and he had this kid with him in the gallery whom he said he'd found at a tube station. He had recognized that this kid was Lucifer.

Kenneth said could I make a jacket for him for this film, anything I wanted to do? He wanted it to be like a baseball jacket but with lettering on the back which said Lucifer. So I designed it and quite innocently I put a pentangle on the back, and coming off that I put a rainbow of seven colours, and the words Lucifer went on them. So it was all numerology and witchcraft. He was besotted with it. He thought I knew. He said, 'You know what these things mean, don't you?'

Anyway, when you came into the gallery, this stack of doughnuts was there and the hole in the middle was finger-sized – it was a stack of large cloth doughnuts. I came into the gallery and there were five doughnuts instead of six and I was mighty mad. Somebody's nicked one of my doughnuts. I then took them apart, because I was going to tie them together with gut – and this gold ring fell out. I thought, 'This is who took it, whoever this belongs to.' Nobody knew anything about it. So I put the ring on my finger. Robert saw it and said, 'Oh, you're wearing Kenneth's ring – he'll be pleased!' Some while later I saw Kenneth and he said, 'You've got my ring!' I said, 'Oh, is that your ring? Did you take my doughnut?' He swore he didn't. However, then he said, 'But how did you know to put it on *that* finger?' So I thought, 'Here we go again . . .'

Letter from P. A. GILLINGHAM, St Anselm Development Co. Ltd
Dear Mr Fraser,

I am sorry to have to tell you that we are again receiving complaints in connection with the disturbances being caused at very late hours of the night by the volume at which music is being played in your flat. I must ask you to take steps to ensure that other residents in the building are not inconvenienced and annoyed in this way.

Dear Mr Gillingham,
I was surprised to hear from you that you have had complaints about the

volume at which music is being played here late at night. If you could please tell me from which direction the complaints are coming . . . up, down, or sideways . . . it would help me to do something about it.

J. PAUL GETTY Then I made another financial mistake with Robert. I sublet a flat from him in Mount Street and he took another one, further down Mount Street. Bit of a disaster. I was rather slow about moving into it and he took full advantage of that, by living in it, putting his friends in it. I arrived back from Rome once to find the Living Theatre living in the flat. We arrived from the airport, all ready for a hot bath and a good night's sleep, and there was the Living Theatre all over the flat. Coming in, wanting to put your feet up, and there's the Living Theatre. God almighty. It's not as if we knew them. They weren't in the least apologetic. They took things for granted – and when I say 'took', I mean *Took*!

Talitha had wonderful clothes and for weeks, months the Living Theatre rifled them, and we'd go to louche London nightclubs and see people wearing her clothes. Mostly men.

RUFUS COLLINS I was on tour with the Living Theatre for a long time and I'd come back to London and visit. If we were playing in London, I stayed with Robert. The Living Theatre was really a group of travelling gypsies. When we came to London the government shut us down, paid us off, then I stayed at Robert's because I thought I was going to do another play. But there were problems with visas, permissions, etc. and it was too difficult. So I went off to Rome to join the Living Theatre again.

The flat on Mount Street was wonderful, 120. The whole flat was semicircular, rooms off, rooms off and back again.

I'd always had this thing of not wanting to be an American and wanting to speak real English. So when I met Robert – well, he was *the* English gentleman, and I liked him immediately. We became very good friends and a very long friendship it was, from '64 until he died. We constantly talked. When I was in London I saw him a lot.

CHRIS JAGGER Robert was practically Hindu then. He spent a lot of time with that Dutch guy I didn't really like. Olivier Boelen. Very overtly gay. Had lots of money, could buy whatever he wanted, including boyfriends. Rufus was very much part of that. I was in the theatre with him later on. He was the key player in Robert's life. When I was in the theatre, Robert was very supportive. Rufus and I did some plays and Robert came to see them. He was amused by them. He found amusement in things that others wouldn't.

DAVID COURTS The first time I saw Rufus he was with Robert (I think he was staying at Robert's). He came sailing into Vesuvio, Spanish Tony's club in Tottenham Court Road, this handsome guy wearing this marvellous long, flowing cloak.

J. PAUL GETTY Yes! That was probably *Talitha's cloak*!

KEITH RICHARDS I do remember Spanish Tony's club. Helping to paint it even, including Robert. Nobody ever went there except us, and played music loud, and we'd say, 'When it's finished this place'll be great, Tony.' Of course, it was no Copacabana. It was like an old disused office building or a warehouse. Probably previously for hot cars for all I know. 'We've got some space here.' Tony was a bit like that. But knowing Robert opened up another world for Tony too, top clients. In those days you had your pet toy junkie.

But Tony became very much affected by Robert and the people around him as well. Otherwise he may have remained just basically a London dealer/hood – an enforcer too in his time. But Robert opened up his world. He would never have had the idea of the club if he wasn't hanging round with this circle of people.

Then there were all the cats involved in the Living Theatre – Rufus Collins, etc. Rufus – a big black guy. Very well spoken, well educated, out of NY. Whether Rufus or Robert bonked each other I've no idea. But gays never bothered me. You come on to me once, you get a slap on the wrist, then it hurts. Robert came on to me in his own way, but it was never so overt I would remember it. It would be, 'Sorry, Robert, you're not my type.'

DAVID COURTS Rufus was travelling with the Living Theatre, but when he came here he stayed with Robert. He was definitely Robert's friend. I don't know if it was friend or boyfriend. But the more I think about it, the more I think about how much Rufus learned off Robert. For example, his attitude with houseboys. He liked the idea of having them and treating them badly. That was very Robert – to have these houseboys and treat them badly – I'm sure Rufus learned that off Robert. He's terrible with young adoring guys – treats them like slaves!

RUFUS COLLINS Robert certainly loved the low life too. But he was very singular in that aspect. He wouldn't think of inviting me to go with him. But I went to some party and they gave me a pipe of hashish to smoke. I took a great big drag and next moment I was lying on the floor. Didn't know what happened to me.

I was infatuated with London, the way of speaking, the jokes. And through Robert I met a lot of people. That whole period was so sixties. Robert and I would go to the Ad Lib, and there you'd see the Beatles, David Bailey with tickets from everywhere hanging out of his jeans, Lee Radziwill and her husband. Robert knew everybody of course. And he was on top of everything.

JIM DINE Robert was living with Rufus Collins in the old Ken Tynan flat at 120 Mount Street, with two sons of a Brazilian diplomat. Somehow they got these kids, without passports, into the country, and I guess they were fucking their brains out. They were kind of slaves. I couldn't believe what was going on. I'm from Ohio, not that sophisticated. But Rufus was great and it was a jolly time.

3–15 MARCH 1968: WILLIAM BOWEN, 'SERIES ONE'

15 APRIL–25 MAY 1968: RICHARD HAMILTON, 'SWINGEING LONDON '67', 'PEOPLE', GRAPHICS, 1963–68

Clive Barker, Esq.,
3, Dartmouth Road,
London NW2
I'm showing some of Richard's things (he calls them 'Swingeing London '67' and 'People') in the gallery at 69 Duke Street. We're opening on April 15. Hope you can come.

RICHARD HAMILTON The *Swingeing London* thing I did while Robert was in jail. I had an idea I could do something, and I'd gone to the gallery and asked if there were any press cuttings. Susan, who was sitting there alone, handed me this enormous bundle of cuttings, which I began to sort and then made collages of them. Then I worked on a painting. That had strange repercussions. The Tate was due to buy one, then I learned they couldn't buy it because the mother, who was then chairman of the Friends of the Tate, had said, 'No, they mustn't buy it.' She didn't want her son to be remembered in these circumstances.

Robert, when he heard this, was very angry and told her to mind her own business. So they bought it. But she wasn't happy about the picture. I didn't know her at all.

I don't think there's anything damaging about the picture from Robert's point of view. It's become quite a famous picture. I made a version of it for Release, the drugs organization, which was very successful in getting money for them. It says a lot for Robert really, in a way, as a symbol of the treatment that was meted out to people in those days.

MRS MORRIS Cynthia had felt decimated when Robert went to prison. It was terribly sad and traumatic, but she was marvellously brave about that. And when they had the exhibition at the Tate, they had a large blow-up of Robert going to prison and they phoned Cynthia to see if she objected and she said, 'No, not at all. It happened.'

RUFUS COLLINS His mother would ring up while I was in London: 'Is Robert there?' 'No, he's not.' 'Oh.' And she'd hang up. And one day she called: 'Is Robert there?' 'I don't think so.' 'I didn't ask you to think, I asked you whether he's there!'

Then I met her, a little lady in a big chair, with her feet hardly touching the ground. I went with Leo and some others. Leo had long Italian hair and she kept whispering, 'His hair is *greasy*, isn't it!' Another time there was a gathering for Mookerjee at Robert's house, and his mother looked across the table at me and said, 'Rufus, what kind of *tea* do you think this is?' 'I really don't know.' 'Well, it's about time you did!'

CHRISTOPHER GIBBS I think his mother's Christian Science beliefs annoyed him most of all. That deserves going into. He coped with her very well – rudely of course. He fought it off. He saw it as ersatz, and I think he saw the spirituality of India as much more productive to him personally.

DRUGS CAN'T DO IT!
A person may think that he can experiment with narcotics and psychedelic drugs, believing that they can help him find the meaning of life. He may think that this type of adventure or experience will take him beyond the ordinary limits of the five senses. But do the properties of matter really expand the thought processes of anyone to the point where he beholds unseen truths?

Mrs Eddy, who discovered the scientific truths underlying the extraordinary healing experiences of Christ Jesus, says of him, 'Jesus of Nazareth was the most scientific man that ever trod the globe. He plunged beneath the material surface of things, and found the spiritual cause.'

Jesus saw reality. He knew who he was and where he was going. But there is no record that he ever used drugs or recommended their use as an agent for opening the human consciousness to perceive reality. Being physical elements, drugs cannot carry us beyond the material state. They merely affect the physical body through a false belief that mind is mortal, centred in brain and nerves.
(Madeline Montgomery Dale, Christian Science Monitor, 1 March 1969

SUSAN LOPPERT His mother always used to send him things from the *Christian Science Monitor* and he'd say, 'Urrgh, *God!*' and throw them in the bin. There'd always be messages. His mother would ring up and say, 'Please get Robert to ring me.' There were always financial crises and it was always his family who got him out, but he couldn't be bothered to ring back. He literally would say, 'Tell her to fuck off!' I'd have to ring back and try and smooth it over. I don't know why I felt the need to do so, but one does, you know. You can't bear that sort of thing – a mother having a son saying, 'Oh, fuck off.' Robert had an unbelievable temper. Unexpected things would trigger it off. But then, never an apology or anything like that.

I have to say that, although I loved Robert, I didn't like him. And I left because I just couldn't stand it any more. Because it was so erratic and unpredictable working for him. I was tired of making excuses for him, of smoothing things over. You know, this was taking it out on my health. When you're twenty-four or twenty-five, or whatever I was by then, it was too much of a burden to act as his mother without being his mother. To be everything, his amanuensis, for no reward whatever, and certainly no gratitude. I mean, in spite of this 'God is love' business, there were *weeks* when I didn't get my salary and I needed it to live on. And for many of the artists it was the same.

He did write me a letter when I left, thanking me for everything. I think he had flashes of *such* originality and flashes of such importance in terms of the art world. I learned an enormous amount from Robert. I mean, I was trained as an art historian, which he wasn't, but I really believe that he taught me how to look. He had this instinctive feeling and that was what was so wonderful. It was an incredible apprenticeship for someone like me. But he was such a difficult man. And when you saw the people who were his close, close friends – or people who called him Bob Fraser, all the Americans, you know – well, *they* saw a different Robert altogether, one I never saw: convivial, gregarious. I mean, somebody I can't imagine. As I said, one I would hear on the phone saying to Terry Southern, 'Hi, Tell, we're g-g-grooving!'

29 MAY–JUNE 1969: JIM DINE, '2 PAINTINGS'

JIM DINE I loved him. I considered him a wonderful, highly unusual friend who, as often happens with friends, went a different way. He was taking classes on Indian dance in the Cromwell Road, then he went off to India to dance.

Drugs really diminished Robert's personality. Before, he was just an occasional pill taker. When he started to do heroin it was the end for him. He was never very interesting after that. The thing that killed Robert finally was his shallowness. He had the potential to be a profound human, but he couldn't get above style. Shallowness was his one flaw.

2 JULY–20 AUGUST 1969: PETER BLAKE

PETER BLAKE Well, its interesting that I was the last show because (and this is one of the pros of the situation), I think he actually stayed open another month to give me the show. I have always suspected that. I think he wanted to close the gallery but I was just in the process of buying a converted railway station in the country and I needed another £3000. Robert put that last show on and got me exactly £3000, which paid for it, the building. So I think he stayed open a month longer than he might have done. Which was one of the positive things about him.

Old Etonian Robert Fraser, who bought pop art to London when he started his Mayfair gallery in 1962, has now closed up shop . . . Says Modish Mr Fraser, 'I've closed because I didn't want to become a middle-aged art dealer and I felt I had had enough. I'm looking for something new in art.' (The Times)

CHRIS JAGGER The straight businessman side of Robert he kept separate – like on his trips abroad. I think the Duke Street gallery was quite important to him, that he was quite proud of it. I remember him saying he had to pay £8000 a year on outgoings before he could make any money. He said, 'Fuck them. Why should I sweat my bollocks off to make them money, because I've been successful so far under my own steam?' Presumably the rent had been reasonable at the beginning. That very much disillusioned him, having to close Duke Street down. He didn't want to be just a business guy making money out of his art, he wanted to enjoy his life and do things on his own terms. Not be a slave to a Rachman. So he closed it down. And it was the best, most avant-garde gallery for miles around.

RICHARD HAMILTON Robert's was the best gallery I knew in London, the best of the post-war years. There's been nothing better. There was something about his gallery which was unique, marvellous. Although there were difficulties as a result of my change of finances, I've always been grateful to him for getting me out of that rut of teaching. And I've never looked back, never needed money since. Never had to go out and look for it, I mean. So I owe Robert a great debt.

Letter from **MARIO AMAYA**
Dear Robert,

Thank you for your note. I am very sad about the closing of the gallery. As you know, I have always felt it symbolized an entire decade of artistic activities in London. I do not know what will happen in London now, but think your decision was probably the right one under all the given circumstances. In any case, what you did was a brave and marvellous thing and it will never be forgotten by either the art world or your friends.

Do try and come to see us some time in Toronto.

1969, ROBERT FRASER IN THE YEAR OF CHANGE

Look at the second half of 1969 and it's beginning to look like the yin–yang sign of completion and the year of change – although no one's too certain about just how that change should be consolidated for the future (in this case, of art). But whether or not we can see precisely how what has to be done can be done we and Robert Fraser can certainly recognize that the state of art and the position of galleries in relation to the showing of art have altered radically over the last decade. So along with the other signs of the alteration down at the ICA's Conceptual Show right now and at the Hayward Gallery's Pop Re-examination recently, the shutter's have gone up on 69 Duke Street – as if that number held the key.

Robert Fraser was rare amongst dealers in that the responsibility for what was shown was totally his own – there was no fear of backers who with the power of ownership could put the finger on any apparently dangerous direction the gallery took. It was totally an expression of his own art and life interests. Although he largely showed Pop he had the kind of freedom to show work outside the limitations of one type of art which can only come from a one-man interest. So alongside Peter Blake, Richard Hamilton and Jim Dine were shown the reduced colour painting of Ellsworth Kelly; geometric light structures of Derek Boshier (a one-time pop image painter); Jean Dubuffet's earth pictures and Bridget Riley's optics. We only saw what Fraser felt was relevant to the moment, regardless of style. Although it's easy to mourn the closing of one of the few outlets in London for advanced art or adventurous art this is no cause for regret so long as that closing leads to another opening up of new possibilities. Seven years ago when Fraser came out of the electricity and care of the New York scene to invest London with some kind of scent of the possibilities for a grey and largely indifferent London, the new image makers who were involved in shifting the local vision were still ignored and unwanted. He provided their only outlet. In this sense his gallery was an English oasis for the new image painters from both Europe and America.

It is significant that the last show, which opened on 2 July and in the presence of Jim Rosenquist, Claes Oldenburg and George Segal (some of the grandfathers of American Pop, who were seen to be still alive and well), should have been that of Peter Blake – the one English painter who had been most involved in producing pop objects for the commercial pop world – notably the Beatles' Sgt Pepper *cover, which he did with his wife, Jann Haworth. Thus the revolution (if it was one) is over and, as Fraser says, 'the wheels have come full circle' as Pop (the art), which once fed off Pop (the culture) is now being used by, and incorporated back into, the pop culture. With this situation where 'the artists have become public property' the role of the Fraser Gallery was diminished if it was to remain visible. Recognizing the absurdity of continuing in an area which was fast becoming stagnant and that 'this is not the time to be involved in static situations', Fraser has left the wheeling doors open to lesser and more historically minded dealers to move into, for the moment, a less active and more contemplative state of considering the present implications. So he's back in the ferment, considering, in the light of the inability of galleries to make art available to the maximum numbers, the alternatives ('in Cuba, artists are putting paintings into empty store windows, in the street, keeping them for a month, then changing them').*

When I asked him about the English art scene, and in particular about the prospect of the kind of patronage (like Robert Scull – and others – in New York) which is totally concerned with supporting the new, Fraser told me that he knew of one (later qualified to one and his son, two) collector in England who was involved in accepting, using and supporting frontiers – most of his support came from Europe and America. As he put it, 'There has never been any desire on the part of the English people for new things.' Although he attempted to make, certainly to allow for, some kind of change in this situation, 'to the English the gloss of age is too comforting'. Nothing has really changed in seven years.

Fraser is currently involved in Tantric Art but doesn't want to show it as yet another specified historical art show separated for the life it is involved with. Art should be concerned with the living – not with killed images capsuled on the wall. Tantra is an inclusive system that takes in everything, from the grass at your feet to the limits of the universe – before it and beyond it – and that like Robert Fraser is concerned with India and the future – and that's another story . . . (Richard Dunn, Rolling Stone, *18 October 1969)*

Robert Fraser and friends, 1968, photographed by David Bailey.

NIGEL WAYMOUTH At that time people were looking East, the time of the Maharishi. The party as such was coming to an end. The end of the sixties was a bit of a hangover. The ideal had not come about in any great form. Things had become much more aggressive and political. The buzz was fading fast. And in come the religions and ologies and isms. Some of us were quite cynical about it. It got a bit out of hand. But Robert needed to recover I think. He really was reeling. Needed to find himself, or something, get away. And he did.

LARRY RIVERS Then Robert became very weird. He went to India and came back with a totally changed personality. I think he even gave up the art thing. Suddenly he wanted to be a dancer. I couldn't figure out what he was doing. But he lost interest in being a gallery owner. I thought, Well, he has a good figure for dancing. I was very interested in dance. But I did think, This is weird, Robert's going to be a dancer? I thought he was going a bit off the deep end. What's happening to this guy? What happened to his interest in art?

John Lennon and Yoko Ono, *You Are Here*, Duke Street gallery, 1968, photographed by Michael Cooper (MIDDLE ROW LEFT: John Dunbar lends a hand).

Kenneth Anger, Robert and friends in India, photographed by Michael Cooper.

Kenneth Anger's message to Robert.

the final
solution to your
stuttering

Spanish Tony and Robert, photographed by Michael Cooper.

Robert and Bill Willis.

Robert out and about with Gilbert and George on Mount Street, 1968.

Jim Dine painting.

1970–1975

Robert's one trip to India had been in some ways unsatisfactory, but what he had seen convinced him that this might be a place to disappear to for a while. It was sufficiently strange to appeal to someone for whom ordinary life was not enough; and as a substitute for the drugs he intended to give up, there was the possibility that mysticism might provide the added dimension needed in his life.

Characteristically, though, his re-appearances in London during the four or five years he was away shed little light on his actions and whereabouts other than conveying his increased enthusiasm for all things Indian.

Robert in India, 1970.

CHRIS JAGGER He'd gone to India because he found himself in a bit of a box in London. He said modern art and England had nothing to say to him any more.

GILBERT AND GEORGE We used to send out these small postal sculptures to different people – 300 in the art world. Every week we'd send out a different one with a different title. The first group was called *Lost Day*. Some people wrote back. But Robert wrote back from India with a photograph of himself on a colonial veranda somewhere saying, 'This is my lost day.' ■

Young man resident West End requires experienced Hindi teacher for private lessons. Please phone HYD 3918 Robert Fraser.
(*Advertisement placed in* India Weekly)

RUFUS COLLINS The whole idea was Robert, Olivier Boelen and myself were going to India, to find a place where people could stay, then I would come back and bring them over. We stayed in a hotel in Bombay, then with a friend of Robert's, an Indian who was an absolute horror. He was a Brahmin and as dark as I am, but he considered me to be lower caste and before I sat down he'd put something on the chair, so I didn't touch it. Then afterwards wipe it over. It was hell. But when we got to Shantiniketan, Ajit Mookerjee gave us a run-down house. The house was just off the university grounds.

MADHU KHANNA Shantiniketan is the great university town. Ajit had this big house there inside the university. It's a huge campus, thousands of acres. These people were all in and out of Ajit's house and I was doing some research work for him. That's how we all met and we instantly liked each other.

Along with Robert came a whole generation of youngsters. There was Rufus Collins, Vivian, who's married to Chris Jagger, then there was Olivier Boelen from Amsterdam and a whole lot whose names I don't know. They came on a personal quest. They had come to India for adventure, but also to look for some spirituality. Robert was the leader, the luminous point. He was the one who brought all these people together.

HARDEV SINGH (GLOGI) Shantiniketan – this was founded by Rabindranath Tagore, the poet. It's open air, you sit under the trees. Robert was there four or five months. What was he doing there? Buggering boys.

MADHU KHANNA Robert and Olivier were very good friends and had this idea of a kind of dance-drama, creating a play and also a film on tantra. So the dance-drama had to be around tantra, taking certain concepts from tantra.

There's a scene I can never forget. There was Rufus, Robert and a whole lot of men were going to practise this great play they were going to create. First, they were going to miss Ajit very much because he was a guru figure for them. So they picked up things from his suitcase, one a hanky, one something else. We'd gone to the station to leave them and there they were, carrying baskets full of honey, two peacocks and birds, plants, and I'm sure a lot of hash also. I'll never forget that scene. 'What are you going to do with all these birds?' 'We're going to create this paradise with them' – the birds, pure honey, health food, etc. Eventually they all fell ill because they had too much of everything.

They were in Shanti for a year, coming and going every three to four months, getting their play together. Finally they did present something, but it was so way-out. That was the first time I met Olivier's mother, who had specially come from Amsterdam to see the performance. Poor lady, everything went over her head. She said, 'Olivier, I don't know what you're up to, but anyway I'm very happy, you've done something.'

I'm writing this in Shantiniketan, it is eight o'clock now but I've been up for about two hours already and have had my bath, done all my exercises etc.

I have been feeling very depressed of late, remorseful for the past, closing the gallery, previous mistakes and omissions, throwing away so many opportunities, such a waste of everything, inability to decide anything, or know what the future holds, although the other part of me says that there is no point in regretting all that – just go forward into the future. Self knowledge and a study of philosophy and absolute values will help and the future will plan itself accordingly with changes in personality and outlook. Never the less, most days I am not happy!

Despite the unconventional aspect of a man of 33 spending a year in the East apparently at a loose end instead of applying himself to a career for which he is suited, I do not feel I am wasting time. One has to follow intuitions as far as possible. My feeling was, and still is, that I could only remodel my life by coming to terms with the inner aspects of it which have caused me so much unhappiness in the past and have been my undoing. To do this I had to go away, leave England or the West, anyway that environment for a while. When I return it will be (I hope and pray,) to perform my functions in life in a harmonious fashion and to use such talent as I have, rather than be constantly *abusing* it as in the past. One must conduct a research into oneself however, to find out why the abuse seemed so inevitable; it is when one has realised the potential and force of evil that one will be able to discover the nature of good and one's relation to the divine force which makes good possible.

RUFUS COLLINS Robert didn't stay till the play's end – he went on, travelling to other parts of India. The others eventually went back and I stayed there. At one point Robert came back to Shantiniketan, either by himself or with Olivier Boelen. Then he split off again and went back on his travels within India.

GLOGI Robert was a very mystical person. He was, in the real sense of the word, trying to find inner peace, you know, doing that spiritual number. He really worked at it. Desperately looking for it. I don't think he ever found it. And there's a reason for it, which I always told him, because of this tantra business. He didn't realize that it's all gimmicks – you don't find anything in it. But he kept trying.

RUFUS COLLINS Robert became extremely calm during the Indian period. There was an ashram in the south, lots of French nobility go there, and it was brilliant. I just went for a visit once. The monastery was so peaceful. Robert gave me a massage with this oil which relaxed you and it really did seep into your system. Robert got lost in India – lost in the art, music and dance – and he didn't want to go back to England. In the meantime he'd rented Mount Street to Kenneth Anger.

KENNETH ANGER Robert was out of London for a good long time. I can't say exactly how long, but he left his furniture. One room was used for storage and it had a lot of paintings from the gallery. And he had a wonderful Moroccan mirror – which is in *Lucifer Rising* – hexagonal shape. Then the red lacquer walls. He'd put up wooden Moroccan shutters in his bedroom, which give that wonderful mottled light in the mornings. I used those in my film too. Basically I used the flat as my set for *Lucifer Rising*. I also shot in Egypt, but the interiors are all Robert's flat. I had Marianne Faithfull stay over now and then, during her homeless period. The legend has it she was sleeping on the streets – she didn't really do that, but she was without a real address and she stayed at Mount Street a number of times. She always left the bathroom a complete mess.

RUFUS COLLINS I know Robert went back to England briefly during this time – something to do with a tantric show he was putting on. I think he helped with it, mostly from India though. Anyway, there was some sort of 'set-to' with Kenneth over this show, I believe.

JOHN DUNBAR Kenneth went through a barmy time. Robert put on a tantric show and all these monks were there. Kenneth ripped off his shirt and showed this huge tattoo – the Great Beast 666. Yes, he really got pretty flaky.

KAY GIMPEL Robert put on a wonderful show – he was the adviser for it – at the Hayward. A series of one or two or three people all making love – ludicrous and terribly pornographic. But Robert advised them and it was a wonderful show. He was very, very, very good at his job.

'Tantra Revealed'
The exhibition of Tantra on show at the Hayward Gallery from 30 September to 14 November has been an event which could be a catalyst to the formation of new conceptions as to the purpose and direction of the art of the future. In this instance I mean art taken as a global entity, not as something divided up into Western art or Eastern art.

MADHU KHANNA That was the most fascinating part of Robert's personality, that he could enter into that conceptualization without really studying philosophy. Certain kinds of people can do that. He had the absorption and receptivity. When you read the article Robert wrote – 'Tantra Revealed' – you'll know what I'm talking about. He couldn't look at tantra as an insider, obviously, he's an outsider, yet finding something extremely relevant in it. He never consciously studied Indian art history, but he could get into the bones of it, just as a response. That means he was already there. He had a genuine quest, I could see that.

The basis of all Tantric iconography is function; although tantra is based in the expansion of consciousness (Sanskrit root TAN expand TRA) its purpose is to provide and explain methods by which the expansion is to be achieved. There have been many different schools of thought on this subject and the reason for the seemingly baffling complexity of Tantra is that it touches upon so many different levels and approaches to Sadhana; philosophy, science and ritual are all involved in what was originally one system of thought based in Vedanta. In recent centuries cults have grown up which have advocated specialized approaches, of which Tantra Asana is one; it is this one approach that has in the present day been identified most closely with Tantra, and its over-emphasis has given Tantra a notoriety which is based upon misconception of its full range. Nevertheless, in this show all this enormous variety of imagery and symbol has been brought together under the umbrella of various methods towards the pursuit of Sadhana and man's relation to the universe.

KEITH RICHARDS Marlon was born. Robert was his godfather. He organized a tantric baptism. He was lying in his little red rocking Indian crib. There's Indians there with great turbans, red dots, laying out herbs and rice, making a beautiful garden all round the crib. (Robert's going: 'Pretty grand, that.') Then they started chanting, two or three of them. What a way to get baptized, better than getting dunked under the water. He was given the full name of Marlon Leon Sundeep by the priests. But the baptism went on and on. Just as we thought it was finished they'd go, 'Oh, lah-lah,' there'd be some more stuff.

MADHU KHANNA Robert was a great lover of India, with a great eye for art. That was one of the things that brought him close to Mookerjee. He could look at thousands of pictures and just pick up one and that would be it, and Robert was the same. I could see them coming together. There was something between them unsaid, not discussed.

Robert was very, very important in the Anglo-Indian network. Ajit looked upon him as his son, his confidant. Ajit was a very simple man with two lovely daughters and his wife was a great religious adept, more like a yogi, all the time praying and chanting mantras. Robert used to love that. Even Ajit's wife adored him. She almost adopted him as her son. He was part of the family, the inner group. She related to his gentleness. She was an aristocrat, she was related to Tagore, and she could recognize the aristocracy in him. He had sensitivity and a love for India, and he would mix with us as one of us. He would sit on the floor, would wear Indian clothes. Sometimes he would buy musical instruments, another time paintings. He would ride rickshaws, wouldn't ride in a car. He didn't come here as a tourist. He was here on a quest. That was apparent from his movement, his gestures, the way he spoke to all of us. He was always searching and discovering.

GLOGI You know, he never used to talk about art. This was the very nice thing about the chap. He never used to talk about something that's somewhere else. He lived here, he was here now. All what was around here would interest him, as opposed to talking about something that happened two years back, in some other place.

MADHU KHANNA Robert didn't have the problem of commerce. That's a very big thing. If you start marketing this thing, then you're catering to a taste which is perhaps vulgar or whatever. But Robert wasn't marketing tantra, he didn't need Indian icons to make him rich. For him it was a love for tradition, because he found something new, and he's voicing the reaction of thousands of others all over the world who've found something in tantra.

GLOGI Re tantra, the five things you must get over are lust, anger, desire, attachment, evil. So how do you get over them? Meditate, this and that. The Buddhists have the same thing. The other thing the tantrics believe: do it all, do it to excess. Have sex in 5,000 ways. This is a tantric text.

VISHU Robert certainly witnessed rituals in different parts of the country, but from an academic point of view, not that of becoming a practitioner. I don't think Robert intended to further his study of tantra through me. I was a practitioner in my own right and later we would discuss various things, but I was not guiding him in any way.

GLOGI Robert went quite far with tantra, but he was not a believer in it. I know it. Not mentally, you know. He would say, 'Oh, I've done this, I've done that.' He lived in a cave for a while, some sort of underground situation with corpses. In the tantric script there's a thing of mind over matter. It's a long story. It's a cosmic thing, but they reduced it to a kind of sexual thing. Of course there's a lot of philosophy behind it. But at the end of the day, you practise sex with all that rotating in your mind. So he was into that. He used to do the sexual things and all that. But I don't think he really believed all of it.

He told me about some underground place, with corpses – he didn't do it, but the tantrics used to. They would eat the corpses; basically to overcome fear, whatever.

VISHU Tantric rituals with corpses and cannibalism? Nonsense! Nonsense!

GLOGI He did follow tantra through the whole way, believe me. The sex part of it – all these boys and stuff like that. Getting wilder and wilder. I said to him, 'Robert, if there was anything there you would have found it by now.'

I think he was a very lonely person, frankly, in a sense. He knew the world, but inside, you know, in his heart he was looking for something more. That's when I came to the conclusion that I didn't think he would ever find it. The sex gets more and more obsessive, and if it was satisfying, gratifying, then he'd have been content. The fact that he had to have it all the bloody time shows that something didn't work. Didn't end up with anything happening really, for the mind.

VISHU We would all go to the Tarpit and all take part in rituals there. That was at a particular point in time only, not part of our lives. You grow out of it and go on to other things.

Robert was a modern version of a Victorian dilettante who wants to know about lots of things, has a certain knowledge of lots of things, and has a specialist knowledge of particular things. Not a practitioner of the arts as such. He was definitely ahead of his time. He was into tribal art, in the Punjab, for example. He loved old photographs and things, the poor people of India.

GLOGI You know, women didn't play much of a part in the whole scheme of things. Robert was fascinated by Sikhs. If Robert found a Sikh boy, he would go bananas. I don't know why. Must be something there. And he had this thing about getting young chaps. Part of the tantric ritual was to become 'brothers'. I don't know what the sense was. Maybe he just liked them. So he got into a bit of trouble in the Punjab. These boys tried to blackmail Robert. They came up with this sum they wanted and he said, 'I don't know what to do.' Might stop him from coming to India. So he called them over one day when I was there. I said, 'I'll break your bloody bones if you try anything.' They were minors, you see. Age of consent is I think eighteen, but it doesn't really work that way.

VISHU Maybe when he was in Madras he was involved in some sect or another, but I have no knowledge of it. As far as I know, when he was in Madras he was trying to put together a sculpture collection.

OLIVER MUSKER Sometime in the seventies, I went to India with Marianne to make this film and we were lent the Maharajah of Mysore's palace at Bangalore to get over our jet lag. So we invited Robert to stay. He turned up. I was very surprised he turned up and he was more surprised to find we were actually there. He'd been in India two years by then. He wasn't with Karma Dev then. I think he was living in Madras, therefore he must have been doing his dancing and going to health farms. He was off smack – clean as a whistle. What was he doing? Being mysterious.

MARIANNE FAITHFULL I did feel a big difference in Robert in India. He wasn't that different really. It's only looking back, I suppose. I see that he had a real confidence and was much more sure of himself, and it might have had something to do with him being on a spiritual path. We didn't talk about that much, it was just understood. But he was very open. I think it's something to do with India – people are really pleased to see you, because they haven't seen you for so long.

Anyway we went off to Mysore and did the film – all shot in palaces – and we met up with Robert in Bangalore. It was just magic. Oliver Musker and Robert got on immediately. Oliver made Robert laugh and vice versa. They were born to be friends. So that was wonderful. It was just a very happy time. Robert took some wonderful pictures of me at that time. Robert was with Dutch Olivier Boelen.

I think Oliver Musker was excited to meet Robert, because Robert was a legend and Oliver knew people who'd known him. And I can't say it too much: Robert *was* a legend.

OLIVER MUSKER Anyway we were in Bangalore and Marianne made this dreadful film. We'd decided to stay on in India – it was summer holiday time – and I was rather hoping we'd go up to Kashmir, but Robert and Olivier of course had other ideas – everybody goes to Kashmir, just like Blackpool – and so we went to Delhi, where we met them.

MARIANNE FAITHFULL Cynthia, Robert's mother, was coming out to see him in so many weeks, and they'd been thinking of going on a trek in the Himalayas, and we arranged to meet up with Olivier Boelen and Robert in Delhi. That was the plan. And go on from there really. Then at some point Cynthia joined us and she was enchanting.

OLIVER MUSKER We travelled very luxuriously, only two in the back of each car. We visited things like the highest cricket ground in the world – a picture of which you'll find in Glogi's suitcase – and we ended up in Manali. We stayed there in a place called Sunshine Orchards, which Robert had read about in a guidebook published in 1910. It was lovely, run by a man named Mr Banham. This guidebook said that if you walked into the Lahaul and Spiti valley, you'd crawl in like a rat and spring out like a mountain goat.

MARIANNE FAITHFULL This was a serious de luxe trip, the opposite of the hippie trail – the best of everything, the best hotels, the best transport, best food, beautiful clothes, nightclubs, all that stuff. No roughing it. In the Simla hotel there was a little band and I'd brought some tapes Nigel Waymouth had made up for me, mainly of Billie Holiday. I'd been listening to them a lot, and it turned out that the hotel band knew one of the songs. It was the first time I sang a Billie Holiday song in public – for Robert. He loved it. And so did the two Olivers. That was fun, singing Billie Holiday in the grandest hotel in Simla. I think the song was 'Some Other Spring'. Then we pushed on. Robert was determined that we were going to go mountaineering.

OLIVER MUSKER Then we had the inevitable brush with authority. You had to get trekking permits and they were two hours' drive away, and because there was a squiggle on Robert's mother's passport which wasn't on ours, they said it was invalid. Before we could have our permits they'd have to write to the Foreign Office – it would take two years. Anyway, we had a long row and got our trekking permits.

MARIANNE FAITHFULL We all had to get proper mountaineering boots, except Robert, who'd already bought his, at the best boot place in the world somewhere. Olivier Boelen had very fancy boots too and they had all the right gear. And Oliver and I couldn't get such fancy gear, but we had to get gear.

OLIVER MUSKER Then we had to get trekking equipment from the government trekking centre. We had it all ready, all our lists. They said, 'When do you want it?' We said, 'Tomorrow.' 'Oh, we thought you wanted it next year.' So, of course, Robert got cross again.

MARIANNE FAITHFULL So this was all planned – sherpas were hired, it was going to take ten days. I'd come off heroin just a little while before that. It didn't cross my mind that this trip might be quite difficult. Because I trusted Robert. Robert had come off heroin quite a long time before me, and Olivier Boelen too, quite a long time before. They'd been mountaineering already in Nepal – Robert was doing a lot of this stuff. It was very much part of his spiritual path. I really understood that, and I understood even better when I got to the Himalayas.

OLIVER MUSKER Anyway we set off and after we'd been walking for about an hour Marianne was bent double, and at this point we were going up a road and up to the top of the Rohtang Pass. There was this small road and they managed to find a car to take them up. But of course it was much quicker to walk.

MARIANNE FAITHFULL Climbing the foothills of the Himalayas had not been on my agenda. I found it hard, it was so cold. Anyway I managed it, but it took me hours, much longer than the others. But Cynthia stayed with me. Her line was: the power of the human spirit and the love of God. Not bad as messages go. That I could do anything if I really wanted to.

OLIVER MUSKER There was a little tea house on top of the pass. Robert, Dutch Olivier and I got there about two in the afternoon and we waited and waited and waited. It started getting dark and we asked the guide, 'What's the last time we can leave in safety to get to the next place?' 'Four o'clock.'

MARIANNE FAITHFULL For me it was terribly hard. I was off dope, had been for about six months, but my muscles were pretty wasted. The others could tear up this mountain, up a glacier, off they cracked, and I could hardly do it. I thought I wasn't going to make it. This is where Cynthia's Christian Science came in – she got me up this mountain with Christian Science. It was so wonderful.

OLIVER MUSKER Cynthia was on a mission to convert Marianne to Christian Science. And when we got back to London Marianne did go to the Christian Science church a couple of times. Got bored with it. Basically Robert thought it was a load of shit. No such thing as a revealed religion.

MARIANNE FAITHFULL When we got to the top there was a little tea house – empty of course, you had to make your own tea. The sherpas were up there already. It was four hours later I got up with Cynthia. So we walked in and the tea was ready – the chai – and Oliver was playing Billie Holliday in this little tea house at the top of the Himalayas. And we all sat down and had a cup of tea. Triumphantly.

OLIVER MUSKER At exactly four o'clock Marianne stumbles in, beetroot red, having been driven. She had to walk a bit of the way. Then she was getting altitude sickness. We wouldn't let her rest. She was livid. The worst bit was downhill, she fell half-way down the mountain. I saw the guide running down the mountain and I thought, 'Nice chap, he's coming to pick up my sack for me' – it had my stereo in it, etc. – but no. He picked Marianne up and ran down the mountain with her on his back.

MARIANNE FAITHFULL It was nearly night by then and we had to get down the other side. I was knackered, seriously exhausted, and they could all see that. One of the sherpas just picked me up, put me on his back and ran down the mountain with me. I was very weedy, very light then. Then at the bottom a fire was lit and dinner was made and we all went to sleep.

I woke up very early the next morning, just at sunrise. Cynthia was already up and dressed and she was sitting in the early morning dawn with her make-up box, which she carried everywhere, full of Elizabeth Arden, putting on her make-up for the day. And every morning of that ten-day trek, there was Cynthia putting on her make-up perfectly early in the morning.

So off we went, and it was the happiest time ever of my life, apart from having Nicholas. It was just wonderful.

OLIVER MUSKER We trekked on for about five days. Robert loved it. I loved it. Cynthia loved it too. On the second day she announced to us all she'd been made an MBE – or CBE or whatever – she'd known all along but wasn't allowed to tell anyone.

MARIANNE FAITHFULL She and Robert got on perfectly. Everyone got on. I really felt I'd found it on that journey. You do feel the higher you go, the closer you get to God. When you're in the valley, there's only a bit of sky, you can only see that much, the rest is all mountains. Then you're going up and there's only sky, and then going down. It was the closest to God I've ever been.

OLIVER MUSKER We went up to a monastery, trekked back, stayed on a few more days, then the whisky ran out. It was Olivier Boelen who had to have his whisky. Then inevitably the money ran out and we didn't have enough to pay the hotel bill. I was left as a hostage and they all went back to Delhi in the cars, promising to send a car back with some money. I was there for five days, with the man in the hotel getting crosser and crosser. But then we were back in Delhi, with normal things like Marianne running off to find some smack.

MARIANNE FAITHFUL I ducked out one day and escaped. They were being terribly holy-holy – both Robert and Olivier were dressing only in pure white Indian clothes, being vegetarian, not drinking – very spiritual. Robert was talking about his guru – it was amazing. I was enjoying all that, but I had one moment where I went off to the Crown Hotel in New Delhi, which was the junkie hang-out. Terrible seedy joint.

Robert realized I would do this at some point and was watching out for it, but I escaped him and was terribly proud of myself that I'd got to the Crown, scored, got high and got back again, none the worse.

Robert said, 'Oh, God, you're such a fool. Anything could have happened. You could have been killed.' Looking back, that tells me a lot about how much Robert loved me. He wouldn't have bothered to say all that if he hadn't loved me.

OLIVER MUSKER Robert snatched the bottle of smack out of her handbag in a taxi and threw it out of the window, but got some of it on his fingers and he suddenly remembered how nice it tasted. After Delhi Robert must have gone back to Madras.

Life is rather boring here – too relaxing really. Karma Dev and I are waiting for the arrival of the Chhau dance teacher who will liven things up. The effects of mountaineering are wearing off so I feel in need of some more strenuous physical exercise which his lessons provide.

MICK JAGGER When he went into his India bit we didn't see much of him. But he threw himself feet first into the India business. He was always there having mud baths, going on treks, and when he came home he'd wear Indian clothes, bells on his feet, etc. Gone were the Turnbull and Asser shirts, Savile Row suits, the carnation in the buttonhole. It was the white dhoti and he even spoke with an Indian accent. Eventually he got tired of the whole thing. But before that he took India and all things Indian very seriously.

During some of that time he had a boyfriend, an Indian dancer, Karma Dev. A made-up name, two gods. I remember a performance given in the church of St James by Karma Dev. Robert was besotted by Karma Dev. Karma Dev was everywhere, and we were always 'treated' to his performances, tinkling of temple bells at the drop of a hat . . .

CHRISTOPHER GIBBS I didn't have to be forced to go and watch a beautiful boy dancing – I didn't make a fuss about that sort of thing! I didn't get terribly turned on by it – but not a privation as far as I was concerned. And anyway, if Robert was keen about somebody, you wanted to be encouraging and try and make it work. But as you know, Robert wasn't the kind of person who was going to let somebody be what they were. He was always going to try to reprogramme the person and tell them that they were doing it all wrong and didn't understand the way things should be done – not wear those silly shoes, 'cut out the eyeliner!' or whatever it was. He always had these great ideas about how people could *not* be themselves.

But I thought it was a good thing for Robert. I thought anything that occupied his head and his energy at the same time had to be a good thing. Because he'd really been in a mess.

CHRIS JAGGER When Robert was in London, he'd have Karma Dev with him then and we would do kuch pudi dance with him at Chelsea Manor Street, Michael Cooper's old studio. Robert, myself and Karma would go. There was a dance teacher too.

Robert was amazingly humble and he really listened to instruction. On one level he'd have no time for people he thought were bullshitting or speaking for effect, but if people were talking about something he was interested in he was quite humble about it.

SOPHIA STEWART Karma Dev came into our lives when I was about six or seven. We heard that Robert was coming to stay – I think it was one Xmas. Mum was very excited. 'He's come back from India, he's coming back to live here and he really wants to see you and he's coming down for the weekend.' I remember being very nervous about seeing him again. I don't know why. I remember the first meeting. He looked just so glamorous. He had kohl round his eyes. I felt in awe of him. He was very gentle and sweet to me. And from then on, whenever I came up to London, we'd do things together. Our first outing was tea in Fortnum's, then he'd take me to see *The Red Shoes*. Things like that. And tea with his mother. From thirteen until I went to live in Italy at nineteen, he was a big influence in my life. Not so much to do with art or anything, he just made me think differently, see things differently. I absolutely loved him.

I remember Karma Dev as being one of the first exotic people who came into our lives, not being able to stop staring. It can't have been Xmas, must have been summer, because I remember him being bare-chested a lot of the time. We had a habit of going into guest's bedrooms, after the maid had brought in breakfast, and he'd always be sitting very still in some lotus position. We were rather fascinated by him.

One day Karma told us this story, all done through the hands. It was about a deer being hunted. It starts off with the deer walking along, then bending down very gracefully to drink the water – he had a very, very long, elegant hand – then he's alerted by a sound, up goes his head, looks left to right. The hunter is coming, the deer escapes off. It *was* fascinating, but after a bit became a bit boring. I started looking out the window, not focusing on that hand. It went on and on – to a child it seemed like hours. Robert was furious that we got bored: 'This is unique, you must listen to this. Pay attention!' And we were quite nervous of Robert – well, I was – and respected him.

They didn't share a room. Whenever we went in in the morning, Karma was alone and holding a position. We must have gone into Robert's room too, but I don't remember. Karma was very, very sweet to us. We were rather nervous of going into Robert.

SAM GREENE I met the dancer only in India, with Kenneth Lane and others I was with. We'd just come from Sri Lanka, we travelled up the coast of India from the south. Robert Fraser met us at some point and took us to Madras, where he was going to live out his life with an exotic dancer! That seemed to be the plan, that's how he announced it.

They lived very comfortably in a house that had been converted to Western comforts, and were a couple. It was the most exotic thing I'd ever seen – here was this person I knew as a London businessman in flowing robes living with an exotic dancer in Madras.

It was quite comfortable. It would be an average Western house, but in the middle of Madras it was quite luxurious, like a separated row of houses in London, with a front yard and a back yard and lots of roof-top activity, because that's where the cooler air was, so they had a sort of tent canopy on the roof. But it was a neighbourhood of houses just like it on either side, occupied by Indians (as Gita Mehta says, that is spot not feather . . .).

KEN LANE I saw him in India, Madras, with the dancer Karma Dev. They had a house on the beach. I remember an absolutely marvellous banana-leaf lunch they gave us.

SAM GREENE He seemed happy and half of a couple, which I thought would *never* happen, and probably never did again. Half of a couple . . . what a derogatory term! It was so strange, his conversion to another life. He was just living another incarnation, from an Indian point of view. It seemed to be that he was on a pure journey of humility and sobriety – probably meditation and yoga. At any case he was clean. It seemed to be under the influence of the dancer; he was so beautiful – not effeminate, but graceful. You would assume he must have exerted a great influence over Robert to have converted him to sobriety. Didn't last long though.

The next time I was in London, there he was again, his life in India had passed and he was back in the back room shooting up.

MADHU KHANNA I don't know why he came back from India. When you live in a country like that, especially when you're the only white person around, you get lonely for the West, for the facilities you have here. And the variety. In India you have Indian food – that's it.

Karma Dev and Robert, India 1974.

I don't want to think about coming back to England. Ever since I closed the gallery I have found life absolutely unbearable there. That is partly psychological as without any raison d'être, life is completely empty for me, and London has not got enough to offer to stimulate one. There is nothing beyond the social round and without my own place I just cannot get anywhere.

The thoughts of living in India are intensely seductive. I do have something going here but I don't know how to make something out of it. At least in the field of contemporary art I know and have the confidence (and reputation) that I can do something better than anyone else or as well, but again this means going through the torture of living in London and being the slave of an ideal. I still have this *wanderlust*. How to reconcile it I don't know.

OLIVER MUSKER To be honest I think Robert got bored rigid with life in Madras. When Rose and I were getting married, he was in India. He came back for that and I said, 'Is this just an excuse to get out of India?' and he said, 'Yes.' That was the late seventies or something. He always got bored with things. I remember he told me the final straw was that he dropped his contact lens in the back of a rickshaw in Madras. He was looking for it on the floor and when he looked up there was a huge crowd of people gathered round the rickshaw to help, jostling each other and him. He said that that was the moment he decided to leave India. He just got irritated by the whole thing, I suppose.

The fears that Robert had had in India, that he would be lost and bored on his return to London, were entirely realized. After years of wandering, London seemed especially hidebound, and his response to this, away from India's calming influence, was to get drunk and angry.

    Knowing that his best bet was the art world, but not being a businessman and in fact having very little interest in money, he was to be as bored by art dealing as anything else. That his taste had been proved right – the works of his sixties artists were now fetching enormous prices – was a matter less of satisfaction than of mild frustration, as he had nothing to show for it other than a reputation as much for notoriety as for excellence. However, finally galvanized more by boredom than by regrets for the past, he moved forward to the next thing.

Jean-Michel Basquiat, *Portrait of Robert Fraser*
© ADAGP, Paris and DACS, London 1999

I think a gallery is something you take up in later life when you want to sit back and let people come to you instead of going out to meet them . . . (1978)

KEITH RICHARDS The last time I saw Robert was on 55th Street, when Patty and I had an apartment, must have been '84. It was about six months before he died. That was the last time I saw him, when he was giving away his belongings. He knew there was no possible cure. But he did make some amazing bouncebacks. There were times when he really seemed to have beaten it. You thought, 'Robert's sick, but if anybody can pull through, it'll be him.' He slid in and slid out. He always seemed indestructible. ∎

LORD PALUMBO Robert and I had been at school together. I always liked him then. He was of course the black sheep, but we always got on very well. I knew his elder brother, Nick – a much different character. Fascinating that two brothers could be so different. Robert was always very lively and funny. Way ahead of his time. One of those figures who help define a culture.

I hadn't been into collecting that much, contemporary things anyway, until the middle to late sixties. Then I'd suddenly seen the light, got rid of all my classical things and started again. So although I did go into the gallery in the sixties, I'd seen more of him at the end of the sixties, because my interest had been awakened in the things he'd been so brilliant at developing.

In between galleries, when he was dealing from home, I would buy odd things from him. The first thing I bought was a watercolour by Jim Dine, one of the heart series. Then I bought various other things, quite a number by Peter Blake. I bought the tantric drawing which Robert brought back himself from the first Indian expedition. I also bought a beautiful self-portrait by Ellsworth Kelly, who was a friend of Robert's, and a big painting by Richard Hamilton called *Glorious Techniculture*. I bought quite a bit from Robert. This was all in the seventies.

I trusted him because he was a friend, always someone I could talk to, to define/refine my own tastes. He was wonderful from that point of view. He was ideal. If you think of the gallery owners of today, good though some of them are, none of them have his taste, his eye, his instinct and ability to spot a trend or a talent ten to fifteen years in advance of its time. He did seem at a loose end then, though, when he was in between galleries. In hindsight he was destined for the end that came to him. I think he was bored. He was one of those people just too far ahead of their time who get so way ahead they lose the rest of the field and then become lonely and bored and frustrated. He was a polymath figure. Superb eye, instinct, wit, sharp tongue. Not too good with the finances. But much loved. That's the thing. If you talk to people now, they all think of him with great affection, despite his deficiencies in ever paying anyone. Well, they don't hold it against him.

Robert's contribution to the art world? He helped very much to form the cultural side of London in the swinging sixties. He was not only there, very much part of it, but also gave it that international flavour and characteristic. But he was a meteor who just flew across the sky. In hindsight, you could tell he was going to burn himself out, to just disappear.

CHRIS JAGGER After India Robert dealt privately. People didn't see what he was doing and share in it. He was just doing deals on the phone, shoving bits of art around. You'd say, 'What have you been doing, Robert?' 'Oh, just selling some picture in Düsseldorf.' That wasn't much of a story. So he separated that part of his life off from the other – more of a businessman than an entrepreneur. That aspect of him was marginalized and a lot of people didn't know what he was about. Then he opened Cork Street, but it was nothing like Duke Street had been. And that must have been expensive.

BRIAN CLARKE When I first met Robert I was still living in Derbyshire, early 1976. I met him at the Midland Group gallery in Nottingham. At that time there was a big exhibition of photography on, curated by John Sakowski, curator of photography at MoMA in New York.

There was a tremor of underground interest in the air then in photography as art. So they had to come to Nottingham – that's where the action was, at Trent Polytechnic. Robert was one of the few people whose antennae had picked up the photography thing. That was just before punk rock. I used to dress in clergymen's robes. That day I had on a clerical collar and a leather jacket and tight jeans, and Robert tried to pick me up in the toilets. Well, he chatted to me along the lines of, 'Ah, when were you ordained?' Flirtatious and laughing. Then we came out into the main opening of the exhibition and Ron Kitai was there. He introduced me to Robert. I was really taken aback. 'Bloody hell,' I thought, 'that's Robert Fraser!'

I was interested in the way he looked. He was dressed elegantly but out of date by ten years. He had the long early seventies collars, too long, too wide. The kipper tie. A sixties-style suit. So he looked elegant but out of date. Down on his uppers. He was carrying a plastic carrier bag, which didn't look right. But he sounded important and grand.

MALCOLM McLAREN Oh, I knew of Robert! When I was at art school did I go to his gallery? Many, *many* times, because it was the centre of attraction. It was on Duke Street – it was extremely trendy and hip, and when you found it you were just transported to this other world – a world of possibilities, of adventure, a world of fashion, of hip-looking people and hip artefacts that seemed to be part of the scene that was going on. It was capturing elements of Warhol, capturing all these other pop artists – Clive Barker, Richard Hamilton, Jim Dine . . . It was groovy, wasn't it? It was happening. It was all part of the scene – London was swinging, wasn't it? And Robert was right there, right in the centre of it, always wearing those ubiquitous sun glasses and he looked spookily cool. He looked sometimes like a Hollywood film producer, sometimes like a very high-society drug dealer, and sometimes like an art dealer, I guess. But an art dealer of a certain type – vaguely mysterious and cooler than cool. All that made you look at him in some way in awe and with a certain sense of trepidation and almost intimidation.

So when I met him, I knew all about him – he was a major icon. You were very conscious of what he represented. I certainly felt when Robert was around the presence of someone who was important. Yeah, I hung around with Robert in those days and I knew Robert from much, much earlier than that, from the days of the Sex Pistols, because he was a friend of a guy called Gerry Goldstein and I knew Gerry from the King's Road days, so I would hang out with him then. And he became very much fascinated by the Sex Pistols. He bought a lot of posters and artefacts from the gay fans – that's the best way I can describe them really – fans who hoarded all that kind of memorabilia. Robert bought a lot of it and subsequently sold it to the V & A. I don't think the V & A were that hip in those days anyway – I mean, everybody's hipper than thou these days – and I think Robert was the person who shone a light on that particular part of pop culture, which he felt the V & A should take some serious note of. He was the one responsible for them suddenly waking up to the fact that they weren't living in the Belle Epoque. They did start to buy in a lot of those things. It was Robert's personal intervention and his kind of bloody-mindedness and enthusiasm about this street culture that got the V & A interested.

But I was meeting him at the time when he was a little lost. He was a bit like a rebel without a cause. I don't think he really believed in the art scene any more. For him it had somewhat died. Painting did not have a place at that moment in time. I'm talking about the dawn of the eighties. The seventies were nearly over and I think the eighties looked boring to him. It was Thatcher and the beginings of the corporatization of the planet. High culture was about to become low culture. I think by the eighties art was . . . if it wasn't a product that was useful, it wasn't worth being on the selling block. That was a Thatcherite philosophy or, in fact, dare I say it, a fucking mandate. Suddenly art schools were being closed down, suddenly you couldn't get grants to go to art schools. You know, what's the point of studying art if you can't use it to get a job? I could see that was having an effect. Bob was part of an old era that was not wanted on location any more.

OLIVER MUSKER The art business, which he helped to create as we know it today, was something you had to be very serious about – the money involved is huge – and a good businessman, which Robert wasn't, couldn't be bothered. He was much more interested in the art. He wasn't going to waste too much time being polite to his customers. There was this old friend of Robert's, Alexandre Iolas, who was Magritte's dealer at one time, and Pauline Karpedis was a girl who'd married a rich man in Greece. She needed to get interested in something and thought she'd start an art collection. So she went to Iolas, he advised her, and she bought a lot of things. Then Iolas's health started to fail. There was a sale at Christies's and he couldn't be there to bid for her, so he said, 'I'll get Robert Fraser to bid for you.' Great. Immediately she wanted to have a cocktail party for him. So she rang up Robert and the conversation went something like this: 'Hello, Robert, this is Pauline Karpedis.' 'Yes, I know who you are.' 'You're going to bid at auction for me.' 'Yes, I know the lot numbers, I'll see you after the sale.' Phone down. Went off, bid for them, 'there you are,' and buggered off. Wouldn't speak to her for six months.

Then they became friends and he'd turn up at her house at 1 a.m., blind drunk, and she'd put him to bed and give him breakfast in the morning. A while after that she asked him about his attitude over the bidding and in the subsequent six months. Robert said, 'Well, you see, Pauline, I thought you were middle class. When I found out you were working class, that was all right, I could speak to you.'

BRIAN CLARKE Apparently at that time there'd be opportunities for him to do deals where he could make big money, like selling paintings to Pauline Karpedis. But he always did it for crumbs. Where he should have made £100,000 he'd get an envelope with £2,500 in it, which he would then blow. He was an extremely poor businessman. He actually had no interest in money. He wasn't interested in being poor or in being rich. He had no capacity in his psychological make-up for projections into the future. So if he made £1,000 on Monday, he would spend it Monday night. If he lost £1,000 on Tuesday, he would still spend £1,000 on Tuesday night. He never adapted to his income. He never lived grandly, always in semi-squalor but with grand style. During the time I knew him anyway. So when I first met Robert he was a sad figure, with his carrier bags and frayed collars, like an old Bentley that hasn't been serviced for a few years. He did have the Bentley image.

FELICITY SAMUEL We weren't close friends but I was always pleased to see him and he was often in my gallery. Presumably he liked it. He was a bit like a cat: he'd walk in and curl up and then wander off again. Robert was one of those people who stuck to you like a balloon that rubs against you and then drifts off. He drifted in and out of one's life.

So, we were sort of friends, and then we even talked about going into business together. Then Robert said, 'You don't seem to make much money.' I said, 'No, not very often.' And he said, 'Oh, well, in that case perhaps we'd better not.' I said, 'Fine.'

Then we put on this show, the only one we put on together, Gerald Incandella. Gerald wasn't an artist I was particularly interested in, it was what Robert wanted to do. It seemed like fun. And it did sell well. They were not expensive, just a few hundred dollars. One woman paid just a few hundred pounds instead of dollars – which still didn't make it expensive. Robert as always was incredibly vague. When he billed people in dollars and they paid in pounds, it didn't worry him a bit. He wasn't stupidly vague, but he certainly wasn't a hustling eighties businessman. Just the opposite.

I had no problems at all with Robert over that show. He was of course immeasurably vague, but we were both committed to showing what we were interested in, so there was a joint belief in the work. He had the same attitude to the arts and the artists as I did. You were committed to them and really interested and thrilled by what you were doing. The practical side was a sort of ghastly afterthought. In the eighties it wouldn't have been conceivable, everything had become so high-powered. But the contemporary art world of the seventies was so amateur in a way. It was people who truly cared about art and who weren't obsessed by money – people bought art because they loved it, not because they thought next month they'd make a profit on it.

OLIVER MUSKER Robert started buying photographs long before anyone else did, getting Cecil Beaton to sign all his old photographs. The only trouble was Cecil had had a stroke and his signature didn't match up with the dates. At the Felicity Samuel Gallery Robert did a thing of photographs, and Kenneth had this picture of Chaplin which he wanted Robert to sell in this exhibition, tiny little picture. Kenneth thought Robert hadn't framed it properly or given it enough prominence in the show – maybe Robert hadn't paid him for it either – so Kenneth got very upset.

KENNETH ANGER The thing that disturbed me about Robert was occasionally he seemed rather unscrupulous, or selfish in a way that would hurt somebody else. I became really furious with him.

The only reason I sent him those photos was because I needed money. I'd run out and he said he'd put on a show. Well, indeed he did, and he sold them, and I never got anything. I was ready to fly over and beat him up.

However, he could make things happen, the timing, and it was a kind of magic. Robert was always a sceptic, but at the same time I thought he was a magician myself. And he was, in certain ways. The idea that there's another dimension to life, with currents of energy happening, that intrigued him. But coming from a Christian Science background he always seemed to shy away from organized religion.

OLIVER MUSKER I remember once going to a party in London – needless to say, Robert was drunk – and there were these people in a VW bus with 'Jesus Saves' written all over it and huge beards and they nearly ran Robert over. So

Robert stood in front of the bus and abused them for a bit. Some silly arse, an American, poked his head out and said, 'Jesus loves you.' Another one said, 'You should read your Bible.' Robert shouted, 'Why should I read that shit? There's no such thing as a revealed religion!' Another one said, 'You're drunk!' Robert: 'In vino veritas!'

HARRIET VYNER I first met Robert with Sophia Stewart, his goddaughter. She was always talking about him – you must meet him, etc. She arranged an evening – he was going to take us to see an Adam Ant concert with Malcolm McLaren. He arrived, seeming very angry and rather bored at meeting me. Suddenly he spotted a photograph of my father and said, 'What's this photograph doing here?' It was as if I'd put up a photograph of some reclusive film star. I was rather surprised – because Robert after all was 'Groovy Bob' and Dad was not a very groovy figure. I said, 'He's my father.' He glared at me disbelievingly and then said nostalgically, 'He always had the brightest waistcoats at Eton.' However, even this chance connection didn't help our relationship at the beginning.

I'd heard he was a legendary figure from Sophia, but I didn't know much about him. He wasn't glamorous in the way I'd expected. He seemed little to resemble 'Groovy Bob' – a name that annoyed him as much as it amused us. He was always glaring at me when Sophia and I went to see him, wishing I wasn't there, but there was something about him I liked. For some reason, I didn't take his attitude personally, in fact I found his company rather relaxing. Anyway, gradually he overcame his dislike and we began to see a lot of each other. Sophia had gone back to Italy, so he'd ring me up and we'd have dinner. He didn't reminisce at all or talk in depth about anything, but when I was with him there was an atmosphere of glamour – a feeling that anything could happen.

GILBERT AND GEORGE When he came back from India, we became quite friendly. He used to come and see us here in Fournier Street. We always used to meet here and he'd pull up outside – I must say, always perfectly on time – and we'd meet him on the first floor. At that time no one came to this street in the evenings, so if a car pulled up you knew who it was: 'Oh, Robert's here.' So we'd get ready. And he used to have this hanky. I said, 'Poor chap's got a cold, Lemsip or something?' Of course, he was outside sniffing coke. That didn't occur to us at the time. This was when the house was being redone and we didn't have a lavatory. He said, 'Can I use your lavatory?' 'Robert, I'm very sorry, we don't have a lavatory, but you can go in the sink'. He said, 'I *love* peeing in sinks, I love it. Where is it? Lead the way!' Extremely generous of him.

We went to nightclubs together. A lot of dancing we did together, he was a good dancer. Crazy dancer. The gallery was closed then. We went to gay bars for dancing, because he liked 'chicken'! It was very interesting, because before we knew that, we were in the Regency Bar, which is next to where the Photographers Gallery now is. We just went up these stairs (there was no sign outside or anything) – very grubby little bar where you could meet *anybody*, an archbishop or the latest rent boy from Scotland – it was very classless in a strange way. And we were there, talking and drinking, and Robert was always looking at these extremely young people. Very innocently, I said, 'Do you like young people, Robert?' And he said in the loudest voice (as always), 'LONG LIVE CHICKEN!'

BRIAN CLARKE The next time I saw Robert properly – I had an appointment to meet Malcolm McLaren, who turned up at my studio in Earl Street, and with him was Robert Fraser. Vivienne, who was with him, was chatting away and might have been talking Swahili for all I understood. She was talking to Robert about me and the design of their *Chicken* magazine. She said, 'When he's designing this magazine, he's to think of a giant-sized baby thing,' and Robert added, 'But with an erotic dimension.' I didn't know what they were talking about. They left the room and I turned to Robert helplessly and said, 'How would you describe a giant-sized baby thing with an erotic dimension?' And he said, 'Oh, give them anything, they don't know either.'

Malcolm had all these letters, supposed to be from little girls to Adam Ant, saying they wanted to lick honey off his willie, etc., but which Malcolm had written himself, and he wanted me to illustrate these. So Robert came round with all these letters the next day and I said, 'I can't do that, I'm an abstract artist.' Robert said, 'Well, go along with it for a bit, something interesting might come out of it.'

Then there was the big scandal that hit the papers. What EMI didn't know was that 'chicken' was a euphemism for under-age sex. I've got the galleys somewhere – it was an outrageous exploitation of youth. Malcolm thought it was all very funny. He wanted to do a photoshoot in Robert's bed, a brass four-poster that had formerly belonged to Cecil Beaton. That was in the top flat at Coventry House.

I was making some neo-constructivist Bauhaus-principle designs for this magazine – completely different from what Malcolm expected. He wanted a child porno magazine really. They got two little kids in, a little Asian boy and a little girl, and photographed them in the bed, naked (actually the boy was wearing a little golden jockstrap). It was all a bit heavy, frankly. They were eight or nine years old. But it never occurred to me it was meant to be pornographic. I thought it was meant to be poetic.

MALCOLM McLAREN *Chicken* was a magazine that was to promote Bow Wow Wow, who were a new budding group, signed to EMI and managed by myself and created by myself. One of the methods of promotion was, we were going to issue this very young, under-age sex magazine – a sort of *Playboy* for kids – to be called *Chicken*. It had various photographers taking sexy pictures of young kids, so it had this paedophiliac touch to it, but actually it was totally unintentional – we were utterly naïve! Robert was involved in some way, linked via Brian Clarke, although I can't remember what Brian Clarke's job was on that magazine – may have been the design and layout. At that time I hung around with Robert and therefore hung around with Brian. They were a bit like Bill and Ben at one point.

BRIAN CLARKE Early in my time of getting to know Robert we went to Chez Victor for dinner and coming out he said he wanted to take me to a very special place. That was the Toucan Club in Gerrard Street. As we walked from Wardour Street we passed a Chinese restaurant and just then a Chinese wearing a white chef suit ran out into the street with a meat cleaver and pinned Robert against the wall, cleaver held aloft, and said, 'If you don't pay me my £50 I'll kill you.' We were both a little bit drunk, but somehow managed to push him out of the way, then Robert grabbed my jacket and shouted, 'Leg it! Leg it!' and we ran down the street followed by the man with the cleaver, until he was stopped by somebody, and we continued on to the Toucan Club. Well, I was horrified. What was all that about, I said. Robert said, 'Oh, mistaken identity, obviously.'

If only I had seen the writing on the wall, because of course this event in one form or another continued to take place in all the years I knew Robert, on a frequent and regular basis. There was almost nowhere one could go in any city in the world without Robert being stopped by somebody, threatening him with death or physical damage unless he paid a bill. So this was the first of a series of similar events. Anyway, we went to the Toucan Club. It was a sleazy, low-life, dingy Soho club/drinking bar, frequented by dusty old men and slightly sordid rough rent boys. They were the only kinds of people who went there. But a heady, intoxicating place. I'd never been to a place like that before. But it was not the only visit I made there. That night Robert and I left with two boys from the club and that established a pattern of behaviour that was to characterize a particular part of our friendship for the next decade.

GILBERT AND GEORGE We went to the Toucan with him, all these places. The Pink Elephant was nearly finished then. We went to the Blitz a lot. He always used to say the same thing when the waiter poured the wine for tasting: 'Mmm, Stephens ink. OK.' (That was a popular brand of red ink.)

We went to the Regency once and the Sex Pistols were there – that was the time. I was dancing with Robert – I remember, he was an incredible dancer – and someone was always bumping into us, all the time. So I stopped this boy and I said, 'What are you trying to do, you great cunt?' My God, he was so angry! And Boiingg!! So I fell on the floor, so they had to carry me outside, then I came back in again and then I fainted after that. And that evening Robert took us all over London in his car – totally drunk. You know you always have railings on these roundabouts now? They didn't have any then, it was just open pavement, and he was going all over the pavement and people were sort of jumping out of the way. It was the middle of summer and Robert was saying, 'Bloody black ice – treacherous!' And we said, 'But Robert, hang on! It's not winter!'

CHRISTOPHER GIBBS I found Robert as a friend exhausting. It wasn't that he demanded extra-devoting behaviour or anything like that. It was something about the pace and the stress and the abrasiveness of the situations that he got himself, and therefore anyone who was with him, into. Whatever it was he was in pursuit of, this was never very clear to me. There were various chimera that he was pursuing. And they were all to do with fulfilments of some kind. I think Robert was far too enthralled with his lower nature. I really do think he was seriously indulgent to his appetites. I mean, to a loony degree, he let them rule his head and dull his heart. I don't know what he thought he was getting out of it all – after all, he was very intelligent.

He had this flat. It was on the top of a building near the Swiss Centre and I remember going back there with him one night, to look at the flat and smoke a joint, and then Robert had all sorts of other ideas about how we might carry on the evening: we might go down to see who was hanging about the street or go to the pinball arcade. And we'd already climbed up this derelict building, with sort of birds flying in and out of it and broken windows and the door didn't quite fit. I mean, I've seen many people look for trouble, but I've seen very few pursue 'The Ruffian on the Stairs' quite so diligently. It seemed so unnecessary. There are so many other things to do. I mean, you've got books there, a record player. There was some very dark force he was wanting to be in tune with that he alone seemed to recognize in himself.

BRIAN CLARKE When Robert was in Coventry House, he lived across from Playland, which was a famous pick-up place for rent boys. They would hang out on Coventry Street, and Robert had a telescope which he'd train on them, find the one he wanted, and then he'd ring this big black man friend of his who worked in the amusement arcade and tell him which boy he wanted. Then Robert would put the keys to the front door in a sock and throw them out of the window. On one occasion he knocked a boy out with the keys. It was a big bunch – it hit him square on the head. I was there that day. He was a Welsh boy.

He replaced drugs with sex, and sex became an obsession – had to have sex two or three times a day. He had to. He'd ring me up and say, 'Let's go and pick boys up.' He'd get bored at Coventry Street and ring up the black bouncer at Playland who knew what sort of boys he liked.

JOHN PEARCE I'd known Robert a long time, saw him fat, saw him thin. At this time he'd be in the Roebuck, and other places, drinking pints of ale, ballooned out like a navvy – this great big fat man. I think he was quite pleased to be fat and boozing at that time. That would be the early seventies, the punk era. He was knocking back the pints. He was just a fat boy then.

PAUL McCARTNEY Linda bought me a Magritte for my birthday and it would be Robert she'd go to. She liked Robert a lot. He was one of our friends. Funnily enough, our kids didn't, because he was too arrogant. And he was often drunk, and they were little and they couldn't understand it. And he would say to them, 'Make the fire, will you?' And they would go behind his back and make little fuck-off signs. They weren't intimidated by this slightly overbearing bloke. They liked him when he got on the wagon. He'd come down to our house in Sussex and then he was a changed person and they could handle him very easily then. But it was when he was being himself and a little indulgent – my kids didn't enjoy that. They didn't like Ringo either. Although he's a bit of a darling. But he had the same problem – he had a major alcoholic problem.

HARRIET VYNER I was drinking a lot then, so we'd get drunk together. Every Thursday we'd end up at Gaz's Rocking Blues Club in Soho and stay there dancing all night. Robert's dancing was eccentric and much imitated by myself and others. He would glare and strike a faintly Indian pose and then change it in time with the music every so often. He would, of course, try to pick boys up – sometimes with success – depending on the lateness of the hour and the degree of his drunkenness. Once he'd reached a certain point, he became incredibly rude – about women, black men – sterotyped abuse but pursued with unusual vigour.

Rufus Collins was an old friend of his, but one he treated with this occasional irritation. We'd be having dinner and as Rufus would be talking away about a new play he was directing or whatever, there would be a silence at one end of the table. An occasional glance would reveal the look of a man outraged that life had subjected him to such boredom. Finally, unable to endure any more of this cultured talk from Rufus, he'd lean forward and burst out in genuine fury, 'Just take out your BIG BLACK DICK and show it to us – that's all we're interested in!' Rufus would just laughed politely and carry on. This happened in various forms a number of times.

BRIAN CLARKE Robert was always broke, never had any money. He'd run up bills he couldn't pay. He would open accounts everywhere – taxi firms, restaurants, laundries, printers, photographers – very rarely paid any of them. He used to tell a story about somebody he admired at Eton who at a young age had got his first chequebook and came into the school and held the empty book in the air and said, 'I've written thirty cheques today and they'll all bounce!' Robert told that story many times, obviously admired that. And basically, that's the way he lived.

People say that at that time he was taking a lot of heroin. It actually isn't true. He was drinking a hell of a lot, but he wasn't even taking cocaine then, or smoking grass. Many people contradicted me over this, but it's absolutely not true. We spent every day together. He lived in my house. There's no way he was taking drugs during that time. He was drinking like a fish and always went to bed drunk. He started drinking at lunchtime and would be incapable by 4 p.m. But no drugs. He started on drugs again towards the end of the period of the new gallery.

But he was running up bills he couldn't pay, hiring people he couldn't pay, and he had rent boys every night and got drunk every night. He was a little over the top. He'd go to restaurants night after night, and he couldn't afford it. He probably already had a lot of debts before we started making money together, so some went there, he blew the rest, and then got a tax bill for what he'd earned and had no money to pay it.

HARRIET VYNER He didn't mind paying for dinners with a cheque, but he never had any cash. He treated the need for money as if it were just one more of life's unnecessary burdens. If it came to paying for a cab (after having spent the whole journey shouting at the driver for picking the worst route), he'd look exasperated, like it really was the last straw. Then with the air of a man attempting grace under pressure, he'd be forced into thinking up a practical solution – i.e. who to borrow the money off at three in the morning . . .

MALCOLM McLAREN I remember once he turned up at my house in Clapham. This was when I was still living with Vivienne. I was in bed, it was about three o'clock in the morning, suddenly – bang bang bang – press the buzzer. I thought, 'Jesus Christ, who is this?' So I rushed to the door in my underwear – opened the door and there was Robert standing there! 'Malcolm, could you give me £100?' 'Robert, what are you doing? It's three o'clock in the morning! I don't even know if I've got £100!' So I rushed off. 'No, look, all I've got is £50.' 'Oh, that'll do.' I said, 'OK, here's £50. What are you doing needing £50 at three o'clock in the morning?' Totally Mr Naïve . . .

GILBERT AND GEORGE We never had a business arrangement with him. He was difficult in that way I know. Even on the rare occasions he said, 'Be my guest tonight' – rare because we didn't like to be taken out by people – we'd say, 'No, we're taking *you* out and that's it.' Sometimes he'd say, 'Well, it's my turn tonight.' 'We'll see.' But inevitably it would be, patting his pockets, 'Damn and blast, I've forgotten my wallet.'

One day he'd done some specially good deal and he said, 'Now I'm really taking you out tonight.' He took us to Boulestin in Covent Garden. A sort of basement, very plush plum velvet, pictures of prize cows on the walls – extremely expensive, I'm sure. As we sat down he said, 'They're all millionaires here, you know! Every table's filled with them.'

He did pay that night. Someone robbed him that evening though. I remember him telling me about the robbery – I can't remember the details but it was at his flat. I said to him, 'The secret of entertaining young people like that Robert is . . .' 'What? What?' I said, 'Never have a heavy bedside lamp.' 'I'll remember that. I'll remember that. Thank you.'

RORY KEEGAN I met Robert when I was at Sotheby's. I was at the Impressionist department and he followed me around for two days and wouldn't leave me alone. I was seventeen, quite good-looking, long hair, high heels, clip-clopping about, and Robert used to follow me round. So that's how I met him.

Robert for me was actually a bit of a hero. I mean, a real hero. I think he was the most important dealer for years and years and years. He was ground-breaking. He was a genius. Nice cool genius, with a sense of humour. Strange sex habits though. He had four or five separate lives. He told me that he liked New York because you could have three or four entirely separate groups of friends who would never ever meet and none would know about the others.

GILBERT AND GEORGE Not once did we see him with a boyfriend. Not once. He was strangely cautious about that sort of thing. In some funny way we always felt he had all sorts of different lives. We heard other stories from New York, more scandals. A friend of ours at that time had been lent a flat in New York. He let himself in, made himself a drink, heard some noises, opened the bathroom door and there was Robert on the floor, being buggered by an enormous black man.

He did like black people very much. He gave us a lovely photo of himself in the African Rifles. Him with a rifle and seventeen Zulus. Once he was here, and we were on the second floor, summer, windows open, and I was standing by the window saying, 'Look, Robert, how lovely.' There was a big crowd of Bangladeshis coming along. He said, 'Oh yes, hairy, aren't they? Very hairy. Fuzzy, you could say. I say, fuzzy-wuzzy, *fuzzy-wuzzies!*' Said in a very loud voice. But he didn't mean it in a derogatory way. He was actually attracted to them. He was very extreme in that way. Unbelievable.

JOHN ABBOTT I didn't know Robert very intimately, very well, but we sort of understood each other. Every time he came to New York (I was working at the Sonnabend Gallery at the time), he would give me a call and we would go out and have a bite to eat and we would talk about one thing or another – you know, art-world gossip and then the frustration of trying to find the perfection one fantasized about . . . And then he would very politely say, 'Well, I'm going on an excursion of sorts.' Because he liked Latin men, you know, Latin boys. At that time I was very involved with blacks, but I wasn't involved with any of the Latinos, so we rarely went to the same bars together.

Robert knew a lot of people, a lot more people than I did. He was always courted and invited places. But he would never miss an opportunity to give me a call and we would go out and chat. Because we were both deeply involved in the art world, which just consumes you from head to toe. Then to let your hair down and just talk about insane sexual frivolities is a wonderful way of relaxing! He just did adore these Hispanic boys with elephantine members.

RORY KEEGAN In New York he took me to some really weird places. He took me to the Toilet, the Anvil. I'm not gay, but Robert would wheel me though the door and aaagghh! You know where the Anvil was, it was unbelievable. It was like a vision from Hades. It was damp, a descent into hell. I'd never seen leather-clad muscled people like that. Up against the bar being buggered and there was this guy crucified to the wall, cigarettes being stubbed out on him.

Robert would just say, 'Oh, let's go and have some fun,' and you'd get down to wherever it was and go, 'Aaagghh.' 'Take your shirt off, darling.' Remember, when you're seventeen or eighteen and reasonably good-looking and Robert . . . Everybody knew Robert, so, you know, victim of the night. Come here, little boy.

Robert didn't participate when I was there. He was my host.

At the Toilet you could go upstairs or downstairs, and they'd go up into the gallery and just pee on everybody downstairs. It was horrific. Then there was the Gilded Grape on Thursday night, where there was amateur night out, and you'd get directors of Sotheby's in drag doing karaoke. This is the seventies. It was hysterical.

Robert had these big black boys and big white boys. As long as they were big . . . He would tend to disappear, getting up to his own things. That's what was great about him. He wasn't totally immersed in this scene or that scene. He would make an impression in all of them, then go off and do unspeakable things, whatever it was, because you never really knew. He'd do that all the time. It was one of the beauties of Robert. I really admired that.

JOHN ABBOTT The Anvil and the Toilet, Keelers, which is a leather bar, and even then he would go to a bar in the East Village called the Bar. He really adored New York; he loved the availability twenty-four hours a day of being able to pursue any obsession you might have, that it *never stopped.*

The more decadent one could find, the better it was. If you were a voyeur or just somebody curious in theatre, those bars were just full of exhibitionists uninhibited to the max! And you could just stand and watch these people perform in a spontaneous fashion things that one would not even consider doing in the intimacy of one's own home . . . But he loved it, he loved it, he *loved* it!

TONY SHAFRAZI In the late seventies, I was staying at the Grammercy Park Hotel, putting a collection together for this museum. The Grammercy was quite nice at that time, not so run-down, and one afternoon I was in the lobby, this guy walked by me and I stopped. Robert! He was wearing a beautiful light linen suit, phenomenal suit, dashing as ever, certainly a little bit older but looking snappy, really good. Again with the same magic. I was in love with the guy again.

'Robert, what are you doing here?' 'I'm just on my way to tea. Why don't you come along?' 'Where?' Very near here, come along.' So I went with him, three or four blocks north on Lexington Avenue. A beautiful old building, which was being converted. We go up to the fourteenth floor. There's nobody in the whole building, just sheets, plaster, dust, like a ruin. It was late afternoon. We suddenly went into an apartment – there's one person living in the whole building – and there's beautiful pink light pouring in. The studio of Gerald Incandella, whose parents were visiting from North Africa or somewhere and he's having tea for them. He was a photographer. He had this lovely terrace with pink sunlight pouring in. What a great place. The next day I took the apartment above him. So Robert was instrumental even in where I lived.

Letter to Cynthia Fraser, 1979
New York is still the same with the same magical energy. I've seen so many of the same people one knew years ago, on the art and social scene, it's incredible. But it's still not quite as exciting or fresh as in the sixties – still most people I was associated with then have become rich or successful.

I have seen the galleries and SOHO all boring and nothing as exciting as the sixties. Everything from the 60s art very high priced – I lost my chance of being a millionaire by having to sell mine.

The art that's being done now is very trivial in comparison with pop art of the sixties which was really saying something.

BARONESS FIONA THYSSEN I think I met Robert though Brian Clarke. I certainly didn't know him before I knew Brian. I can't remember the circumstances of how I met him. I remember talking to him one day and you remember how he talked: 'What are you doing in London?' I said, 'I'm looking for a flat. I want a big dining room, big kitchen we can live in, huge sitting room, couple of bedrooms.' Robert said, 'I've got it.' That was it. 'What do you mean, you've got it?' 'I've got the flat you need. It belongs to my brother and I'm living in it.' So I went round to look at it and it was absolutely perfect, so I said, 'I'll buy it.' But as I lived in Switzerland I didn't immediately need it, I said to Robert, 'Of course you can stay. Pay me rent instead of your brother.' That was fatal, because to get £5 out of Robert was impossible.

BRIAN CLARKE Fiona couldn't get Robert out of Queensgate Gardens in the end. I think the landlords threatened to take away her lease because he was doing business from there.

FIONA THYSSEN He created a shambles in my life because he was disorganized and unreliable. Landladies see things differently from dealers and lovers. He was totally hopeless in business. I only saw him socially, except when I saw him wheeling and dealing from my flat, shifting these huge paintings out, then getting the landlords' letters about dealing. I went to Robert and said, 'Look, I'll lose my lease. You can't have young boys carrying all these paintings in and out.' Actually, I think the landlords thought he was running a brothel there, because there were a lot of young boys going up and down.

BRIAN CLARKE There'd been lots of myths and rumours about Robert reopening, because his gallery had been the most exciting thing in London in its day. The idea he might reopen was an exciting prospect. This time, though, I took him quite seriously, because I wanted it to happen of course. But he didn't really have the money to open a gallery. He started talking about finding backing. But nobody took it too seriously and the reason they didn't was because they didn't take Robert seriously any more. He was always pissed.

FIONA THYSSEN I remember one party at my house with Brian and Robert and we were seriously drunk, among a whole lot of other people. Robert came late and he was so out of it I don't know how he got up the stairs. Then at some point Robert was leaning over to tell Brian something and he fell over, fell on Brian, who also fell, and his glass, which broke, knocked me over, and I thought

Robert had killed Brian. There was blood everywhere. Brian was unconscious too. It was absolutely ghastly, like a stupid play. All that happened was this broken glass and one of them got blood on his hands, that was all. But the mess!

BRIAN CLARKE Then in 1980 I was commissioned by Olympus in Hamburg to design the stained glass in the entrance hall and a series of paintings for inside. Robert had heard about this Hamburg work of mine, and the day I got on the plane to go over for the opening Robert was sitting next to me. He was going over to see a photographer, Hans Bockleberg. He came to Olympus, saw the project and we flew back to London together the next day. On the way back he said, 'Having seen this project, I'd like to do an exhibition of your work. Would you be interested?' I said to Robert, 'Fantastic idea, but you don't have a gallery.' He said, 'I'll open one if you'll do the show.'

Around that time I got this commission in Saudi Arabia, a huge commission. My fee was substantial and Robert had a big cut of that. It was the first time he'd earned any real money in a decade, I think. We both made a lot of money that year. Anyway, he opened the gallery.

ROBERT FRASER – AS RENAISSANCE MAN

Cork Street really will be the centre of the art market when Robert Fraser opens his gallery at Number 21 in June. Fraser is an art dealer who has entered the halls of legend, not only because of his involvements with the 'swinging sixties' beau-monde, but because of his entrepreneurial and perceptive qualities as a gallery owner. When he exhibited Jim Dine in his Duke Street Gallery in 1966 the police raided the exhibition under the pretext that the work was 'indecent' and contravened the 1838 Vagrancy Act. The media had a field day as the Old Etonian son of banker Sir Lionel Fraser was fined a few quid. A year later he hit the headlines again when he was busted, along with the Stones, on drugs charges and spent four months in Wormwood Scrubs – not too hard for the ex-Mau-Mau fighter (Kenya) and an incident immortalized by Richard Hamilton in a painting about judicial overkill. Since the close of the Duke Street Gallery in 1969, a sojourn in India and Morocco, and a promotion at Felicity Samuel in 1978 of Clive Barker's sculptures of Peter Blake, Fraser has consolidated his position away from the limelight and now plays the cards close to his chest. At one time he supported Peter Blake, Jann Haworth, Richard Hamilton, Colin Self and Clive Barker; showed interest in Boyd Webb, Gerald Incandella and Hamish Futton; and now launches his Cork Street gallery with Brian Clarke. At 44, Robert Fraser still has the respect of his artists and his friends – there's a promise of good things a-coming . . .

BRIAN CLARKE That art world at time was really tired. Nothing was really happening. But the feeling was, if anything *was* going to happen, it would be at 21 Cork Street.

MIKE VON JOEL: *Are you intending to run the new Fraser Gallery? What address is it going to be?*
ROBERT FRASER: *21 Cork Street, which is interesting because it's twenty-one years ago that I opened the first one in Duke Street. This, incidentally, would no longer be viable because it's too far away: whereas twenty-one years ago the West End of London was a charming and interesting place – people wandered around – now it's a traffic jam.*

PHOEBE BURRIDGE I was his first assistant at the gallery. The first time I met Robert was with Nick Danziger. I'd been working in France and when I came back Nick said, 'The guy who's opening this gallery needs someone to help him and you're just right. Come and meet him.' So we had an incredibly boozy lunch and Robert said, 'Fine, you can start whenever you like.'

BRIAN CLARKE But there was no storage there, nowhere to put paintings. It was typical of Robert not to find a place that would function practically. It had been a carpet showroom I think. I think he stored things in the Mayor Gallery

ROBERT FRASER REOPENS MAYFAIR GALLERY
Personification of Swinging Sixties, Fraser enters the Eventful Eighties. Robert Fraser, London's most noted and distinguished contemporary art dealer of the sixties – his name was synonymous with the decade – is opening a new gallery after more than fourteen years' absence on June First, at 21 Cork Street, London W.1.
  Fraser's art gallery from 1962 to 1969 revolutionized the art scene when he first gave a series of exhibitions that were visual Happenings, whose impact and importance reverberated around the Western art world.
  Fraser brought to Europe for the first time the work of Jim Dine, Andy Warhol, Roy Lichtenstein, Jasper Johns, Yves Klein and a firmament of international artists. At the same time he presented to an astounded British public some of their own talent: Peter Blake, Richard Hamilton, Eduardo Paolozzi, Patrick Caulfield, Gilbert and George and other artists largely overlooked and for the most part unexhibited.

BRIAN CLARKE When it was rumoured Robert was opening another gallery, nothing else was talked about in the art world: was it true? Established artists rang me up: 'Is it true Robert Fraser's opening a gallery? Has he got backing?'

Because everybody wanted to be with him. It was fun. It was where the action was at. But they held back because of the past, the unpaid bills, etc. Everyone believed in Robert, but not his handling of finances. He was seen as the one man who just might inject some life back into the art world.

MIKE VON JOEL: *Nobody in England buys paintings. As you're obviously in the business of selling art, why open up in England? Why not New York, Berlin – places like that?*
ROBERT FRASER: *Because I'm known for England. I'm known here in London.*
MIKE VON JOEL: *So you're obviously relating very strongly to the past, showing your sixties people.*
ROBERT FRASER: *No. I'm relating to a future which I think London could have.*

PHOEBE BURRIDGE Then we spent the next few weeks in his flat, writing invitations to the opening, the Brian Clarke opening. Cork Street was closed for the event and the party spilled on to the street.

BRIAN CLARKE When Robert opened, all the other London dealers were very excited about it. Anthony D'Offay was very supportive of Robert and he sent him a lovely big bunch of flowers. They felt it would bring something back to London that it had lacked without Robert. The day the gallery opened it was full of flowers, all from other dealers. Waddington and Kasmin and D'Offay. Everybody thought something might start to happen. There hadn't been an opening like that since the sixties.

Brian Clarke: Robert Fraser Gallery, 21 Cork Street (1 June–8 July)
Robert Fraser's great promotional flair made his Mayfair gallery a phenom-enon of the swinging sixties. After fourteen years as a private dealer he is reopening in Cork Street with the work of this fashionable young painter, whose geometric abstractions appear to be softening into a lyrical expres-sionism. Fraser says he is reopening his gallery after years of private deal-ing because, 'I am so bored by what I see in art galleries and art maga-zines around the world that I am sure I can come up with something much more exciting.'

BRIAN CLARKE The art world at that time was fucking boring, as bad as it was on the rock scene. The top of the rock scene was Rod Stewart, Bucks Fizz, Elton John – there was no guts there. Then Robert came along and suddenly it was a party, a party that lasted about two years, intense, really creative, like a Catherine wheel shooting sparks.

The London art gallery that has most come to symbolize the zest of the sixties has been Robert Fraser's, so it is not surprising that the reopening of the Robert Fraser Gallery after a decade, this time at 21 Cork Street, W1, is welcomed by art dudes old and new as the most energizing event of the year – at least. Brian Clarke is the most sixties character to have emerged in the London art world since the sixties, and appropriately he is the artist honoured with the inaugural show. Best known for himself, then as a stained-glass maker, he here exhibits his latest seven paintings in oil on canvas. Clarke's energy, whether manifested in the form of publicity or the making of objects, is both undeniable and commendably against the English grain, so to say that one or two of these latest paintings display more artistry than he has shown before is potentially to say quite a lot. A year for him is an age for most of us, and he will surely benefit from the sophisticated direction of Robert Fraser. (*John McEwen,* Spectator, *2 July 1983*)

BRIAN CLARKE   Robert was excited then at being back in the flow of things. Very pleased to be seen. Much to everybody's surprise, he was on time in the gallery every morning.

One night at the Toucan Club, after the gallery had reopened . . . My show was still on and was very successful and we'd made a bit of money and we were very happy. Robert was back, and back strongly. If he'd handled it well – which he didn't – he could have been very very successful. Anyway, there we were in the Toucan that night and Robert said, 'I want you to know something. You've brought me back from the dead, because without you I couldn't have done this.' I was really touched.

PHOEBE BURRIDGE   Robert was really excited with the opening of it. Brian was always in and out. He owed Robert quite a bit but on the other hand he put up half the money for the gallery to open.

BRIAN CLARKE   Robert got the feeling – as I did – that it was going to be a huge success, because the opening show was rather successful. He made a third of whatever we took from that. But of course he had a lot of expenses at the beginning. He would do things like, instead of carefully planning what he wanted in terms of letterhead, for example, he would hurriedly order one without thinking it through, it would arrive, he would have to pay for it, but he wouldn't like it and so he'd order another one. A lot of waste went on.

MIKE VON JOEL: *Let's look at the idea of running a gallery, and the people who run galleries and the methods of doing it.*
ROBERT FRASER: *They're mad.*

MIKE VON JOEL: *Are you bringing forward the criteria that you used initially, or have you rethought it and got a new set of values?*

ROBERT FRASER: *No, I don't have any set values. When you have your name outside the door, you're responsible for what's inside.*

MIKE VON JOEL: *How do you go about doing this thing? You've obviously got a stable of artists to show after the Clarke opening.*

ROBERT FRASER: *I don't think that far ahead. I mean, I do have some people . . . but I opened my first gallery in 1962; I didn't have any idea.*

MIKE VON JOEL: *Yes, but it's a bit different now. It's an expensive outing. That can't be true . . . You've got a good idea of who you are going to show, who you're looking at. There is a business aspect to it which everybody has got to face.*

ROBERT FRASER: *Yes, well. I mean, you're selling paintings.*

MIKE VON JOEL: *Yes, but you can't sell any old painting, even with your back-up and reputation.*

ROBERT FRASER: *The idea is to show what you like and pay your bills. If you're doing that then you're OK.*

NICK DANZIGER I think the second gallery weighed on him terribly. The pounds, shillings and pence. He was not only hopeless at it but uninterested, incapable of running a business. His heart certainly wasn't in the business side of it. He went through a succession of assistants at the beginning. He was definitely a nightmare to work for.

Money was a different thing with Robert, but I don't think he was ruthless or uncaring. Money didn't mean much to him, that's the key. The gallery was behind it all though. It was there he started to drink again, all the bad vibes came back. He was in debt to other artists. He wasn't free to do what he wanted to do. He had to put on certain shows. He was no longer in control.

OLIVER MUSKER Robert always said artists were a pain in the arse. When he was about to open the new gallery in Cork Street, he was dreading it: 'All these bloody artists come and see you all the time.'

BRIAN CLARKE The only artist I never heard Robert criticize was Colin Self. In fact he often use to talk about how much he admired the work of Colin Self and Clive Barker, but I remember walking past once and Clive Barker was on the doorstep screaming, with Robert shouting at him, calling him names, then he just pushed him out of the gallery on to the street: 'Fuck off, and don't come back, you whingeing bastard. Moan, moan, moan, that's all you ever do!'

CLIVE BARKER I never think of Robert as a bastard. You had to take him as he was. When he was great, he was great. When he was a pain, he was a real pain. I went to the gallery once and he was absolutely horrible – he'd had a terrible day. 'Right,' I said, 'I don't want to talk any more.' I walked off down the road and he came to the gallery door and shouted, 'Clive, come back, come back!' I carried on walking, got a cab, came home and my wife said, 'Robert's phoned about twenty times, ever so upset.' I said, 'He was absolutely abominable to me and I just decided: that's it, I've had it.' He'd given me a cheque which bounced. Usual Robert. I'd just had enough that day.

COLIN SELF In the seventies. I had done swaps with Robert for bits of Tibetan jewellery, etc., and he was saying then how he was looking forward to reopening. His arrogance was unique then. He was very arrogant and offhand with people, an unknown language that only he spoke. But by the time he opened again in the eighties, it was like every other art dealer had learned Robert's language and it didn't stand out any more.

Robert carved out something distinctive and original in the sixties. Part of the trouble was this envy and almost like what became the Thatcher marketplace. Fine-art van drivers would collect art from Robert's, envy the scene, then think that's what they wanted to do as well, and within weeks they'd have a gallery somewhere in London. In the end there were so many of them, it did detract from Robert.

JANN HAWORTH In the eighties he'd put on so much weight he was just a different person. It was really odd. He was much easier to talk to, though, and much more approachable and reactive.

Well, as soon as he opened – I went to the opening exhibition and we went to the back room and he said, 'I hope we'll have a show of your work by Christmas – or by so and so.' And I said, 'Oh, God, Robert, I can't do it by Christmas. But it'd be fantastic. I'd love to have a show.' And so it was that evening and then I saw him a couple of times subsequent to that, and really it was just a question of deciding a date. And then I got pregnant with Allie and thought, 'Can I get through this pregnancy and produce a show?' and I was not sure.

For a man who didn't respond, he was a terrific responder, if you know what I mean. He didn't visibly give away anything and yet he did things. So it was like he made it possible. He wouldn't sort of laugh or jump up and down or give you an emotional response as though to say, 'I love that work – it's so great, it's fantastic.' He would just say, 'Well, let's have a show.' And of course that made a great deal of difference to you.

BRIAN CLARKE He would spend a lot of time looking at young artists. He was doing the things he loved to do, pursuing interesting ideas, but he wasn't doing anything to pay the daily bills. He never did wildly extravagant things, it was just a combination of small things, the sum of which was beyond his means.

After my show at the gallery, I remember Keith Haring's show. Then the Dali drawings, the Black and White Show – Ellsworth Kelly, Nick Danziger – the Combas show (he was a French graffiti artist), then the Hervé Di Rosa show, Jean-Charles Blais – who's now regarded as one of the greatest living French painters but in those days painted big people rushing about/dancing.

NICK DANZIGER In early '84 I left England, but before that I had a show with him. Previously he had organized a show of my work at the Riverside, before the gallery had opened. I always found he had a lot to say about the work and was on the same wavelength. He was always very keen to know what ideas I had. These conversations were what I'd hoped to find at art school but hadn't. He was always there in the background as a supporter of whatever I was trying to do. If I needed money for something, he would somehow provide it. He was very, very generous. Having said that, when he sold my works later on for quite large sums, I never saw the money.

MIKE VON JOEL: *Where are you going to get the new painters and new art from, are they going to come to you [as a gallery] or are you going out to look?*
ROBERT FRASER: *I think a lot of an artist's inspiration comes from their art dealer, and if you can build up a relationship with artists and you can show them that certain things are happening in your gallery then they'll approach you – and also their work correspondingly improves.*

PHOEBE BURRIDGE When young artists sent in their slides, Robert would put them straight in the bin. As soon as he'd gone out I'd retrieve them and write to the artists saying, 'So sorry, but good luck.' But that's not so much against Robert, all the galleries did it. And we were inundated by people wanting to be represented.

ROBIN DUTT The minute I heard about Robert Fraser, the image instantly came to mind of the handcuffs in the car window. The next thought: 'How exciting. Which gallery director gets busted with the Stones?' That's one of the reasons I sought him out. I thought, 'There's someone rapacious, cheeky.' It wasn't until I met him that I felt this arrogance and dandyism. He was just to me at that point, with that picture, a bad boy. I only knew him by reputation. The famous busted Stones picture – that was the only image I had. I was too young to have known him in the sixties. I just happened to stop by the gallery one day and he was there.

The gallery was obviously not trying to chime in with the rest of things. I noticed that instantly. Especially the Black and White Show. I think that was the first time I met him. Haring was in that, wasn't he? I described the Black and White Show as being 'Afro-fifties'. If I remember, the image they chose to go with the piece was of a sort of robotic African tribal image, which I think was by Haring. It was before the big Haring show. I wrote quite a lot about Robert Fraser. I asked Robert once, 'Which critics come into the gallery,' and he said, 'The only ones are John McEwan and yourself, that's it.' I don't think anyone really paid him a lot of attention. He created a lot of interest, but established, scholarly critics avoided him like the plague.

NICK DANZIGER He'd built this reputation in the sixties. I don't think he was burdened by it, but by the second gallery he was starting anew, moving forward. But there were things like taking a painting out of the warehouse because the bills hadn't been paid, and endless fights with the warehouse owner, ex-Army, and it was like Robert pulling rank – the officer to the warehouseman, a mere soldier. Endless bargaining sessions – like haggling in a Middle Eastern bazaar – which could be exchanged, signatures and cheques going over a certain amount. That became more and more frequent and I think he just gave up, it kind of swamped him.

JANN HAWORTH We sort of have Robert trapped in amber. He's forever green, a beginning, a middle, a short end. What would have happened later? After he closed the first gallery, everybody said, 'Oh, wouldn't it be wonderful if Robert opened another gallery? Like the Beatles getting back together again.' But when he did open the second gallery, where was everybody? He was still putting on very interesting shows, but it was almost a non-event. And yet it shouldn't have been. He was taking up the graffiti artists, he was at the cutting edge, but there was no real response. If he could have carried on, he might have done what he did in the sixties. But maybe not, because of Margaret Thatcher, the mood of the times.

The eighties was a hideous decade for the artist, the academic, the intellectual. Very retro. Robert would have been victimized by that and probably gone out like a damp squib. He would have taken up people like Basquiat, but I don't think most people would have responded, not in London anyway.

PHOEBE BURRIDGE The solo show was really big news at the time, because it was the first of the graffiti artists. It was with Keith Haring. He actually painted the shutters across the windows. They weren't ever sold.

RICHARD HAMILTON I did see Robert at the second gallery, went to a few shows he had. The Keith Haring show I remember. I knew Tony Shafrazi at the time. Robert Mapplethorpe was at the gallery, photographing people, and Shafrazi was treating him like a lackey and insisting he take a photograph of me, which he did with great disinterest.

TONY SHAFRAZI I had started in the early eighties to think of putting a gallery together and then did so. My role-model image and the thing I aspired to would take me back to just before the Pop era or the beginning of the Pop era, those early sixties. And Robert had a lot to do with that.

Robert was very keen and wanted to work with me and show Keith. So we helped organize an exhibition of Keith's there, which was quite exciting – in London, that was. Robert was really starting to get connected to this generation. Keith worshipped him, very impressed with him. So we got reconnected, Robert and I. Keith did a great show with Robert and was very excited. A lot of the paintings were sold.

But now Robert was starting to look up to me. It was a very odd experience for me, to feel that here was my hero and now he's looking up to me. And every time I would give the full credit to him, he would never accept it.

ROBIN DUTT Generally, there was a stultifying corporate boredom to Cork Street. Robert was so refreshing. I remember going to the Haring show and there were break-dancers, two enormous stereos pumping this music, which was unbelievably hip and trendy for the time. Just down the road a gallery was showing eighteenth-century sporting prints. I walked across the road and looked at the two of them and thought, 'I'll never forget this moment,' because it was just such a juxtaposition. Haring was a pleasant chap and he was there signing autographs, giving away little drawings. And yet on the walls his work was marked at thousands of pounds.

What always impressed me about Robert was his sense of being ahead of the time. He would have this sense of knowing what would happen way before it would happen. I was very impressed with him finding the French Pop Art scene. They've lasted. And then Haring, Basquiat, di Rosa, Kenny Sharfe – I think Sharfe showed with him, in a mixed show. At the time people criticized Robert for being a Pop phenomenon hangover from the sixties, but what they didn't realize was that he was a classicist and he was very excited by draughtsmen. And Haring, whether you like him or not, was a draughtsman. He knew about spatial organization of lines on a page, every bit as much as Dürer. The people Robert showed could actually draw. So to me Robert wasn't a punk gallerist.

TONY SHAFRAZI Robert and I did quite a bit of business together. He was a little notorious at the business end of things – he wasn't organized. Ended up owing money. But I didn't care, I'd hate to ask him for any. He'd always show up here at the gallery in New York and we'd do something or another, some business. When we went to London, Robert would find a hotel room, make sure it was the particular room that was the best; all the restaurants he took us to, the parties he arranged. And the same thing in New York when he was here. I took him to all the clubs that Keith knew. I would see Robert quite a bit, he was going back and forth to New York quite a lot.

BRIAN CLARKE I was living with John Harp in New York in I guess 1984, he started coming to New York more often and he liked going to bathhouses. There are baths, saunas there, and a lot of cubicles in which people 'meet'. He told me that one night he'd been with four different men. He liked to be fucked. He was the passive type.

ROBIN DUTT Robert was a dandy. In my definition that's someone who teaches a lesson that cannot be learned, by example, by self-destruction, by fencing yourself off into your own society and really cocking a snook at the rest of society, and eventually probably killing yourself because society isn't what you really want. I do recognize that destructive dandyism, through the drink, the drugs, the sex. It's a gauntlet thrown down at life.

But I think Robert alienated people as well as attracting them. I remember when I went to interview him, and it had to be done over two or three visits because he was always quite gone really, I made a comment and he looked at me though half-alcoholic eyes and said, 'You trying to be funny, or what?' Very violently. I defused it with a joke and it all became fine. But he could be quite sinister, menacing in many ways. People found him quite intimidating, even though his appearance was very English gentleman.

HARRIET VYNER It was exciting for me being with Robert. It fitted my restless mood at the time. I kept wanting something to happen and with Robert I felt anything could. The fact that I never knew what was going on – everything was chaotic – made me relaxed, like I was living in a dream world. Whether it was running into some old criminal friend of his that he'd enthuse about for hours – who'd seemed to me quite dull – going from club to club or just sitting in his flat, listening to 'Ain't Nobody Here but Us Chickens' time and time again, it always seemed like an event. It wasn't so much what happened, it was more the atmosphere round him. Nothing was ever enough for Robert – even when he was happy there was a feeling that more could be got from this – and that suited my mood.

But Robert like me could veer wildly from elation to fury; we had many drunken fights. One night we'd been out together to an African club. He'd picked up a man and we all went back to Robert's place for a spliff. However, as soon as we sat down. Robert lunged at him and they started grappling on the floor. In a unusual attempt to be polite, I said, 'Well, I think I'll go and get some breakfast.' Unexpectedly, Robert's friend jumped up and said, 'I want some breakfast – I'll come too.' I didn't especially want this , I'd actually planned to go home, but of course I said, 'Sure.' However, as we made our silent progress down the stairs, there suddenly followed a passionate stuttering tirade, 'You f-f-fucking sex-mad bitch! I hope you *fuck* yourself to death!!' etc., etc. Robert's temporary friend, rather shocked, said, 'He's cross,' and I said, 'Yes,' laughing awkwardly. But the next day it was, 'I don't know *what* you're talking about . . .'

ROBIN DUTT He was a magnet, a great magnet actually. His private views were always the most fun, most rumbustious and crazy. At that time it was quite rare to have such a complete mix of people. Cork Street was so conservative. I asked Robert once what the other galleries in Cork Street thought of him and he said, 'What other galleries? There's only the Mayor.'

ROBIN DUTT: *How do you get on with other galleries. Any jealousies?*
ROBERT FRASER: *I don't think there is enough going on in London to create any sort of atmosphere, of tension.*
ROBIN DUTT: *What do you think of Nicola Jacobs?*
ROBERT FRASER: *I've never met her. The Mayor Gallery is the only one I keep in contact with.*

JAMES MAYOR By the time my daughter Louisa was born in 1981, he was a constant appendage of the family. I'd known of him previously – what he'd done in London was what I wanted to do when I came back at the end of '73. It was a job that needed to be done, and so I tried to do it. Fill the gap he'd left. When he closed his gallery he left a huge void in the London art scene. He was a legend in his own lifetime. *The* great dealer. But you'd make a deal with him and then he'd break it . . .

Robert was a very special person and I miss him every day. He was one of those gays who didn't prattle about that side of his life to non-gays. Rather pleasant. I loved all his weirdness, etc. I really loved the guy and he became a really close friend. There was a whole area of his life I didn't want to know about. I was amused by the weird clubs and would visit them occasionally. But I don't need to live in them.

I remember having dinner with Robert and Leo Castelli one night, and about

11 p.m. Robert just disappeared. You'd be walking down the street with him, talking, and the next second he was gone.

PHOEBE BURRIDGE There was a very good Dali show, done in conjunction with Mayor. We had the Mae West lips in the gallery and they were selling off the drawings to raise money to preserve Dali's house – or something like that.

We couldn't show all the drawings in the gallery, so he got Mayor in, who was two doors down. So we showed half each. What was agreed was that whether it was sold from one gallery or the other, we'd split the commission 50/50.

BRIAN CLARKE Under the advice of James Mayor largely, Robert started to see the sense of doing shows that might actually sell and doing deals that would bring in money. And James had seen the opportunity through Robert of accessing a whole lot of clients he couldn't otherwise get to. He wasn't entirely altruistic. But he would find important paintings, like the metaphysical nude by de Chirico, which Robert would help to place with Pauline Karpedis for a very large sum. However, Robert only got pocket money out of the deals of this sort.

PHOEBE BURRIDGE Robert had got a smart Heal's leather sofa right in the back office that was in a room so small nothing else would fit in – almost a corridor – and there he would lie in the afternoon, with those airline-type masks over his eyes.

One time the police arrived – this is very early on – wanting to see Robert. Before that he'd said, 'If any parking tickets arrive, send them back Address Unknown or Return to Sender.' So we did, and then one day these traffic police arrived with a computer print-out an inch and a half thick of all his parking tickets. Pages and pages of them. He owed thousands in parking fines. As he'd lost his licence and didn't have a car, that was a waste of money, paying them. But this day I had to sign for these fines, and when he came back from lunch he said, 'What on *earth* did you sign those for?' 'Well, what could I do? I couldn't just say Address Unknown when your name's blazoned across the front of the gallery.'

BRIAN CLARKE There were many opportunities he could have taken that would have helped the gallery financially, and himself, which he never took. For example, we met a New York collector one night in Mr Chow's – can't remember the man's name – and he wanted to buy one of my paintings. The next day I was in the gallery and this man walked in and came through to the back room. Robert was sat there, fed up, hung over. I recognized the man and smiled at him. The man turned to Robert and said, 'Hello, Robert, we met last night.' Robert didn't reply. The man said, 'At Chow's.' And Robert said, 'So what do you want, a medal?' 'No,' he said, 'I said I'd come in and look at paintings.' Robert said, 'Well, that's what people do in galleries, look at paintings. Help yourself, look.' And of course the man walked out.

HARRIET VYNER For some strange reason, in spite of his own apathy, Robert was always getting at me – 'You've got to *do* something', 'What are you going to *do*?' More than once he'd say, 'Why don't you get a job at the London Library?' I don't know why this appealed to him so much, but he always produced it as the ideal solution to all my problems. However, I had no plans to follow this recommendation, so he suggested we go into business, setting up a company for buying and selling pictures that would be separate from the gallery. I thought this seemed OK, but when I suggested putting up what seemed to me quite a large sum, he looked at me as if this were a joke. However, we thought we could borrow the rest and so we went to visit my bank manager, armed with all his press cuttings. Once there, in mid-conversation, he decided to edit out the parts that talked of his prison sentence. The bank manager politely looked away as Robert ripped out parts of the paper – but the loan was refused nevertheless.

However, the company, Vine Art, was set up with my money, which I never saw again – except for £500 one Christmas in cash, which seemed good enough to me at the time. One thing was, Robert never lost the opportunity to complain about the trifling little sums involved.

At other times he was very enthusiastic and grateful. I gave him a Bobby Bland record one Christmas and he'd ring me every morning with it blaring in the background, saying, 'Bobby Bland – he's the greatest!'

PHOEBE BURRIDGE As time went on he often didn't come in for a couple of days. If he came he was either stoned or pissed out of his mind. He was quite nice when he was drunk. You know, those sleepy eyes. My main memory is being left alone there for weeks on end. It was great when the shows were on, fine. But we sold nothing. One of Nick's sold, that was all. A couple of things were sold over the phone to Americans. But really, nothing sold at all. And at the openings every freeloader in London turned up for the champagne. I did feel Robert's heart wasn't in it. He was so excited about the openings, then he seemed to be bored.

BRIAN CLARKE Very occasionally he would have little paintings in the back room that friends would ask him to sell, and he'd make a little bit from those. But the shows were very rarely successful and quite a lot didn't sell anything. The problem people have not identified about why Robert was fiscally such a failure is because he was crazy, nuts and forgetful, but primarily because he got bored. He got through a succession of assistants and secretaries, all of whom loved him but were driven to distraction. I don't know if anybody ever got paid.

PHOEBE BURRIDGE There was an American guy, a real American rich kid, who came and worked there for nothing. It was a couple of his wealthy relations who'd bought things over the phone, and he bought a couple of Harings. He wanted to work in the art world, and also wanted to get a work permit for England. So he worked for nothing and even subsidized quite a bit. He was young. Then he went back to America and Robert was meant to fill in this form to say that he needed this lad to come back to work, that he'd provided Robert with valuable contacts, and this poor boy would phone up every day: 'Have you filled the form in yet?' When the boy would ring up, Robert would say, 'Oh, I don't think the form's arrived yet.' In the meantime, Robert hired Gerard instead. This lad drove Robert potty, because he was so willing, grovelling almost, and Robert couldn't stand it.

I left just before Xmas, which might have been after the Dali show. I can't remember. I couldn't wait to get out. It wasn't Robert. I hated the whole scene. Forty-one weeks I was there – I counted the days. I went off to drama school.

GERARD FAGGIONATO How I met Robert, I was looking for a job at the time and someone rang me and told me about a job at Robert's gallery. I said, 'What is Robert like?' 'Well, he's pretty weird, but it's a very good gallery.' I went to see him on Friday and he asked me what I wanted to do, so I told him. Then he said, 'Let me think about it.' He called me the next day and said, 'OK, you can start work on Monday, on a weekly basis.' I said, 'Fine.' That Monday was the day before Keith Haring arrived for a show, so there was a big brouha-ha. At the end of that first week Robet said, 'Would you like the job? I'd like to keep you.' That's how I came to stay there. I was very pleased.

ROBIN DUTT Robert was very generous as well as very selfish – extremes, polarities. He was either drunk and exciting or he was sober and unpleasant. I've been at the gallery when you could cut the atmosphere with a knife. I'm sure he made Patrice's life hell at times with his demands.

PATRICE MOOR He treated me like a skivvy. He didn't treat people terribly well. Sometimes he could be terribly nice. But I was young, I didn't care. It was just a job. I went in, I worked, I went home. No big deal. It wasn't important to me, I knew I wasn't going to stay there a long time. He was OK. He didn't bother much about me, I didn't bother much about him.

The running of the gallery was shockng. He was really brilliant when it came to painting and artists, but he was never a businessman, had no business sense at all. The financial side of it was always a disaster. Some weeks he paid me, some he didn't, and I always had to chase him for it. There was never any petty cash. The one thing I learned while I was there was how to fend off creditors. We had stacks of bills that clearly we'd never be able to pay.

The whole thing was completely baffling to me with my Victorian background. I was extremely naïve. I didn't know anything about gay people, about drugs, about painters. There I was with my strait-laced background and my history degree suddenly working in this gallery. I was overwhelmed by events most of the time. Didn't know what was going on. It was like watching a movie.

I was visually illiterate too, so even the paintings didn't make an impact. They were just part of this weird scene I was part of. My interest in art didn't start during my time at the gallery, but it might have been an influence. It was all exciting and quite fun, but I felt I was being overtaken by events all the time. I wasn't part of it, and didn't want to be.

He used to lunch with people, but he wasn't really involving himself in the financial side of it, confronting it and trying to resolve it. Gerard always treated me as very much inferior. He was fairly high and mighty. So he didn't discuss any of this with me.

GERARD FAGGIONATO Robert was a personality and you take such people with their good and bad, that's it. You couldn't be indifferent about Robert. He was a great person and he could do things nobody else in London could do. I was his young blood in the later part of his life. I was giving him ideas, stimulating him. That's what he needed. He was always searching for stimulation. He knew I wasn't interested in men and never mentioned anything to me, never made a pass at me. I always felt at ease with him.

There were many great shows, the Paris/New York show and the Pop Art show which was the most sucessful show we did, showing classic works by such great artists as Colin Self, Alan Jones and Richard Hamilton. Robert and I weren't quite partners, but we very much had a dialogue. We went to studios together, I took him to Paris and we went to New York together to visit artists. He liked to have someone to respond to. It became a great relationship.

ROBIN DUTT: *We know about Keith Haring daubing subway walls, but what about the others – Basquiat, Combas, Di Rosa? Were they doing much the same thing on a variety of walls? How did you discover them?*
ROBERT FRASER: *I didn't discover anybody. I was trying to find out a pattern.*

BRIAN CLARKE All the people who are now accepted figures in the art world, who were thought of as ridiculous pranksters then, were showing at Robert's. Like Jean-Charles Blais, Keith Haring, Combas, Jean-Michel Basquiat – Jean-Michel didn't have a show there, but he had work there. It was crap then, nobody was interested. Sandro Chia. Robert was trading in stuff other people were frightened of and horrified by, thought was ridiculous. He was the only one who wanted to show Keith Haring. Nobody else was interested, they thought he was a joke.

And the opening parties at Cork Street weren't like anything else happening in the eighties. Everybody wanted to be there and everybody *was* there. Openings had become po-faced and very serious. Don't forget, Robert came back at a time of earnest abstract photography, minimal art, people doing posters based on semiotics, intellectual shit. And Robert had funny bumblebees made out of tin cans flying round the gallery: Combas, Di Rosa and all that. He got very excited over going up to Edinburgh with Jean-Michel Basquiat, got excited about doing an exhibition with Keith Haring.

But if it was to do with straightforward sales, of being in the gallery, he was just bored. The business side of it bored him rigid. He didn't have the energy for it, wasn't interested. For the brief period Gerard was there, somebody else did that and it started working rather nicely again. But even when there was an opportunity to make money, Robert wasn't interested enough to make the effort. If it meant working with the artists to create something but didn't make money, he'd put the energy into it. He never liked to deal unless it involved fun people. There was a plan to show Basquiat and it was all organized, but whoever was acting for him wanted Robert to buy some of them, and somebody else, D'Offay or Waddington or whoever, came up with a better financial deal. So Robert didn't get the big show.

We had a dinner at Pauline Karpedis's – Robert organized it – with all these people there, for Jean-Michel, a fancy crowd, and Jean-Michel didn't come until we'd sat down for dinner and announced he didn't want dinner with an old bag, all he wanted was sex. He was really rude and awful. And funny, I have to say. Robert wasn't fazed by this behaviour. He probably wanted sex too. Pauline was very upset and said she'd never have him in her house again.

Robert had great style but was always on the edge of being dishevelled. Quite often he'd be wearing a well-cut suit with a shirt with frayed collars. But he started getting a bit more dishevelled and his appearance started to decline. Francesca went with him to Cologne art fair and a number of people told me they'd seen him there, looking like a tramp. I never spotted him smelling badly, but he did start looking run-down and dressing oddly. Once I met him and he had no socks on, although everything else was right. And it was winter. He'd started losing it. I thought he was taking too much drugs or alcohol. But so was I, so I didn't think much about it.

MALCOLM McLAREN I had noticed Robert was getting ill, but I didn't know what it was. I think he was going a bit bonkers at the end, poor guy, and it was all a bit sad. He was so wonderful.

I remember going out with him and Jean-Michel Basquiat over to that guy's place who did all that mad R&B, old-fashioned R&B night – Gaz, who had an apartment on Bayswater Road, to his house and then on to the club. And I remember Jean-Michel Basquiat very sad and *highly* suspicious of me actually! I think because he was a black guy with a huge chip on his shoulder. Who the hell was I? Was I another white man profiting by black culture? Was I another scam artist? And so on and so forth. I always felt that in his presence, no matter how kindly disposed I was towards him – or trying to be, at least. And then Robert sitting in the corner, very meek and mild – happy that there may be some semblance of a relationship emerging, which there actually wasn't. Also he was very fucked up at that time, Jean-Michel Basquiat, very druggy, and Robert was already suffering from that dreadful disease. It was a very odd moment, with Gaz's rocking blues and his little bobbing hat, you know, jumping around, playing his old R&B tracks. I felt totally incongrous and weird. I'll never forget that night.

OLIVER MUSKER We did notice he was going a bit weird. The Xmas he went to stay with Bill Willis he was locked in a darkened room the entire time. Bill was having his annual egg-nog party in Marrakesh and the room was full of Marrakesh queers, and Robert walked in, looked at all these ghastly people and walked out again, and can't remember doing it. So dementia set in while he was still walking around. Not just drunk.

BILL WILLIS Robert's last visit, he stayed here for three weeks, his last Christmas. That was when he was starting to look strange. He was listless. He was messing the bed, or so I learned afterwards. There were parties all over the place and I just thought he wasn't enjoying himself. I said, 'What do you want? Parties? A *boy*? What can I do to please you?' He said, 'Bill, I'm not feeling well. I want to be very quiet and rest.' He was squinting. Obviously not enjoying himself. In such physical pain, I guess.

GERARD FAGGIONATO Robert was ill already and he became very, very weird. He wouldn't show up for two days to the gallery, wouldn't keep any appointment, wouldn't talk, wouldn't do anything. I was extremely fed up, but nobody told me what it was. Nobody talked about it – no one knew what the symptoms were.

BRIAN CLARKE Then he moved to the flat in Holland Road. What an awful flat. But by the time Robert moved in, he no longer cared. I visited and I remember the flat smelling bad. Robert was losing his grip. He wasn't interested in anything – not alcohol or drugs. He was too ill. All the fire and spirit went out of him. He was a shell, a walking corpse.

PATRICE MOOR There was one night when Gerard and I looked everywhere for Robert, and we found him in his flat in a pretty dishevelled state. A squalid flat in Holland Park somewhere. Robert was such an extreme person. And the squalor in which he lived was just mind-boggling. He was seeing all these fantastically wealthy people at the same time. It was so bizarre.

GERARD FAGGIONATO The episode with the flat – where he couldn't answer the phone – you know, we had to send the police. You know, complete nightmare. He was staying in his flat, wouldn't answer the telephone. We didn't know where he was . . . It was very traumatic.

BRIAN CLARKE Then the decline manifested itself in more serious ways – in business, for example. He started believing the most extraordinary fantasies. That was the height of my problem with alcohol but, even though I was pie-eyed, I could see Robert was living in a complete world of Oz. A point came where it was absolutely clear that the gallery couldn't possibly work because Robert was not on the planet any more.

GERARD FAGGIONATO I left because Robert had become so weird, not coming out of his flat, not coming to the gallery – where was he? etc. We wouldn't see him for weeks, had no idea where he was. He wouldn't answer the phone. It was really strange. Or he'd come to the gallery, sit in his chair and do nothing the whole day. So I decided: I've got to get out of here, there's no point staying.

HARRIET VYNER Some time before this I'd been away from London somewhere and had picked up a newspaper – it had a story inside about a new gay cancer that was baffling doctors in California. It had pictures of some of the skeletal victims and the article said it was incurable and fatal. I had felt momentarily terrified, thinking of Robert. However, it was still so vague and far away, I managed to push it from my mind.

Next time I saw Robert it was a month or so later at Chez Victor. I was very drunk and speedy and he was very tense and silent, looking at me as if he wanted to say something. I said, 'Let's go clubbing.' He said angrily, 'Don't you understand, I'm ill – I don't feel like clubbing.' I said, 'What is it?' and he considered me for a split second, then answered, 'I don't know what it is, but it's not that new thing, AIDS.' I just said, 'Good,' deciding to take him at his word. Unfortunately, he'd picked a poor confidante. Why couldn't I have let him tell me? I still feel bad about this.

GILBERT AND GEORGE Then we saw him in Tottenham Court Road, very near the YMCA, which he loved. He went there to swim – at least I hope it was to swim – hopeless swimmer. This time it was rather surprising. He had his collar turned up, with dark glasses on, looking as though he didn't want to be recognized. Hurrying along. So we said, 'Robert! Robert! How are you?' 'Oh, fine. Recurrent malaria you know, recurrent malaria.' Isn't it sad? Didn't want to say that bloody word. That was the begining. Nobody knew about it. I think that was probably the last time we saw him. He had sort of bubbles on his face.

OLIVER MUSKER I knew he was ill because he'd sit there not talking to anyone, with these spots on his face. This must have been – I can't remember. But I remember Christopher Gibbs and I going to see him, and Dr Gibbs and Dr Musker decided it was his liver that was the problem. So we arranged for him to see a liver doctor, but the liver was all right.

CLIVE BARKER He said he was going to hospital. We'd made plans to meet and he said, 'I have to go to hospital tomorrow for some more tests.' And I said, 'OK. Well, you know, we'll do it another day then.' And he said, 'Let me call you . . . It's just a few tests.' And I said, 'Oh, is it your liver again?' And he said, 'No, Clive, I wish it was, I wish it was.'

JANN HAWORTH When I went in I thought, 'He's not well.' And then thought, 'Oh, shit – I know what it is.' I knew immediately what was wrong with him and I thought, 'Oh, my God.' You know . . . And I called somebody and said, 'Robert looks dreadful. I know he's not well. Do you know if he's all right?' And it was Bernie Jacobson and he said, 'He's been playing too hard.'

PAUL McCARTNEY I remember seeing Robert outside Cicconis, this posh Italian restaurant, and he was then hanging out with James Mayor, who'd become a logical successor in a way. That was the last time I saw him. He seemed OK, a little quieter than usual. I remember Linda kissing him and noticing marks on his face. It was AIDS. I thought it was quite brave of her to kiss him. That was the first year anyone had heard about AIDS and nobody really knew how to deal with it. So my final memory of him is him walking away from Cicconis towards Cork Street. I waved and he turned round. I said, 'Bye. See you, Robert.' He turned away, didn't look back and turned the corner. And I got a horrible feeling. I said, 'That might be the last time I see him.' And in fact it was.

ROBIN DUTT When you went to Robert Fraser's Cork Street gallery in the past it was a very tangible atmosphere. You could tell something electric was going on, something irreverent, something eclectically crazy. When you went in the latter months there was almost like a void, you almost heard your own footsteps although the walls were full and the sculptures were on the floor. His last exhibition, when he was so ill, he sat there as if he was holding court. I remember this procession going up to meet him, as if he were a king leaving. A really bizarre phenomenon.

CLIVE BARKER The last time I actually saw him at the gallery he asked me to go and meet him at eleven o'clock. I got there at eleven and a taxi stopped and out got this little old man with a walking stick – and he took ages to get up the kerb. And I realized it was Robert. I mean, it was the worst – probably one of the worst days that I'd ever seen him anyway. And a lady – an American whom I knew only by reputation – came in and she said, 'Is Robert Fraser going to be in today?' And he was standing like that. And he must have made some motion and I said, 'Well, I'm waiting for him as well.' And she'd no idea. From America – from when he was in America as well. She was a collector. And he just stood right by her and she didn't recognize him. He was in very bad shape that day.

RORY KEEGAN As you know, Robert used to hit the bottle. I hadn't seen him, but we'd been talking on the phone, once a day, every two or three days, and I noticed that he'd be a bit slurred, and I thought he'd hit the bottle again. Then I went round to have a meeting. I'd seen him about a week beforehand. I couldn't believe how he'd deteriorated in a week. That's when I realized. He was in a complete state, but it wasn't because he was hitting the bottle, there was something really, really wrong. And over the next two weeks he went from being Robert to being an eighty-year-old man. It was dreadful.

I'll always regret this. We were going off to see John Paul Getty, their accountants in the City, and Robert said to me, 'Just get me some money and get me on a plane to Switzerland. Forget going into hospital, let's just go up and out.' I always regret not actually doing that. I went to that terrible flat, that was horrible. That's when I got so pissed off with the family, because if he'd kept all the stuff – there was a couple of hundred grand's worth of stuff that wasn't in the records, no one knew who they belonged to, and if the family had just kept those, he could have popped those. All the guys down Cork Street would have done a deal with him, taken stuff off him, given him some money. At least then he'd have lived in some comfort. But Paul Getty helped him a bit; put his hand in his pocket for a hundred grand. A remarkable thing to do. And it wasn't the first time he'd helped Robert out.

ROBERT FRASER GALLERY LIMITED: DRAFT REPORT ON THE
CURRENT FINANCIAL POSITION AND THE WAY FORWARD
6 March 1985
Trading Position
The following information is based on the accounts for the year ending 1st
March 1984, as accounts are not presently available for 1985.
Important salient features:
Weekly loss £1,472 (we believe that the current losses are much higher).
The main reasons for this are as follows:
Increase in overhead expenses due to opening of the gallery.
The increase turnover generating insufficient profits to cover these over-
head expenses.

Future Running of the Company
The manner in which the company has traded has produced significant
losses in the past. Clearly there must be a drastic change in policy to
enable the company to make profits in future.
This area will need careful planning by the directors but initially we
would recommend the following:
• Appointment of a part-time Financial Director.
• Appointment of someone who has had the experience of running a
gallery in the present market environment to supply business support to
the existing team.

Conclusion
If the funds outlined above can be obtained the company will be able to
continue trading with a clean bill of health and sufficient working capital to
enable it to trade successfully. However, it is essential that a plan is formu-
lated to ensure that the company will trade profitably in future, and imme-
diate and careful consideration must be given to this.
Signed*: Keith Hayley, FCA; Rory Keegan*

CHRISTOPHER GIBBS Paul did a wonderful thing there. The pressure on Robert was extreme. I mean, he was in a frightful mess. If you live that way and you know there's a mountain of unpaid bills, it's not very good for your peace of mind.

Robert was to a considerable extent in denial about his predicament. I brokered the deal whereby all his debts were paid and that was very, very tricky because he was very unstraight about that. And didn't seem to understand that . . . I don't know, it was very difficult. It was very difficult and not a lot of fun. I got absolutely no thanks from either party. My hand was severely bitten by both.

RORY KEEGAN I was very impressed with Mr Getty. He didn't ask any questions. 'He's my friend, he needs help.' The only thing he was concerned about was that Robert wasn't going to get himself into any more trouble.

He'd turned into an eighty-year-old man and it was after that meeting, we put him in a cab and Getty's accountant, a lady, can't remember her name, pulled me off to one side and said, 'Do you think Mr Getty should do this refinancing?' I said, 'No, actually, he should bale him out, just get out.' Robert wasn't capable then. Gerard had been there at the gallery and had been very, very helpful, very, very good. But he was very young at the time. He couldn't have carried it on without Robert. Specially with the backlog of debt. It was just a complete can of worms, trying to work it out. Robert had this amazing ability to get people to do things. He was extraordinary. The deals he'd get people into. Amazing. That's why he was such a good art dealer.

PAUL GETTY I may have helped Robert here and there with keeping the gallery going, but that wasn't a major thing. He never talked to me about having AIDS. He wouldn't accept it for quite a while, he really wouldn't. But then when he did, he just didn't want to talk about it, and I don't blame him.

CHRISTOPHER GIBBS He'd already got these spots all over his face and he was refusing to go to the doctor. I did realize what it was, would have all these conversations, try to make him go to the doctor – all pretty good hell. And then there was this terrible moment when Mario Amaya came to see me in my shop and he'd just seen Robert and had realized what had happened to Robert and also that he was in the same boat. And he was absolutely ashen and trembling. Nightmare, the whole thing. It was a ghastly time, people remembering scenes of wild druggy depravity in New York – ghastly – ghastly – and everyone was terrified, kept on having blood tests (and then being rather cross when they were negative – 'Oh, these doctors have snarled up again!').

OLIVER MUSKER He never confided in me about AIDS because we didn't know what it was. He kept saying, 'I can't keep any food down.' Robert was shattered, though, when he began to realize what it was, he shut himself away, wouldn't let anybody come near him. Nobody knew why he was doing this to himself. Eventually, it all came out and he was taken to hospital.

HARRIET VYNER I remember the day very well. It was very sunny and I was lying in bed thinking that everything seemed to be going quite well. Then out of the blue I got a call from Patrice at the gallery, crying uncontrollably, saying, 'Robert's been rushed to hospital – he's got AIDS.' I felt sick with horror and got blind drunk before going to the gallery, supposedly to help. There was an atmosphere of chaos and gloom – far from being a help, I ended up shouting hysterically at one of the *many* people who were ringing that day to demand to know what would now happen to their owed money/paintings.

BRIAN CLARKE When I was in New York, Cynthia called me, before I went to Italy, and told me Robert was dying. She said he had an illness 'that's a kind of cancer that affects sexual glands'. That's what she thought AIDS was. That's how it had been explained to her. I asked what it was and she said, 'It's called AIDS.' Then I spoke to Nicholas, who said, in an unusually cheerful way, that Robert was dying. Sort of: 'He's had a pretty extraordinary life. Amazing he's lasted this long.' I didn't know how to deal with that, he was so laid-back about it. That was '85, I'm pretty sure. I left for Italy in July, so it must have been in the spring.

I remember walking through Grammercy Park and I suddenly realized Robert was going to die and I burst out crying and couldn't stop.

GERARD FAGGIONATO When I'd left, I'd gone back to France. Then his mother called me, saying, 'Robert is extremely sick. Could you come back, do the last show and close the gallery?' 'Of course,' I said. So I went back.

It was pretty traumatic at the end. I was really sad. I had plans for the gallery, there were some people interested in it, to make it into a proper gallery, to take over the business side – with Robert and me on the art side. If that had happened, Robert's gallery would still be the best in London now. No doubt about it.

Robert didn't need an office like a dealer, he needed a space in order to show – to get an exhibition together. That's the difference between a gallerist and a dealer. Robert needed a space to show what he had in mind – to show, you know, what was going on. And you cannot show what's going on if you're just a dealer. I am *convinced* Robert would have had one of the best galleries in London now if he were alive. I've no doubt about that, no doubt.

JOHN PEARCE He was so far ahead of his time. I don't think we knew he had AIDS. I was downstairs at St Mary's with meningitis when he was upstairs with AIDS, in the glass room. I learned he was there and was off up to see him when I was stopped by a nurse: 'Where are you going?' 'Oh, I'm off to see my good friend Mr Fraser upstairs. He's got meningitis as well.' Which is what we thought he had. The doctors reacted: 'Oh, you know Mr Fraser?' Then all kinds of quacks were coming in to have a look at me. It was too early for the penny to drop. But they kept taking my wife aside and asking, 'Is there anything you'd like to tell us about your husband?' She said, 'Why don't you ask *him?*' I would go up while we were in hospital and have a chat with him. But I was getting better and he was slipping away.

LORD PALUMBO Robert never discussed his AIDS. I remember going to see him at Cork Street once and I was absolutely shocked at the way, he looked. He had to sit down all the time. A few weeks before he had seemed fine. He said, 'I've got to go to hospital for treatment.' I said, 'I'll come and see you.' Which I did. I went to hospital to see him a couple of times. Took him a bunch of grapes.

We had long chats. I forget how it arose, but I asked a priest to go and see him. Robert wanted to talk to someone. I suggested John Foster – a very caring, lovely man – and he said that yes, he'd like to see him. I didn't see Robert again. He died very shortly after that.

RICHARD HAMILTON I didn't see Robert when he was ill, but I was in touch with Peter Palumbo, who said he saw him him every week, or very regularly. So Peter kept me informed. I hate hospitals and sick rooms, and I wouldn't have gone out of my way. But I felt deeply about what happened.

Letter from RICHARD HAMILTON
Dear Robert,

I've recently heard that you are very unwell. It was sad news. This is by way of a 'get well' card.

You are often in our thoughts, ever since you did me the good turn of getting me out of teaching and into painting – I will always be grateful. The opportunity to show in the best gallery London has seen in the last fifty years was a real privilege.

See you soon.

Much love from Rita and your protégé Richard

STASH KLOSSOWSKI When the Stones where recording in Paris I organized the writing of a card to him. I remember Keith saying, 'Yes, we have a friend who's on the big slide and what do you do and what do you say?' So all the Stones signed it, and myself.

Then one day Keith and I were at Simon Kirk's house, and walked from his house all the way back to Kensington – we couldn't find a cab – and we went to my apartment, the last one I had in London, in '88, so this must have been '85, and we discussed going to see Robert or calling him, and Keith was saying, 'What if he says he wants to see us, can we face it? We shouldn't risk it.' Then people said, 'You'd better not see him. Better keep your memory of him.'

BRIAN CLARKE After the call from Cynthia, I came to England and met Robert's doctor, Anthony Pinching. He's the AIDS doctor at St Mary's, Paddington, one of the world's top men in AIDS. Absolutely regular, stand-up professional doctor, the kind you want if you're poorly. I went to see Pinching and he explained to me what AIDS was, what the prognosis was, and he told me Robert was going to die within six months.

I then went to see Robert and said, 'I've just had a meeting with Pinching,' and he changed the subject. He did not want to talk about it, did not want to know. This was when he was in hospital. And we never ever discussed it.

Then he moved to another hospital – was it the London Clinic? I went to see him, and Christopher Gibbs was coming to see him the same day. I arrived second. Christopher had brought him a bottle of old port and I brought a pile of gay porno magazines, which I thought he would find amusing. Robert took the magazines, looked at them, said something like, 'Oh, very amusing,' and put them in the bin. In one movement. Well, it was a stupid thing to do. Christopher thought it was a very crude and common thing for me to do. He looked at me and for the first time for years I was very conscious of my accent, felt I was considered to be very vulgar. In my embarrassment I suggested we open the port and they both looked at me as if there was some ritual about bringing port that I wasn't acquainted with, because I was too common. They made me feel very working class, uncouth.

OLIVER MUSKER His huge nurse got very angry with the hospital because they were just experimenting on him, trying out all these things. She thought it was not improving the quality of his life. That's why she insisted he went home. I'm sure the whole time he was in hospital he was trying to get into a private room.

MRS MORRIS I went to see him in hospital. Very sad indeed. Then Cynthia had him home and looked after him there. She cared for him herself, nursed him, bathed him, lifted him. I told her she mustn't try to lift him, he was too heavy, even though he was very light at that time – Cynthia was not very big and certainly not very young. It was a very hard time. But she just didn't allow the fact of it to affect her sense of care and love for him. She was remarkable during that year, which seemed like for ever.

BRIAN CLARKE He never discussed the issue with me on any level at all and the word AIDS was never ever mentioned. Robert got sicker and sicker, and still didn't want to talk about it to me. He did speak to a number of others about it, but not to me. Which was very odd. I felt rejected a bit by that. An intimacy he did not want to share with me.

The next thing I remember is Robert at his mother's. That was heavy-duty big-time depressing.

JOHN PEARCE He must have been the first guy in London that I knew who had got AIDS. That was Robert: fashion victim par excellence. After I got out of hospital and was making what was probably his last suit, I put two and two together. He was probably laid out in that suit. He was living with his mum at that time and wearing this wonderful scarlet-flannel dressing gown. It was a beautiful spring day and the heating was at full blast, to keep him warm. Very sad. Then again he had cash. He was telling me about a painting he'd just done a scam on and went to the safe and pulled out cash. *Déjà vu.* So even terminally ill, he was still Robert.

OLIVER MUSKER I went to see Robert one day and he said, 'Do you know anybody who can sort out VAT problems?' I said, 'I do as a matter of fact, but what the fuck are you doing, worrying about VAT? Don't worry about it.' That was the only conversation that even touched on the fact he might be dying. The last thing I remember of him is lying in bed shouting at the television. He was in terrible pain. He was paralysed.

BRIAN CLARKE He moved into the back bedroom at Cadogan Gardens and then it really was as if he was waiting to die. His suits all hung on him. He was very fragile, very weak, walked slowly. He became a very thin old man very quickly.

CHRISTOPHER GIBBS It's an extraordinary life. And he was first in on everything, including the last bit. That was very rough. It was terrible at that time, at the beginning of that. Ghastly. Him banged up in that little room and that ghastly yapping dog of his mother's, and his irritation at having to be there. And the dementia. It was very bad. I thought his mother was very good about it. She was wonderful, great. I used to go and see Robert quite a lot. Not so much for dinner. I used to take him flowers from the country (which he hated). I used to give them to Cynthia, who loved them.

MRS MORRIS Robert was always in trouble, one way or the other, from the start. But always charming, always amusing, ready to laugh it off. He didn't even realize what he was doing to his mother really. He was killing her really. It ate into her soul, what Robert did. And then the end was so terrible. Who wants to go though that. If you're his mother you love him, so it's doubly hard. The umbilical cord is a pretty hard thing to cut.

BRIAN CLARKE The Terrence Higgins Trust helped take care of him at home.

They sent people round and the people told me, at the time he died, that Robert was the first person to have AIDS in England who died at home.

When he came back to Cynthia he never wanted to leave again. He loved it. He was at home. She was taking care of him. At times he thought his father was still alive.

For a brief period he seemed very happy. All the worries and anxieties dropped from him and he took enormous delight . . . And another thing, he had a nurse looking after him, big woman, strong, no-nonsense kind, and there were certain things Robert wouldn't allow her to do for him that he insisted his mother should do. And he insisted his mother cook certain meals. Cynthia didn't cook. But I think for the first time in his life, Robert had a mother, when he was dying, and he liked it very much. She washed certain of his clothes herself, she made certain meals for him, she sat next to him, holding his head, stroking him, and he was very, very happy. And he called her Mummy, but it was the intonation, the way he said it, just like a little boy. Appealing and sometimes naughty: Mummy. He went into a second childhood briefly there, but one characterized by happiness. He really was happy his mother was taking care of him. He was very happy when the end came, he really was. And Cynthia told me that although it was very, very upsetting, it was also happy for her. She said she'd never been as close to him as when he was there in her flat, at the end. They played out a role they'd never played before but obviously hungered for.

J. PAUL GETTY I saw quite a bit of Cynthia in the last months of Robert's life. I used to go round there a lot, because I felt very sorry for her. She had a small poodle. Dreadful dog. But Robert, it was terrible for her to come to terms with. Not pleasant at all. Because Robert's last days were very uncomfortable for everybody. Not pleasant to dwell on. He never got old, poor Robert.

BRIAN CLARKE She took great delight in giving little dinner parties for him. I attended most of them, Rifat one or two, Nicholas Serota came to one, and Gerard and Nick also. Just before Oscar Wilde died he had a dream that he said was like supping with the dead. And that's what these parties were like – supping with the dead. Not cheerful affairs. And Robert made no attempt to make them cheerful. Once he said everybody had to leave because he and Mummy had things to do. And we'd just stated the main course. 'You'll have to be quick. Mummy and I have things to do.'

I know they were very, very close in that period. Robert used to talk about his father a lot too. There was one occasion I had to get somewhere and he said if I waited I could go in his father's Bentley, because, he said, 'My father never rides in the Bentley, he walks alongside it. So it'll be empty. Save you walking.'

Cynthia was there and after she said that was true, he would walk to the office and the car would follow him. But she said Robert often thought his father was still alive. And he was constantly asking if his dead sister was coming to dinner. Whenever anybody went round, he would get up and dress and very, very feebly walk from the bedroom to the sitting room, talk with someone for ten minutes, then lose interest and Cynthia would say, 'It's time to go back to bed now,' and then he'd have tea and cakes with Cynthia. She would undress him and put him back to bed, with the nurse, and come back and join you. That was the pattern. Sometimes you'd be sitting there with Cynthia and he'd shout, 'Mum-my, Mum-my!' and she'd say, 'I think you should leave now.'

I went many, many times to visit him there and on several occasions he didn't know who I was. Which I found very, very upsetting. I was upset at losing him, at what would happen to me without him, and I felt angry with him. He was abandoning me. Not because he was dying, but because he didn't seem interested in me any more, then didn't know who I was. He asked me once what I wanted, why was I there.

The only thing that remained intact was this little boy with his mother game. That's how it seemed to me. Cynthia was under a great deal of stress, but she never expressed it, she was always very stiff-upper-lip, talked almost jokingly about the practical difficulties of having to deal with a big man like Robert.

He physically diminished, substantially – his hands were thin, the veins standing out – and his collars were big around his neck. He'd lost his mind as well as everything else, and his eyes lost their colour. There seemed to be nothing behind them. He was like a corpse.

James Mayor called me to tell me Robert had died. And very nicely, he did it very well. James loved Robert. He was as upset as anybody. When he phoned he said, 'I'm sorry to tell you that we've lost Robert.' The fact he said 'we've' lost Robert made it somehow less painful. That was very nice, touching. There was a tremor in his voice, he was near to tears. The only person who really rang to commiserate and treat it like the end of an era was Tony Shafrazi. And Lee Eastman, Linda McCartney's father, he said in his letter to me that Robert was a great man who deserved a better fate. (Except his secretary typed 'faith' instead of 'fate'. I didn't understand and rang Lee up. I've still got that letter.)

HARRIET VYNER Brian rang me to tell me that Robert had died. I knew it was coming but I still felt that terrible feeling – now there's no hope. He then rang me a few days later to say that Cynthia wanted me to come to the funeral, which was to be very small. All I remember of the funeral was the small (and rather odd) group of people who went back to Cynthia's flat afterwards and stood around. I was feeling and looking so desperate I suppose that my friend Rifat took charge – poured out my large glass of sherry and somehow replaced it with brandy he found on Cynthia's drinks tray. On the way home the brandy had got rid of any reserve I might have had and I was crying so much that the taxi driver refused payment. This was the only time that I had no means of coming to terms with a friend's death. I *couldn't* believe it. Robert had meant so much to me and somehow I felt he was the best thing in my life, though I couldn't have explained why and still can't. It just had something to do with the fact that being with him, whether he was in a good or bad mood, was always to feel life suddenly held the promise of great things. I've never felt that way with anyone else since.

J. PAUL GETTY He deserves to be remembered, Robert. He really was an icon of his time and I think that when he died there wasn't an obituary in any of the major papers. Which is a shame, because he certainly required one. He was a figure round London. If there had been a war on at the time you'd have expected him to turn up as a character.

LORD PALUMBO Robert was a mixture of the old world and the new. His father was an establishment figure, and so is Nick. And his mother was very traditional. So he came out of this very straight background, but gave it his own interpretation. I wasn't surprised at the prison episode – I was never surprised at anything that happened to Robert. We used to meet at the Windsor races under cover when we were at Eton. He had little bottles of gin and whisky, paper cups, and we'd sit sipping, watching the races. Nothing Robert did ever surprised me. Very much a live wire. Rules weren't for Robert. Or they were there to be broken. Which was rather exciting. Life was lived very much on the edge.

There was sadness that he died the way he did, but on the other hand he'd run his course. I didn't think that at the time, but I think so now. He'd done it all, nothing left to do. Been there, done that, move on.

MALCOLM McLAREN We're left with all those memories now. I'm not sure if the new generation of art dealers have that much understanding of Robert Fraser. They're too square to start with, and hustlers too. Robert was part *bon viveur* and part art dealer, part music fan – he was all of those things and I think at the end of the day business was not at the top of his priorities. Every time he walked into his office in the morning, it was probably a priority to figure out what was going on after the gallery closed. Once you'd got that together, then you'd work backwards to where you were at ten o'clock in the morning. I think that was how Robert operated a lot of the time. Because it was all part of the scene, but the sixties could afford all of that because it was not a pragmatic era;

the exact opposite – it was a romantic era. We now live in that era when all those kind of people are either dead, like dear old Bob, or they've been driven out to the hinterlands. Robert was part of a moment in pop culture, part of a time which could afford to have such romantic figures, because that's what he was – he was a romantic figure. Probably without him a lot of the glamour would have been lost. I think he probably acted as a catalyst – he made people more glamorous than they really were, by his charm and his manner and his ability to pull people up, corral them, make stars. He had no interest in business but definitely an interest in creating stars. Those English artists that he worked with, whether it be Peter Blake or so and so – he did try to make them all appear *much* more groovy than they really in effect were. I think it was in association with him that they became groovy. Any bit of stardust that fell off Bob's jacket during the day at the gallery on to someone else, an artist wandering through, might suddenly turn them into a star. It's a very particular talent, you know, and it's a talent other entrepreneurs have – they do make ordinary people feel like stars. If it makes them feel like stars, they in turn become stars.

I certainly loved him for his romantic air and in many respects found him to be a great friend, a great friend always. I loved him for all those things, even eating ridiculous Chinese meals late at night on Wardour Street. It all seemed much more romantic with him than without him. It made you feel like you had potential, made you feel like you could do something. He was that kind of guy, he gave you that sort of sense. It's a wonderful and rare talent. He was a wonderful man.

BRIAN CLARKE When Robert died it *was* like the end of an era. That's easily and frequently said, but when Robert died it was definitely a turning point. Something bigger than Robert had ended for me and for quite a few people. From then on the art world seemed like a very serious place. It changed its image. The art world seen through Robert's eyes was simply a rather clumsy vehicle through which you expressed your artistic ideas, was the publicity machine for getting the art out, just a clumsy tool. While Robert was alive, he saw the art world rather humorously, never took it seriously.

All those dealers thought Robert was a fucking legend, although they'd deny it now. They regaled each other with stories of his excesses, his outrageousness. Many of which were invented or exaggerated.

What they admired, but criticized him for, was his close liaison with so many famous people. He had access to a lot of very glamorous people. A lot of other dealers didn't and they envied him that. He was the ultimate glamorous art dealer. He didn't sell to dry old collectors living in Belgravia. He sold to groovy rock stars and movie stars. Robert did say to me that the only reason he was famous as an art dealer was because he'd given up. He said, 'It's easy to become a legend: you give up something when it's going well.'

KEITH RICHARDS One of the reasons we're talking about Robert, he was a one-off. There were so many facets to him. I only know some of them and I knew him pretty good. I've only brushed over the surface of Robert. In a way he reminds you of Sir Richard Burton, East African Rifles, you know. I always had the feeling he wanted to cut that whole thing off. He'd done his bit, gone to Eton, in the Guards, boom.

There must have been something in Robert's upbringing that made him feel he'd been restricted into a corner of the world, privileged, separated in the upper strata of society. You went to Eton, did all the right things. But he felt that he was under-privileged because he wasn't allowed to know what was really going on on the streets, and that was one of the fascinations for him, knowing what life was really all about for others, and he wanted to share and join us.

When I got out of school I said, 'I'm never going to have a boss. Fuck it. You put me right off. You tried to educate me. I've learned a few things, but you failed to break the spirit, which is the whole point of schools. You have not got me in the herd.' Maybe this was also true for Robert, although he had to go on longer, given the fact it's Eton, that strata.

This is my speculation, but I felt Robert felt he'd done his time for the establishment – Eton, the Guards, East African Rifles. He'd been there, done that, seen what a shabby set-up it was, especially in the fifties and sixties, hardly prime time for England. He did his bit, what was expected of him. Did the military bit. Then fine, no more yes sir/no sir. It's not often you meet a captain of the East African Rifles actually yearning to be an art connoisseur. It's once again one of those Victorian things, where officers would be wonderful water-colourists. You know, 'My paint's not dry' but at the same time, 'Oh, shoot him, him and him.'

He was caught between two bits of England, and he wanted to go forward into the new one, having done his bit for the old one.

I'm a lot richer in my life for knowing him.

OVERLEAF: Keith Richards and Robert, Morocco, 1966
photographed by Michael Cooper.

Acknowledgements

I owe an immense debt to those whose words, spoken or written, make up a large part of this book, and who contributed with great generosity. For reasons of structure, the following people who were interviewed do not appear in the book, but their time and help is much appreciated: Toni Basil, James Bendon, Madame Cecile Boelen, Susan Bottomley, Matthew Carr, Jess Collins, Tony Curtis, Nancy Dine, John Edwards, Llyn Foulkes, Gerry Goldstein, James Hogg, Walther Hopps, John Jesse, Sam McEwan, Gaz Mayall, Gita Mehta, George Melly, John Michell, Barry Miles, Mark and Catherine Palmer, Naveen Patnaik, Morris Payne, Dr Hubert Peters, Mark Shand, Rita and Inder Pratap Singh.

Susan Loppert has generously allowed me to reproduce sections of her interviews with Clive Barker, Peter Blake, Jim Dine, Richard Hamilton, Eduardo Paolozzi, Bridget Riley and Bryan Robertson which originally formed part of her 'Robert Fraser Gallery' Radio 3 programme, broadcast on 5 May 1993.

I would also like to thank the following, whose help included advice, contacts, loans of photographs and books, typing, transcribing and necessary encouragement: Mick Geyer, for all his editorial help; Kenneth Anger, Hercules Bellville, Martin Booth, Clare Conville, Violet Edge, Gerard Faggionato, Nicholas Fraser, Bella Freud, Lucian Freud, John Gibbs, Robin Hardy, Liz Hopkinson, Dennis Hopper, Peter Hunt, David Jenkins, Fiona Laing, Angela Lange, Heather Laughton, Elle Lewis, Alastair Londonderry, Linda McCartney, David MacMillan, John Maybury, Robin Muir, Sally Munton, Karma and Laila Nabulsi, Beatrix Nevill, Hiroko Onoda, Rifat Ozbek, Hali Procter, Anna Pryor, Perry Richardson, Jaqui Roberts, Tony Shafrazi, Margaret Vyner, Charles A. Walker, Baillie Walsh, Stella Wilkinson.

At Faber and Faber I would especially like to thank Jon Riley, Lee Brackstone, Rafi Romaya, Charles Boyle, Judith Hillmore, Joanna Mackle and Walter Donohue.

And Brian Clarke, who first suggested the idea of writing about Robert and to whom this book is dedicated with love and gratitude.

H.V., July 1999

The publishers wish to acknowledge the following for permission to reprint previously published material: Blake Publishing Ltd for extracts from *Up and Down with the Rolling Stones* by Tony Sanchez and John Blake; extract from *Enemies of Promise* by Cyril Connolly, © 1983 and 1948 by Cyril Connolly, published in paperback by André Deutsch, reprinted by permission of the Estate of Cyril Connolly, c/o Rogers, Coleridge & White Ltd, 20 Powis Mews, London W11 1JN; Robin Dutt for extracts from an interview first published in *Inside Art*, supplement of *Ritz Newspaper*; News International Syndication for 'Who Breaks a Butterfly on a Wheel?', © Times Newspapers Limited, 1967; Perry Richardson for extracts from *The Early Stones* (New York: Hyperion, 1992) and *Blinds and Shutters* (Genesis / Hedley, 1990).

Index

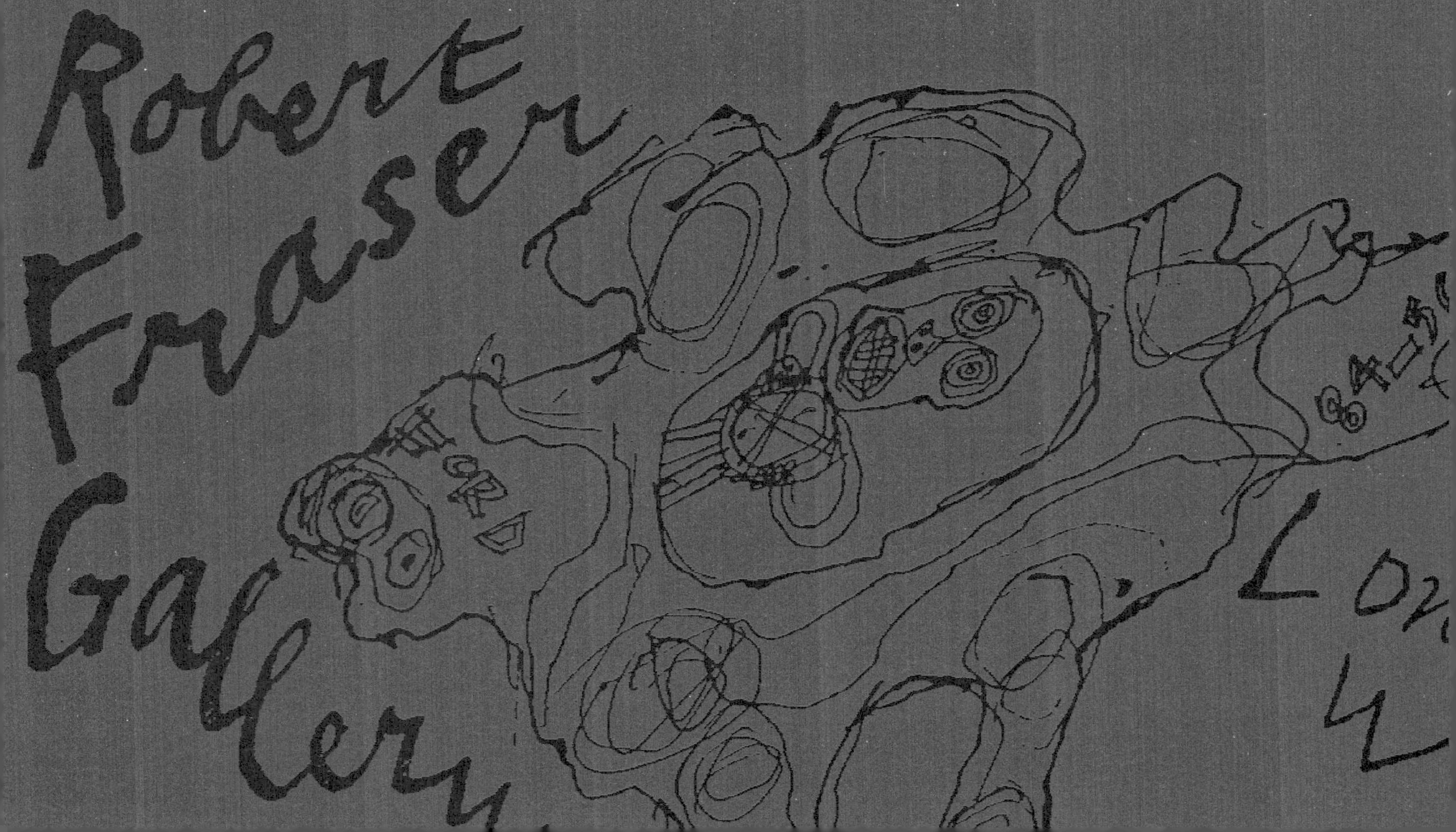

Endpapers: Jean Dubuffet, untitled sketch,